It's another Quality Book from CGP

This book is for 11-14 year olds.

It contains lots of tricky questions designed to make you sweat — because that's the only way you'll get any better.

It's also got some daft bits in to try and make the whole experience at least vaguely entertaining for you.

What CGP is all about

Our sole aim here at CGP is to produce the highest quality books — carefully written, immaculately presented and dangerously close to being funny.

Then we work our socks off to get them out to you — at the cheapest possible prices.

Contents

Section One — Life Processes and Cell Activity

Section Two — Humans as Organisms Part One

Section Three — Growing Up

Section Four — Humans as Organisms Part Two

Section Five — Plants as Organisms

Section Six — Variation

Section Seven — Organisms in Their Environment

Section Eight — Materials and Their Properties

Section Nine — Solids, Liquids and Gases

A few pages have got a splodge like this one where bits have been taken out of the syllabus.

This stuff shouldn't come up in the SATs, but it's still really important so we left it in.

Published by Coordination Group Publications, Ltd.

Typesetting and layout by The Science Coordination Group
Illustrations by Sandy Gardner e-mail: illustrations@sandygardner.co.uk

Compiled by Paddy Gannon.

Contributors
Ellen Bowness, Tom Cain, Katherine Craig, Kate Houghton, Rose Parkin, Katherine Reed, Laurence Stamford, Jane Towle.

ISBN: 978 1 84146 239 4

Groovy website: www.cgpbooks.co.uk
Also thanks to CorelDRAW® for providing one or two jolly bits of clipart.
Printed by Elanders Hindson Ltd, Newcastle upon Tyne.

Questions on the Microscope

Q1 Below is a typical microscope found in the lab. Join up the *label* with the correct *letter*.

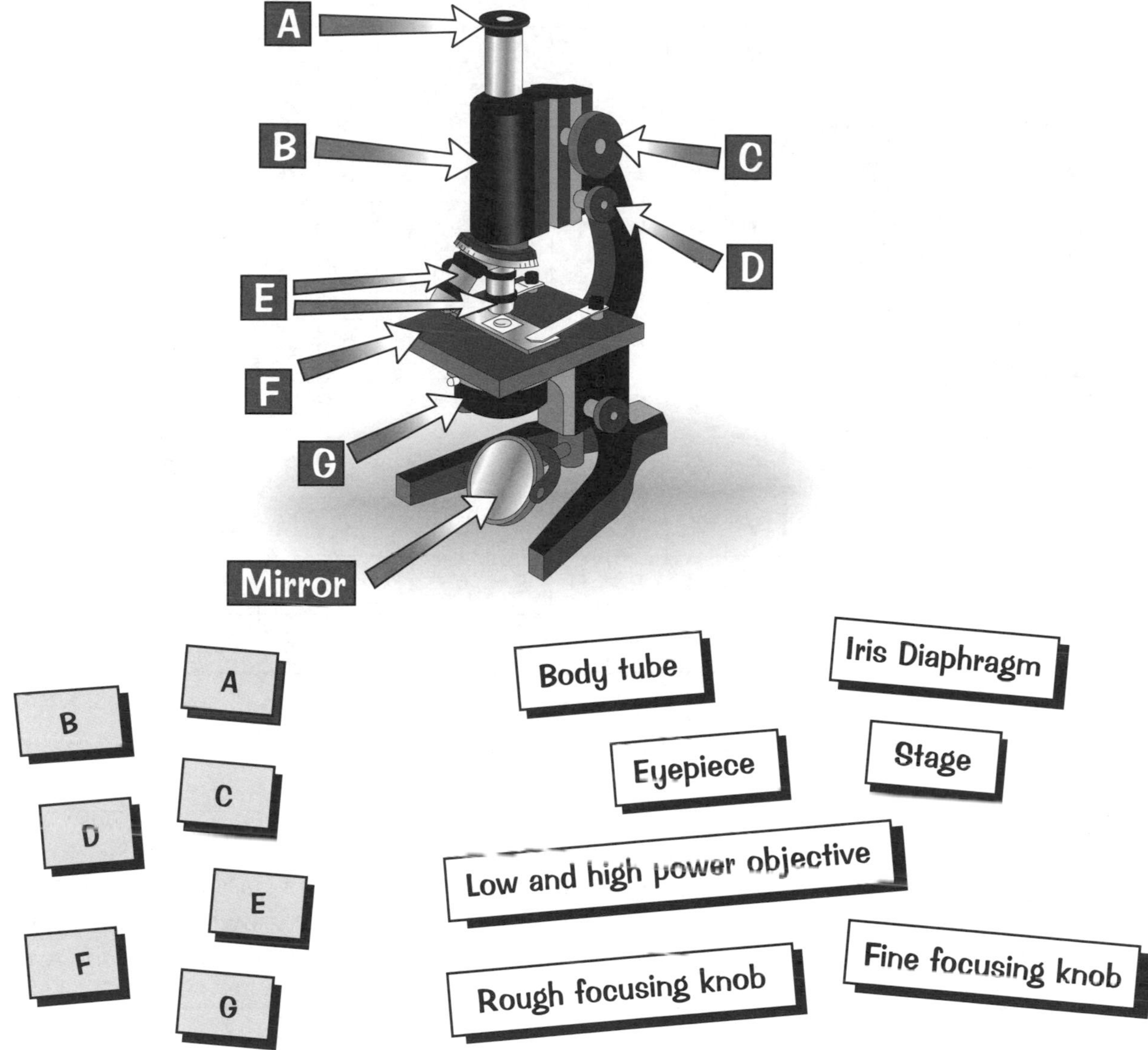

Q2 State what job each bit of the microscope does.

A ....

B ....

C ....

D ....

E ....

F ....

G ....

Questions on Life Processes

Q1 **a)** Complete the following *word search* using the words below.

Words:
reproduction
respiration
excretion
nutrition
movement
growth

N	O	I	T	C	U	D	O	R	P	E	R	G	N	C
W	U	V	P	G	Q	W	C	C	Q	N	C	O	C	D
V	E	L	J	I	L	B	K	G	P	E	I	M	N	U
T	D	K	T	H	E	B	Y	W	X	T	U	U	X	D
N	Z	O	C	L	Q	C	L	C	A	V	T	M	Z	H
E	S	C	L	J	X	M	R	R	T	R	M	K	F	V
M	F	C	J	I	G	E	I	W	I	Q	X	S	I	B
E	O	Y	Z	A	T	P	J	T	K	A	X	R	T	I
V	X	G	F	I	S	T	I	M	H	T	W	O	R	G
O	U	B	O	E	A	O	F	H	F	L	D	Y	T	I
M	S	N	R	I	N	N	P	E	I	K	J	P	B	H

b) Which *life process* is not in the word search above?

....

Q2 *Life Processes* are the things that both plants and animals do to be classified as being alive. Life Processes which are common to both plants and animals are shown in the table below. Match up the name of the *process* with its *meaning* by drawing a line between the two.

Life Process	Meaning
Growth	The ability to produce more of its kind
Nutrition	The ability to move all or part of the organism
Respiration	The increase in size and complexity of an organism
Excretion	The ability of an organism to respond
Movement	The ability to take in oxygen and give out carbon dioxide to make energy
Sensitivity	The removal of waste materials which the cells have made and may be poisonous
Reproduction	The ability to take in food or raw materials to support other life processes

Questions on Cells

Q1 The following diagrams show:

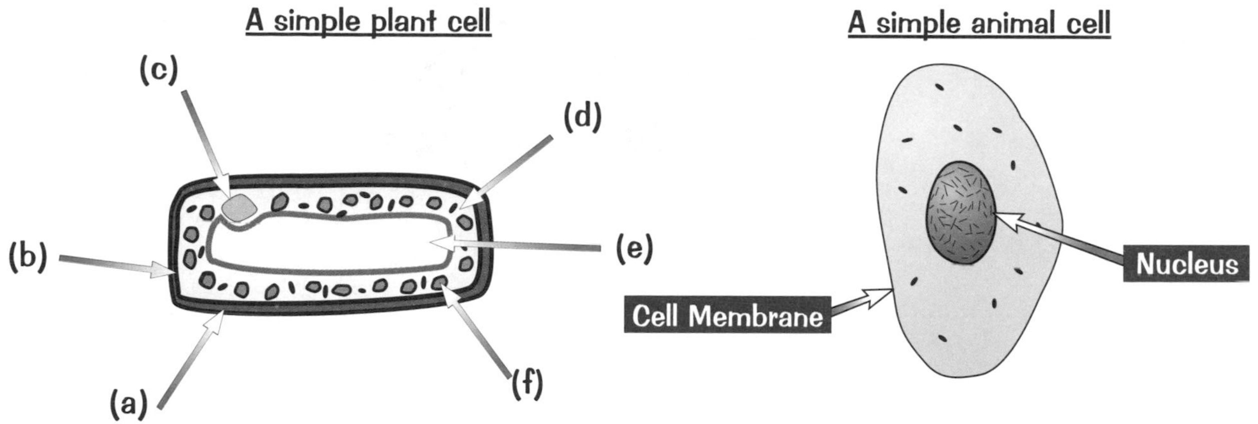

Name **a)** - **f)** in the above diagrams, then fill in the table below:

a) .... **d)** ....

b) .... **e)** ....

c) .... **f)** ....

Both cells have	Only plant cells have
1)	1)
2)	2)
3)	3)

Q2 Which part of both cells passes on information to new cells?

....

Q3 Which part of the plant cell absorbs the energy from the Sun and uses it in photosynthesis?

....

Q4 Complete the table below by placing a tick in the boxes where the cell parts are present in the cells listed.

	Cytoplasm	Nucleus	Cell wall	Vacuole
Leaf mesophyll				
Sperm				

Questions on Cells

Q5

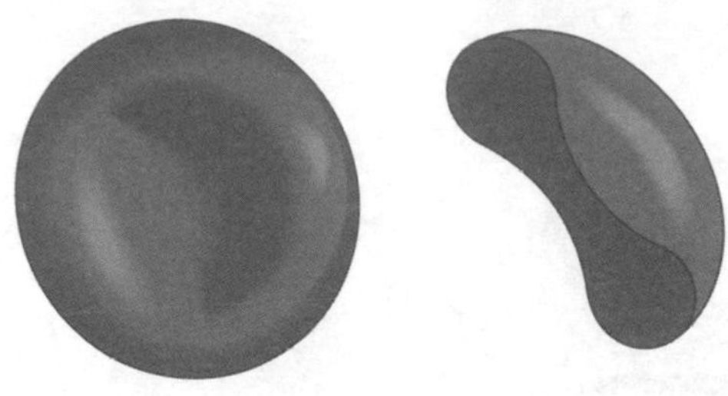

a) What is the name of this type of cell?

b) What job does it do?

c) Why is it shaped with a dimple inside?

Q6

a) This is a plant cell. What is it called?

b) What job does it do?

c) Where in the plant would you find this cell?

Q7 This is a nerve cell.

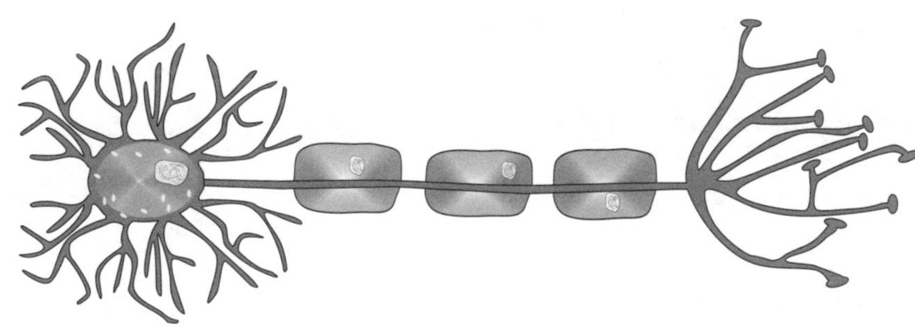

What is the function of the nerve cell?

Questions on Specialised Cells

Q1 Match each *cell structure* with the *cell function*.

Cell Structure	Function (job)
An epithelial cell with hairs on its outer membrane surface which waft or beat	Carries oxygen around the body
Contains the red chemical substance called haemoglobin	Carries information (impulses) round the body and joins other impulses
Is a cell made with an extension (the tail)	After a journey it joins with an egg cell
Has a long cell cytoplasm and has many branches at the end / ends	These cells are found in main body tubes like those near the lungs and help to trap germs and dust and clean the air

Q2 The drawings below (**a)** – **d)**) show a variety of animal and plant cells.

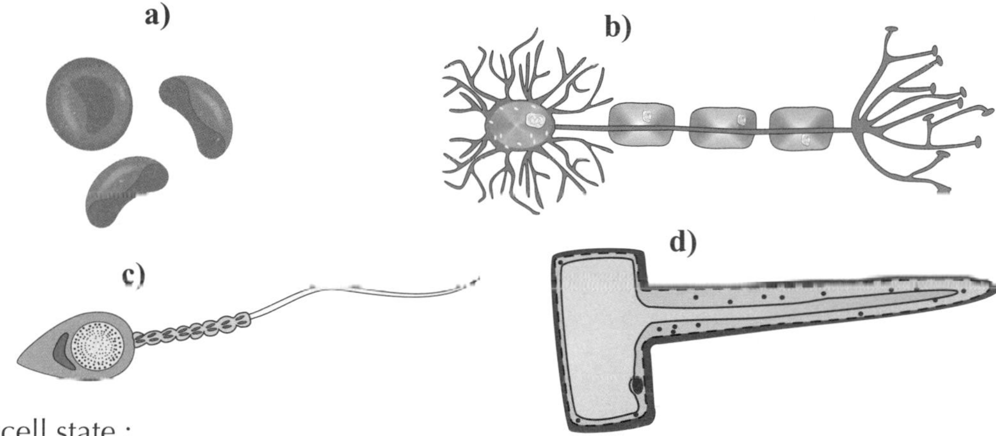

For each cell state :

i) the name (type) of cell.

ii) the life process(es) in which it is especially involved.

a) ....

....

b) ....

....

c) ....

....

d) ....

....

Questions on Plant Organs

Q1 From the diagram of the plant, name parts S to X and record their functions in the table below.

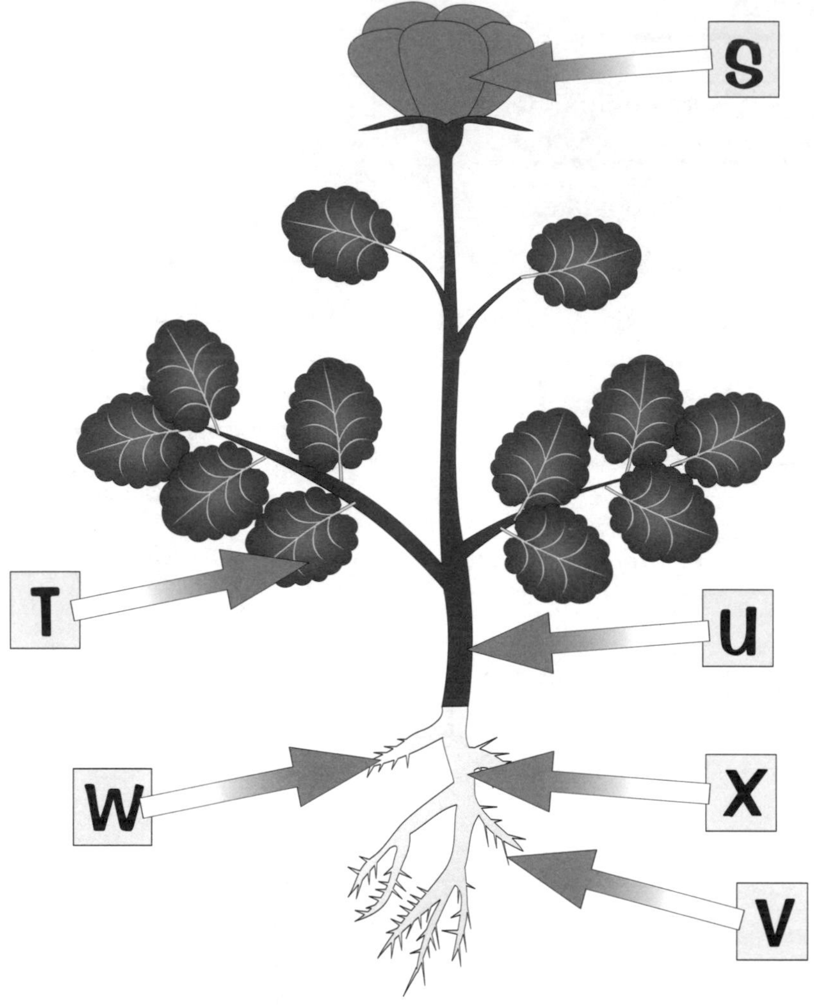

Letter	Name of Organ	Function
S		
T		
U		
V		
W		
X		

Questions on Plant Organs

Q2 Replace the letters in the chart below choosing from the following words to show the transport of water from the soil to the leaves:

shoot, bud, root, flower, root hair cell, stem

Soil → A → B → C → D

A .... **B** ....

C .... **D** ....

Q3 The following jumbled words are all parts of a plant.
Solve each word using the clues given.

a) *wrofle* — reproducing part of a plant ....

b) *plate* — part of a flower ....

c) *flea* — part which makes food ....

d) *mets* — support structure above the ground ....

e) *roto* — takes in water and minerals ....

Q4 **a)** What process takes place in the leaf of a plant?

....

b) Which two substances are used in this process?

....

c) Which substances are produced in this process?

....

d) Could this process take place in the dark? Explain your answer.

....

....

e) Write a word equation for this process.
(Words to use: **carbon** / **oxygen** / **sunlight** / **glucose** / **water** / **dioxide**)

__________ + __________ (__________) → __________ + __________

Questions on Human Organ Systems

Q1 Name the *systems* below which have some of their letters omitted. There are some *clues* to help you.

a) This is the system which includes the *heart*, *blood* and *vessels*

c _ _ c u l _ t _ _ y.

b) This is the system which involves the *lungs* and *airways*

_ _ _ p i _ _ t _ _ _ .

c) This is the system which involves the *stomach* and the *intestine*

d _ _ e _ _ i _ _.

d) This is the system for producing offspring

_ _ p r _ _ u _ _ i v _.

Q2 Complete the table below by naming the organs **a)** to **e)** and for each one state in which system they are included.

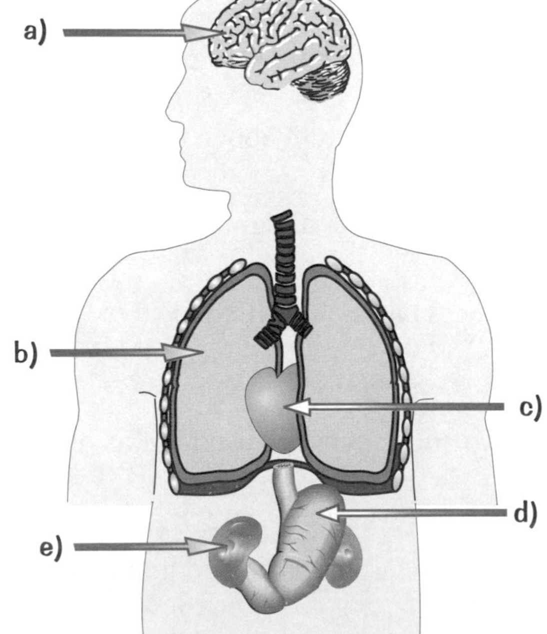

Letter	Organ	System
a		
b		
c		
d		
e		

Questions on Human Organ Systems

Q3 Match the *organ* in Box A with the *function* (job) in Box B by writing the correct letter next to the numbers listed below. (E.g. 1) t) or 2) u)).

1) ....
2) ....
3) ....
4) ....
5) ....
6) ....

A	B
1) lungs	p) to provide information about the environment
2) brain	q) to take oxygen in/to remove carbon dioxide from the body
3) stomach	r) to cause movement
4) kidneys	s) to control and organise the body's activities
5) muscles	t) to digest (break down) food
6) sense organs (eyes, nose, etc.)	u) to purify the blood and remove waste products

Q4 **a)** What do we call a part of the body with a special function?

....

b) What do we call a group of organs which work together to carry out a particular function?

....

Q5 Look at the four diagrams of *human body systems* and state the name of each system (there are two in diagram D).

A) ....

B) ....

C) ....

D) a) ....

b) ....

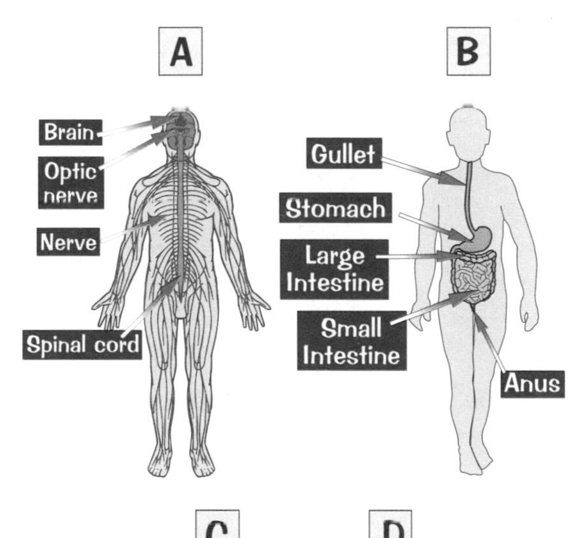

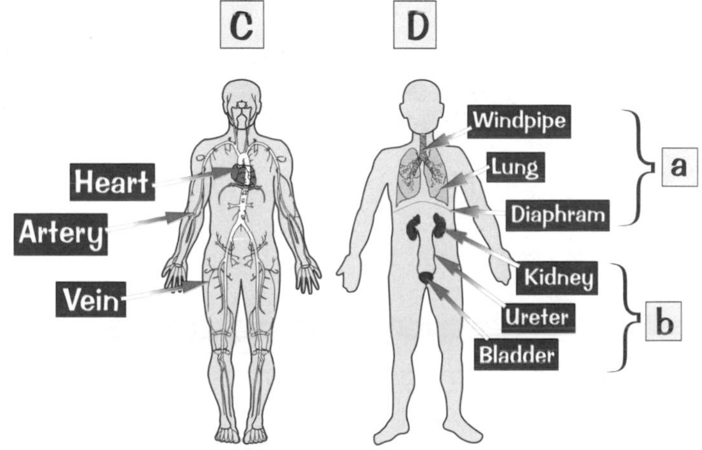

Questions on Nutrition

Q1 **a)** Complete the table which shows the *function* (job) of each food group.

Carbohydrates		Fats		
	Used for growth and repair		Usually needed in small amounts to help make certain parts of the body	A large group of substances needed in small amounts to prevent many diseases like scurvy

b) What does the word '*nutrition*' mean?

....

....

c) Water is not a food but without it a person would die within several days.
Even though water cannot be stored in the body it must be taken in and lost every day.
State what *percentage* of the body is water.

....

d) What is a *deficiency disease*?

....

....

e) What problem would occur if you didn't have enough fresh fruit and vegetables in your diet?

....

....

Q2 Peter is going on a 50 mile sponsored walk and he knows it is going to take him a long time. He really likes sausages for his tea so he thinks it would be a good idea to take some to give him lots of *energy*. He puts all the following food on the table ready to pack.

a) Why should he not take the sausages for energy on his walk?

....

....

b) Which *main ingredient* is missing from his pack?

....

Questions on Nutrition

Q3 Study the three pie charts showing the food groups of breakfast cereals.

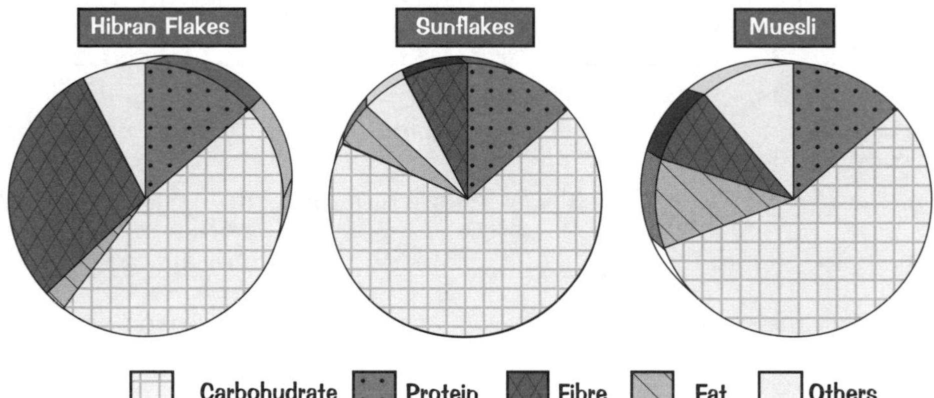

a) Which food group is the largest in all 3 cereals?

....

b) Which cereal has the largest fibre content?

....

c) Why do we need fibre in our daily diet?

....

....

d) A *balanced diet* is good. Does this mean eating equal amounts of all food groups? Explain your answer.

....

....

Q4 **a)** Cells in our bodies use the food we eat in the process of respiration to give us energy. The energy is used in many ways. State two of them.

....

b) Which of the following people of the same age needs the *most* energy and why:
a *computer operator*, a *builder*, a *bus driver* or a *teacher?*

....

....

c) Fill in the sentence by choosing appropriate words from the list below.

respiration	growth	food	nuclear power station
fuel	nutrition	substance	repair

Food is used as a ____________ for the process of ____________ and as a raw material for ____________ and ____________ .

Questions on Digestion

Q1 Complete the introductory sentences below with words from the word list (some words will be left over).

small, insoluble, egestion, small intestine, small, large intestine, soluble, large colon, digestion, nerves, bloodstream, enzymes, large
The process of __________ is the breakdown of food into __________ substances, and the passage into the __________. The food molecules are too __________ to pass through the walls of the __________ and need to be broken down by special chemicals called __________.

Q2 **a)** Use the diagram of the *digestive system* to fill in the chart showing the names and functions of A to F.

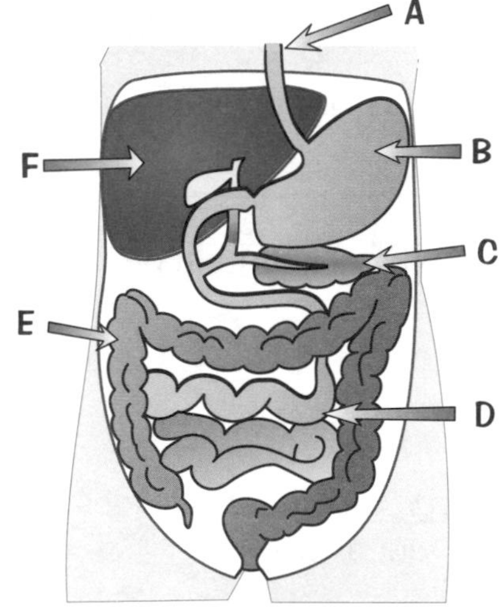

Letter	Name	Function
A		
B		
C		
D		
E		
F		

b) Match each *digestive part* to the *enzymes* it produces by drawing a line between the two.

Digestive Part	Enzyme(s) produced
mouth	Proteases in acid, which digests protein
stomach	Salivary amylase
pancreas	Protease, carbohydrase and lipase

Questions on Digestion

Q3 The pupils in Priesthorp High School performed an experiment to try to show why *digestion* must take place. They set up the experiment as below using *visking tubing*, which is *semi-permeable* and achieved the set of results given. Use the results to answer the questions.

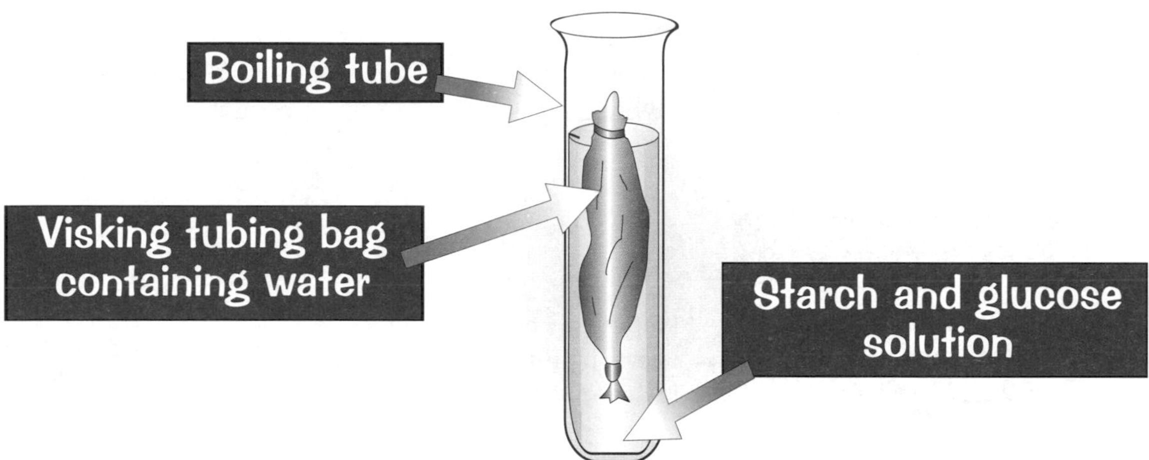

Water inside visking tubing	Starch present	Glucose present
At start	no	no
After 25 mins	no	yes

a) Can starch *pass through* the visking tubing? Explain your answer.

....

....

....

b) Explain why glucose could pass through the visking tubing.

....

....

....

c) What *part of our body* acts like the visking tubing?

....

d) In the experiment which substance in the body does the water represent?

....

e) What is the starch and glucose mixture supposed to represent?

....

Questions on Digestion

Q4 Find the missing words in the diagrams, which show *enzyme action* on large molecules.

Digestion of Carbohydates

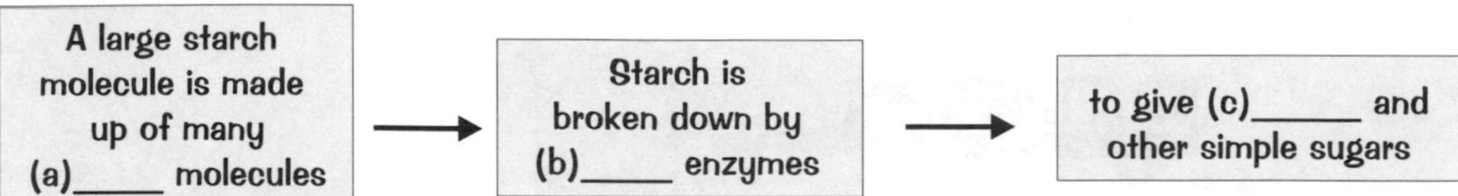
A large starch molecule is made up of many (a)_____ molecules
Starch is broken down by (b)_____ enzymes
to give (c)_____ and other simple sugars

Digestion of Proteins

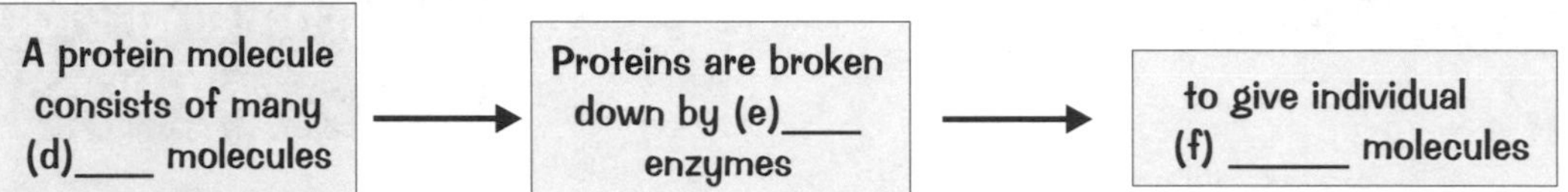
A protein molecule consists of many (d)____ molecules
Proteins are broken down by (e)____ enzymes
to give individual (f) _____ molecules

Digestion of Fats

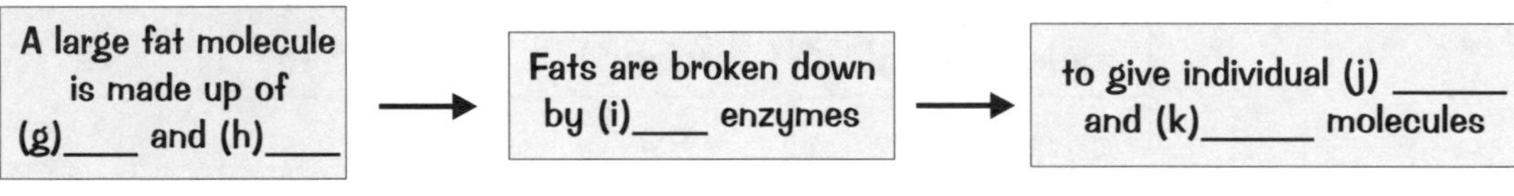
A large fat molecule is made up of (g)____ and (h)____
Fats are broken down by (i)____ enzymes
to give individual (j) _____ and (k)_____ molecules

(a) .... **(g)** ....

(b) .... **(h)** ....

(c) .... **(i)** ....

(d) .... **(j)** ....

(e) .... **(k)** ....

(f) ....

Q5 Once the food has been broken down into smaller soluble molecules it needs to be *absorbed* from the alimentary canal into the blood.

a) In which *structure* does this process of absorption take place?

....

b) Name the special structures we find in 'a)' that aid absorption.

....

c) State two ways in which the structures named in 'b)' are adapted for their job.

....

....

Questions on Absorption and the Kidneys

Q1 Where do the particles of digested food go?

....

Q2 What is the name of the process which takes digested food through the small intestine wall?

....

Q3 State three reasons why *villi* are ideal for absorption.

....

....

....

Q4 **a)** Circle the word which means the removal of *undigested food*.

excretion , *renal* , *egestion* , *contraction* , *filtered*.

b) Which word is the organ from which waste undigested materials leave the body?

....

c) Name an organ which excretes **i)** *carbon dioxide* and **ii)** *water*.

i) ....

ii) ....

Q5 Some of the foods are *stored* in your body after absorption. Give the names of two digested food substances, state where they're stored and what they're used for.

1) ....

....

2) ....

....

Q6 When the kidneys work they *absorb* all the useful and all the waste products, filter out the waste and put the useful products back into the blood.

a) State two *useful substances* which the kidneys might absorb again.

....

....

b) Give the name of a *waste substance* from the blood which the kidneys get rid of.

....

Questions on the Circulatory System

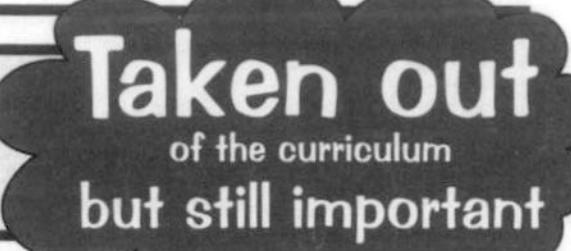

Q1 Complete the introduction by filling in the gaps, using the words in the box.

oxygen	nutrients	grow	heart	transport	waste

Blood is the __________ system of the body. It carries __________ and __________ to all parts of the body. It is pumped round the body by the __________ . It also takes away __________ products.

Q2 a) The following diagrams show components of the *blood*.
Complete the table below by naming them and giving the function of each.

A 

B 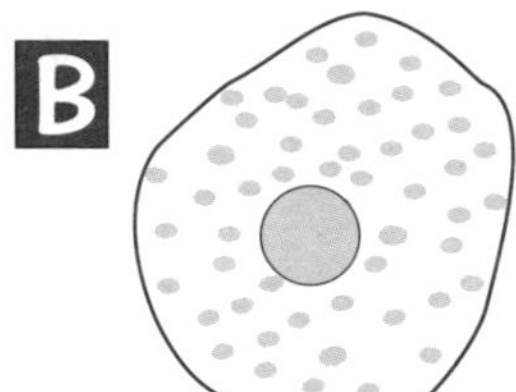

C 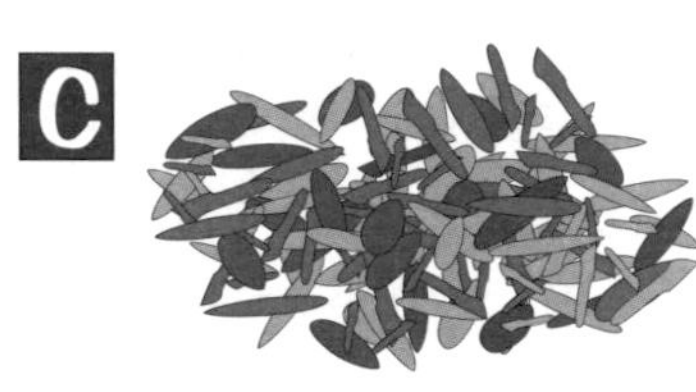

Letter	Name	Function
A		
B		
C		

b) Explain two ways in which *white blood cells* work.

....

....

....

....

c) Other than these three types of cells, what makes up the blood?

....

....

Questions on the Circulatory System

Taken out of the curriculum but still important

Q3 Draw in *lines* to match the statements on the left with the information on the right.

Plasma	Fight against disease occurring
Capillaries	Can be produced by a certain type of blood cell
Red blood cells	Contain haemoglobin
White blood cells	Help the blood to clot and so prevents invaders
Antibodies	Narrow blood tubes
Platelets	The body's blood pump
Heart	The liquid portion of the blood

Q4 Which cells in the blood do not have a *nucleus*?

....

Q5 What is the name of the pigment which makes red blood cells red?

....

Q6 Look at the three blood vessels below. For each one, name the vessel and explain its features.

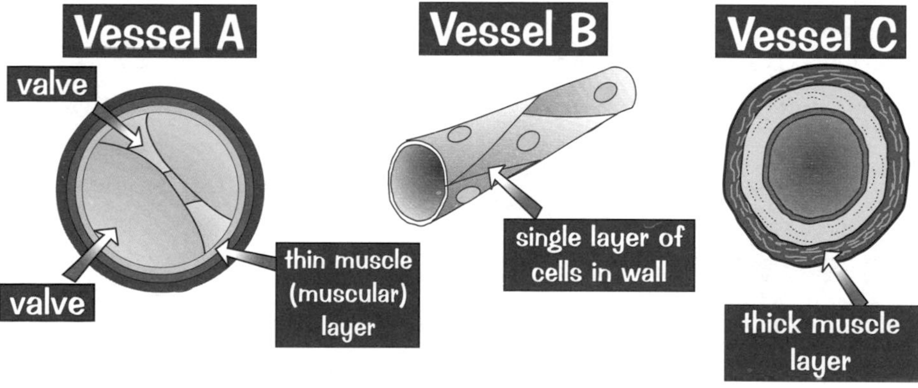

Vessel A ....

....

Vessel B ....

....

Vessel C ....

....

Questions on the Circulatory System

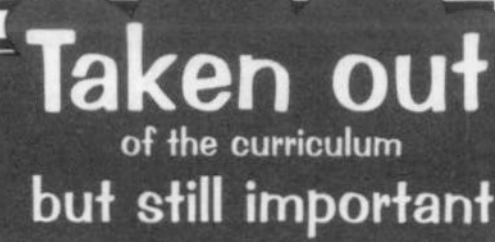

Q7 **a)** Which side of your heart (when facing the front), left or right, contains deoxygenated blood (blood without oxygen)?

....

b) Which side, left or right, puts the most pressure on the blood?

....

Q8 Look at the diagram to the right.

a) Starting at B place the letters that label it in order to show the *complete flow* of blood into and out of the heart.

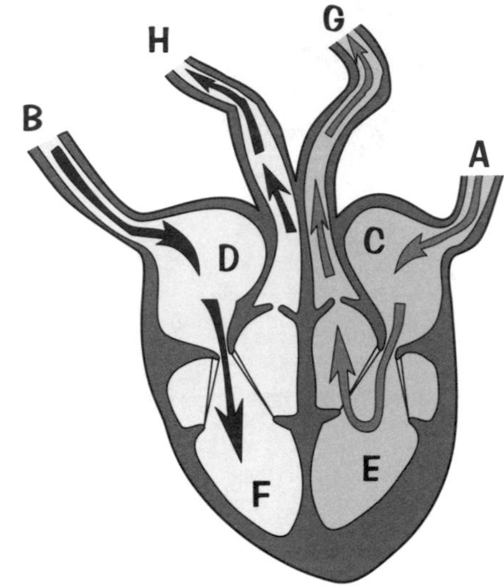

B → __ → __ → __ → __ → __ → __ → __

b) Label four valves on the diagram of the heart.

c) Why are valves needed?

....

d) Which blood vessels, *arteries* or *veins*, carry blood away from the heart?

....

e) Complete the following sentences using the letters from the heart diagram above.

.... is the part of the heart where the deoxygenated blood comes first.

.... is the main artery in the body and carries blood with oxygen away from the heart.

.... is the left top part of the heart.

.... is the blood vessel which carries blood with carbon dioxide from the heart to the lungs to pick up oxygen and remove the carbon dioxide.

.... is the blood vessel which brings back blood with oxygen from the lungs to the heart.

.... is the part of the heart with the thickest walls to put the blood under the most pressure.

.... is the blood vessel which carries blood from the tissues to the heart.

Questions on the Skeleton, Joints and Muscles

Q1 Fill in the missing words. Some letters have already been put in to help you.

The b _ _ _ _ in your skeleton protect many important o _ _ _ _ _ in your body.

Bones also allow m _ _ _ _ _ _ _ to occur at joints and they also s _ _ _ _ _ t

the entire body.

Q2 **a)** Using the diagram below place the parts in the correct order to form a figure of a skeleton.

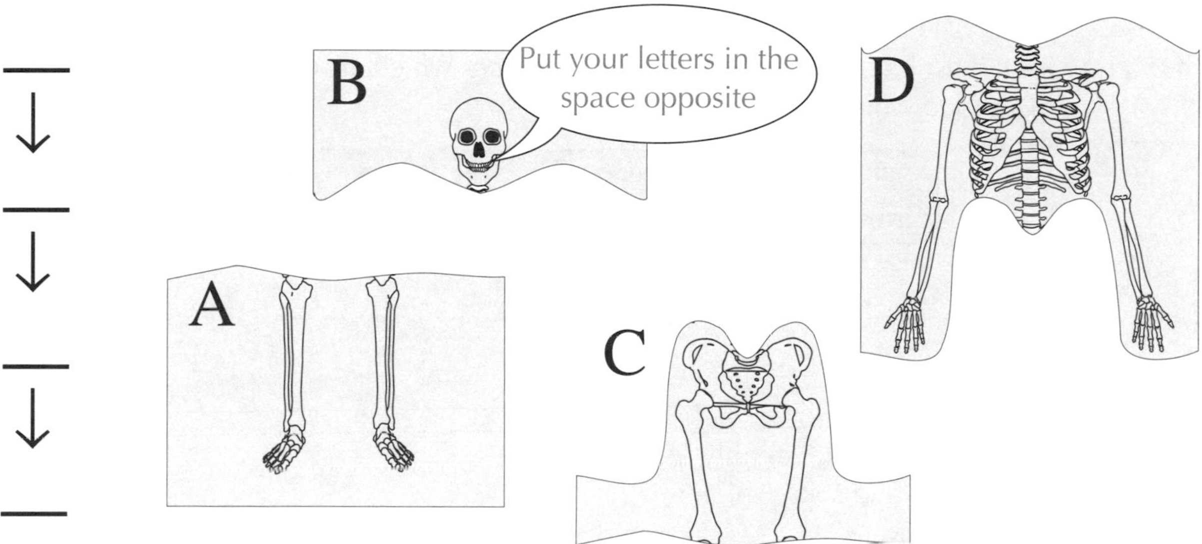

b) From the skeleton diagram complete the following table of *names* and *functions*.

Clue	Name	Function
1) The main head bone.		
2) The bones which are involved when we breathe.		
3) The column at the back of the body.		
4) The upper arm bone that is not funny if you lift things in the wrong way.		
5) There's a pair of them, and they have long bones and large joints.		

Questions on the Skeleton, Joints and Muscles

Q3 **a)** Why is it important that bones are **i)** *strong* and **ii)** *light*?

i) ....

....

ii) ....

....

b) Why are two pairs of ribs called the *floating ribs*?

....

Q4 **a)** From the list below name the *pair of substances* which are needed for healthy bones, and name a food which contains both.

calcium and vitamin C	vitamin D and calcium
iron and vitamin D	vitamin C and iron

....

b) The two diagrams show a *male* and *female* pelvis. Look carefully at the two diagrams and state which is which and why.

A

B

....

....

....

....

Q5 Complete this paragraph using the words in the box.

fluid	cartilage	joint	ligaments

Wherever bones meet a ____________ is formed. Bones are held together by strong fibres called ____________. The bones are prevented from rubbing on each other and wearing away by smooth ____________ and there is also a ____________ which fills the joint.

Questions on the Skeleton, Joints and Muscles

Q6 Look at the *knee joint* diagram opposite and answer the questions which follow it.

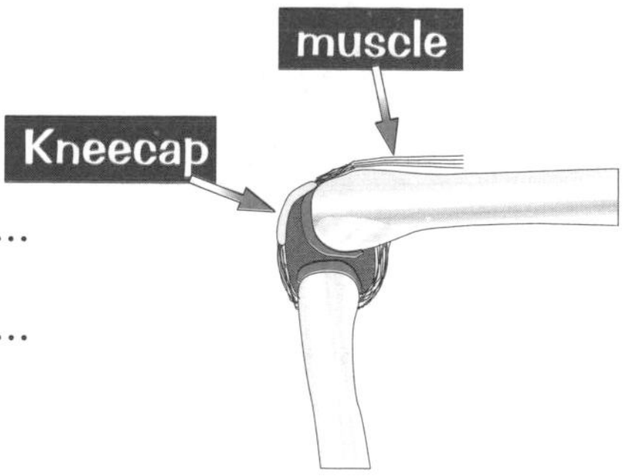

a) The knee joint is a 'freely movable' joint.
Name **i)** a slightly movable joint, **ii)** an immovable joint

i) ....

ii) ....

b) Which part of the diagram represents the *cartilage?*

....

c) Why is it necessary that cartilage is present in all moving joints?

....

....

d) Explain what might be the cause of a rugby player finding it painful to bend over in scrums.

....

....

Q7 **a)** Look at the diagram and name the labelled parts which show the arm as a hinge joint.
Use the words in the box below to help you.

Radius	Biceps muscle	Triceps muscle
Ulna	Humerus	Elbow

A ....

B ....

C ....

D ....

E ....

F ....

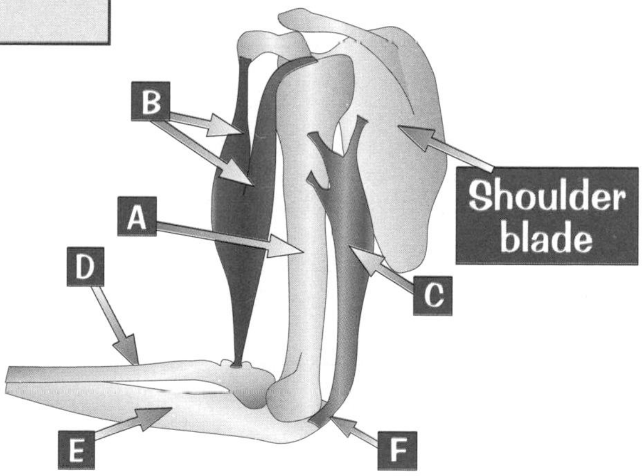

b) A *flexor muscle* bends a joint; which is the flexor muscle in the elbow joint?

....

c) An *extensor muscle* straightens a joint; give the name of one in the elbow joint.

....

d) Name the structures which join **(A)** and **(B)** and all muscles to the bone.

....

Questions on Growing Up

Q1 Fill in the spaces from the word list below to show how humans *develop*.

sex organs	ovaries	sperm	puberty	reproduce
eggs	testes	sexual	genetic	fertilisation

Children, like all young animals cannot ______________ because their ______________ have not fully developed. In order to produce offspring the female ______________ must produce ______________ and the male ______________ must produce ______________. The process of reproduction in humans is called ______________ reproduction where the ______________ material in the male sex cells combines with that in the female sex cells when ______________ occurs. The stage of life when human sex organs begin to develop is called______________.

Q2 During this important stage of life many physical and emotional changes occur which are controlled by *hormones* carried in the blood.

a) Look carefully at the statements below. In each box put either an **M**, **F** or **B** to show whether the statement applies to males, females or both.

- **A)** The testes start to make sperm. ☐
- **B)** The male sex hormone is made. ☐
- **C)** Hair grows around the sex organs. ☐
- **D)** The female sex hormone is made. ☐
- **E)** A small amount of blood is lost every month when the lining of the uterus breaks down. This is known as a period. ☐
- **F)** The body becomes more muscular and the shoulders broaden. ☐
- **G)** Your emotions change a lot. ☐
- **H)** Erections happen during this time. ☐
- **I)** You often feel and think differently. ☐
- **J)** The hips become rounder. ☐
- **K)** The breasts develop. ☐
- **L)** An egg is released once a month. ☐
- **M)** The ovaries produce eggs. ☐
- **N)** Glands make hormones to start the body changes. ☐
- **O)** Hair grows under the armpits. ☐
- **P)** The sex organs begin to grow. ☐

b) What is the name of the period of life between puberty and adulthood?

....

....

Questions on Growing Up

Q3 The following are very important key words regarding *Growth and Changing*.
Explain the meaning of each word below.

puberty

....

....

....

ovaries

....

testes

....

sex hormones

....

....

adulthood

....

....

....

Q4 Find the following seven words in the word search connected with this section on Growing Up.

Sex hormones	Ovaries	Testes
Physical	Puberty	Adulthood	Adolescence

S	E	N	O	M	R	O	H	X	E	S
T	H	I	S	I	S	H	A	R	D	T
X	A	D	U	L	T	H	O	O	D	Y
J	B	A	D	C	E	F	V	G	U	H
J	P	H	Y	S	I	C	A	L	K	L
T	M	I	N	P	O	Q	R	S	T	U
V	E	W	E	X	Y	Z	I	A	C	E
B	A	S	C	P	U	B	E	R	T	Y
F	I	B	T	G	I	B	S	H	I	P
J	A	B	K	E	G	L	I	M	B	S
E	C	N	E	C	S	E	L	O	D	A

Questions on the Menstrual Cycle

Q1 The *menstrual cycle* concerns egg release which occurs every month in females. In the following set of sentences fill in the missing words from the box below.

menstrual cycle	uterus	fertilised	bacteria
month	ovary	blood	menstruation

The egg cell is released normally from an ____________ once a ____________. Each time an egg cell is released the ____________ gets ready to grow a baby. A thick lining full of ____________ vessels slowly develops. If the egg is ____________ it passes into the uterus and becomes attached to it. The uterus grows a fresh new lining every time an egg is released because the environment in the uterus provides excellent conditions for ____________ to grow and so it must be replaced. If the egg is not fertilised the breakdown of the uterus lining occurs and this is called ________________. The whole sequence of making a new uterus lining and an egg is called the __________________.

Q2 Match each term on the left with the explanation on the right.

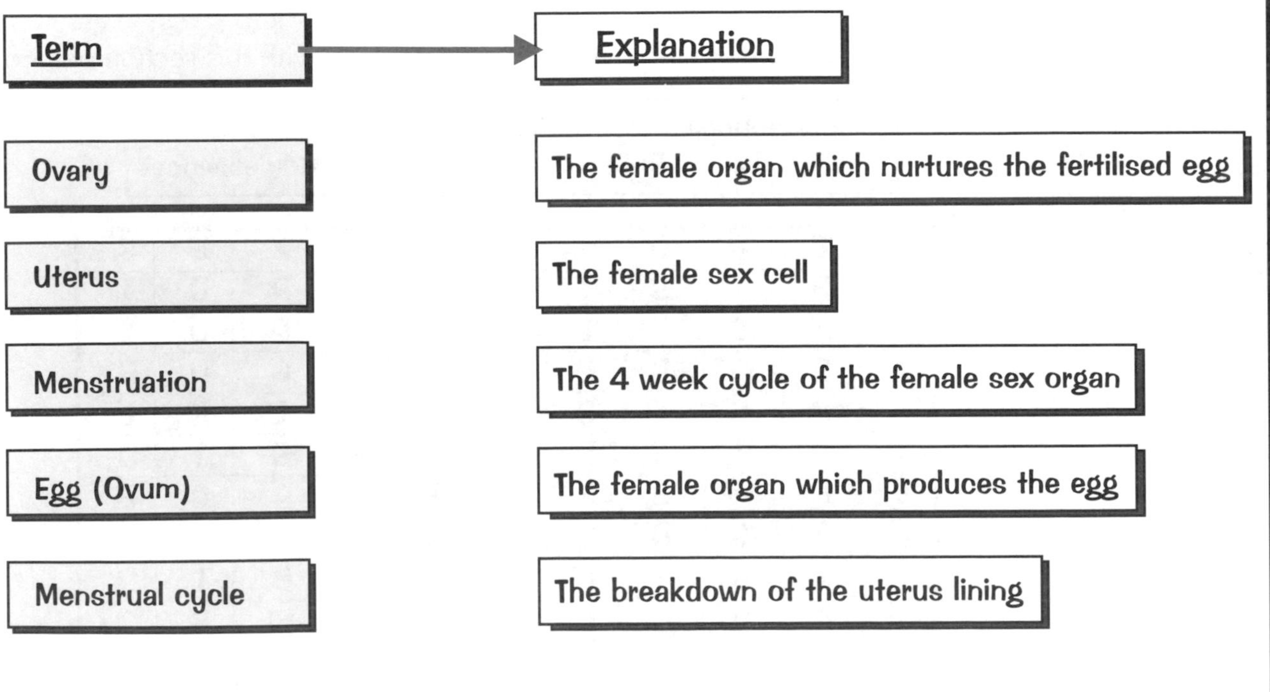

Term
Explanation
Ovary
Uterus
Menstruation
Egg (Ovum)
Menstrual cycle
The female organ which nurtures the fertilised egg
The female sex cell
The 4 week cycle of the female sex organ
The female organ which produces the egg
The breakdown of the uterus lining

Questions on the Menstrual Cycle

Q3 Study the following diagrams showing the menstrual cycle.

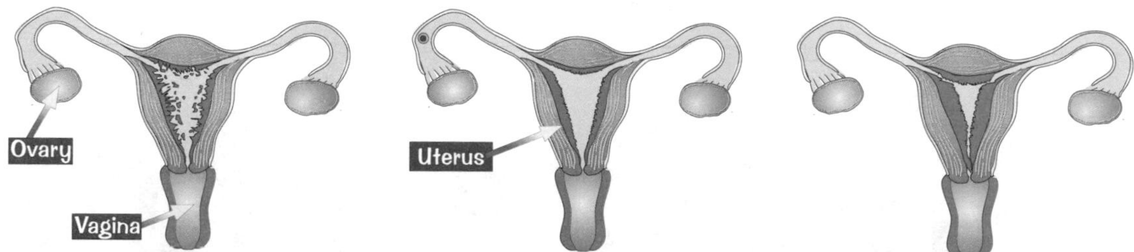

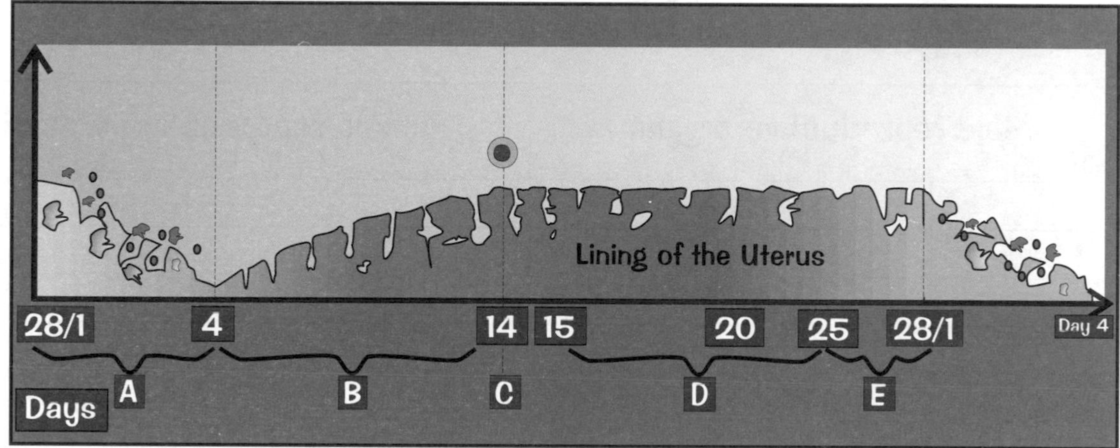

Key
= blood and lining
= egg released from ovary

For each sentence below, put the corresponding letter from the diagram in the box.

1) The lining of the *uterus* is very thick and full of blood. ☐
2) The lining of the uterus builds up. ☐
3) The egg is released from the *ovary*. ☐
4) The egg is travelling down the *oviduct* to be fertilised. ☐
5) The thick lining of the uterus breaks down and blood flows out (menstruation). ☐

Q4 **a)** Why does the lining of the uterus need to become thick?

....

....

b) How long does it take the uterus lining to build up again after menstruation?

....

c) At which point in the menstrual cycle is the egg released?

....

Questions on Having a Baby

Q1 In order to have a baby the male and female *sex cell nuclei* with *genetic information* must join. You must understand the male and female reproductive organs and what they do.

a) Complete the table below:

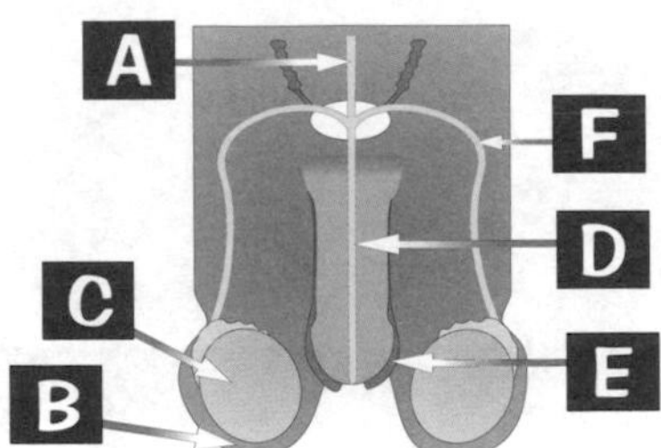

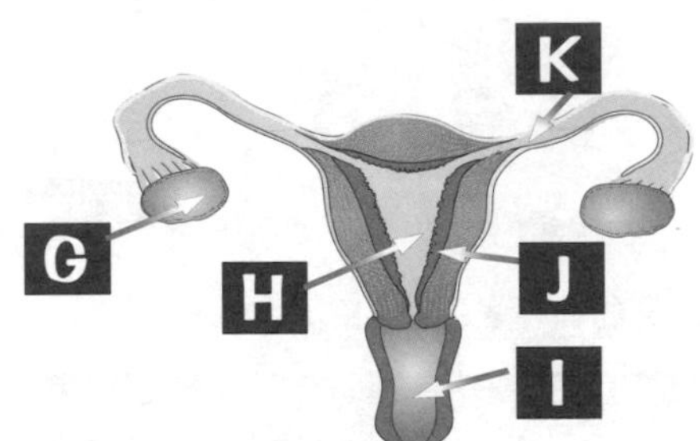

Male reproductive organs		Female reproductive organs	
	Name		Name
A		G	
B		H	
C		I	
D		J	
E		K	
F			

b) Following the release of sperm into the vagina during intercourse, what must happen for an egg to be fertilised?

....

....

c) Where is the female egg fertilised?

....

d) What type of *genetic information* does a new baby contain?

....

....

Q2 **a)** Which process places millions of sperm in the female?

....

b) What happens to all the other sperm when a sperm enters the egg?

....

....

c) Where does the genetic information in a fertilised egg come from?

....

....

Questions on Having a Baby

Q3 **a)** Once the egg is fertilised and it implants itself in the uterus lining, it must have room to grow. There are 3 other things that it requires. Name these.

....

b) Place the following diagrams in the correct order to show the *development* of a *fertilised egg*.

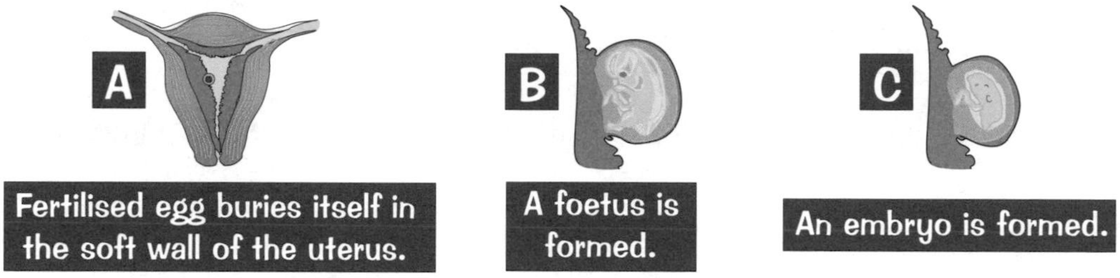

A — Fertilised egg buries itself in the soft wall of the uterus.

B — A foetus is formed.

C — An embryo is formed.

__ → __ → __

c) State the first structure that the fertilised egg makes.

....

d) What is the word which describes a female carrying an embryo? ....

e) Is it true that periods occur as normal after an egg is fertilised? Explain your answer.

....

....

Q4 The diagram to the right shows a *foetus* developing in a uterus. Name the labelled parts on the diagram from the word list.

Word list :cervix, amnion, uterus, placenta, vagina, amniotic fluid, umbilical cord.

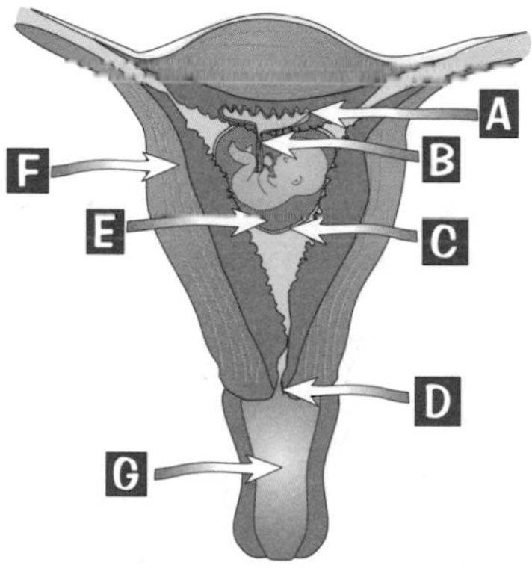

A ....

B ....

C ....

D ....

E ....

F ....

G ....

Q5 The diagram to the right shows the *blood supply relationship* between the mother's blood and that of the foetus.

Is it true that the mother's blood mixes with the foetus's blood? If not, state what does happen?

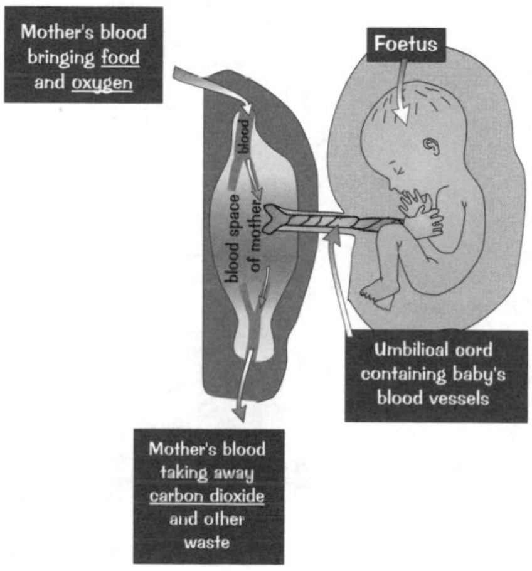

....

....

Mother's blood bringing food and oxygen

Foetus

blood space of mother's blood

Umbilical cord containing baby's blood vessels

Mother's blood taking away carbon dioxide and other waste

Questions on Having a Baby

Q6 **a)** How many months after fertilisation is the birth of the baby?

....

b) Does the diagram in Q4 show the foetus ready for birth? If not, why?

....

c) What must be cut to separate the baby from the mother after it is born?

....

....

....

d) What is left inside the mother after delivery? What happens to it?

....

....

Q7 Complete the word search by finding the following *key words:*

pregnancy, gestation, reproduction, intercourse, menstruation, fertilisation, oviduct, placenta, embryo, uterus, ovum, sperm, penis, vagina.

a	i	r	g	o	v	a	g	i	n	a	a	u	t	t	x	o	g
i	n	d	e	x	b	c	d	e	f	o	g	h	t	i	j	v	k
f	t	l	m	p	n	o	p	q	r	s	v	t	u	e	v	u	w
e	e	x	y	m	r	x	a	b	c	d	e	i	f	g	r	m	h
r	r	i	j	e	k	o	l	m	n	o	p	q	d	r	s	u	t
t	c	u	g	n	v	w	d	x	y	z	a	b	c	u	d	e	s
i	o	f	e	s	g	h	p	u	i	j	k	l	m	n	c	o	p
l	u	q	s	t	e	r	r	s	c	t	u	v	s	w	x	t	y
i	r	z	t	r	m	a	e	b	c	t	d	e	f	p	g	h	i
s	s	j	a	u	b	k	g	p	e	n	i	s	l	m	e	n	o
a	e	p	t	a	r	q	n	r	s	t	u	o	v	w	x	r	y
t	z	a	i	t	y	b	a	c	d	e	f	g	n	h	i	j	m
i	k	l	o	i	o	m	n	o	p	q	r	s	t	u	v	w	x
o	y	z	n	o	a	b	c	c	d	p	l	a	c	e	n	t	a
n	e	f	g	n	h	i	y	j	k	l	m	n	o	p	q	r	s

Questions on Breathing

The *respiratory system* is the name given to the system made up from the body's breathing organs. Oxygen is taken in from the air and carbon dioxide and water vapour breathed out.

Q1 In the diagram below label the *breathing organs* by placing the correct letters in the table opposite the name.

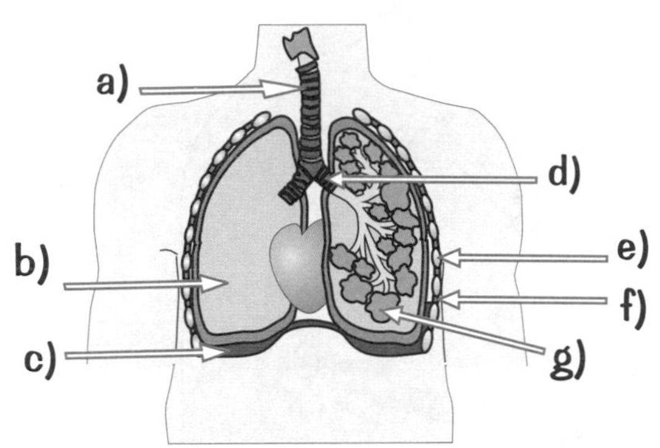

Name	Letter
Lung	
Windpipe (trachea)	
Bronchus (plural: bronchi)	
Alveoli	
Diaphragm	
Ribs	
Rib muscles (intercostal muscles)	

Q2 Use the following words to fill in the missing spaces:

blood lungs breathing oxygen air carbon dioxide energy

The ____________ we need to stay alive comes from the ____________.
The waste gas, ________________________ , and water vapour go out of our body. This total process is called ____________.
The important gas we take in enters our ____________ and is used with sugar in the cells to release ____________.

Q3 Match up the sentences on the left with those on the right to show how air is brought in and out of the lungs in the process of breathing. (One has been done for you)

Rib muscles contract	Rib cage moves downwards and inwards
Diaphragm contracts	Diaphragm becomes dome-shaped i.e. moves upwards
More space is formed in the chest	Air is forced out from the chest space
Rib muscles relax	Rib cage moves upwards and outwards
Diaphragm relaxes	Diaphragm becomes flatter
Less space is left in the chest	Air enters to fill the extra room

Questions on Breathing

Q4 A piece of apparatus was set up as shown in the diagram. The idea was to show how breathing works. You get to explain how it works by answering the questions below.

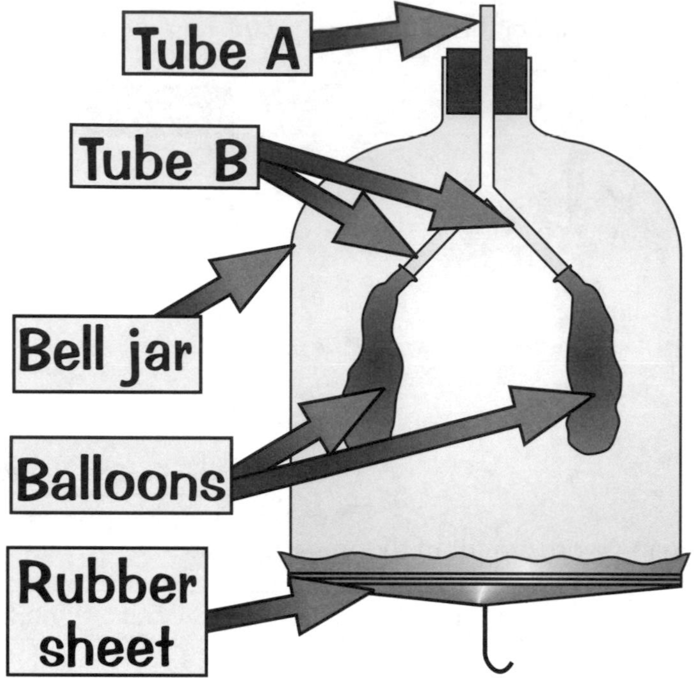

a) Which *organ* in the body do the balloons represent?

....

b) Which main tube (A) brings air into and out of the body?

....

c) What is the name of the tubes (B) which take air in and out of the lungs?

....

d) Which *two muscles* control breathing?

....

e) Name the muscle which the *rubber sheet* represents.

....

f) What structure in the body does the bell jar represent?

....

g) What happens to the balloons when the rubber sheet is pulled downwards?

....

....

h) What part of the breathing process is this?

....

Questions on Breathing

Q5 The diagram shows the end of the small tubes — the *bronchioles* in the lungs

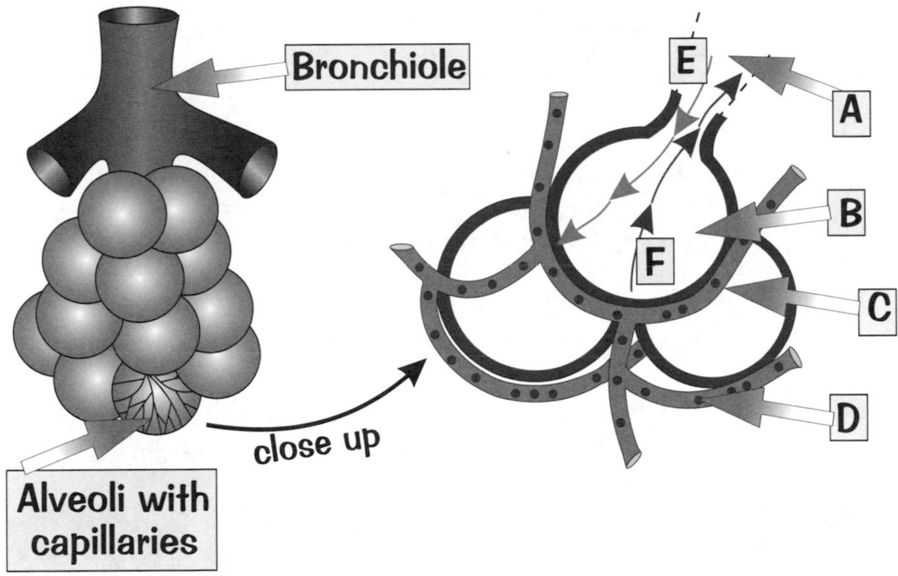

a) What is the name of the small tube (A)?

....

b) The small tube (A) ends in a tiny sac. What is the tiny sac (B) called?

....

c) The lung has to exchange the two gases *carbon dioxide* and *oxygen* from the cells. Name the part of the body (C) in which the exchange occurs.

....

d) There are certain cells (D) in blood which are very important in this exchange process. State what they are called.

....

e) Why does the lung have many of these air sacs?

....

....

....

f) What do the *alveoli* and *blood capillaries* have in common, and why?

....

....

....

g) Name gases (E) and (F) which enter and leave the lungs.

....

Questions on Smoking

Q1 Write the introduction to this section yourself by placing the words from the word list into the paragraph below:

windpipe	lungs	air	cilia	mucus	swallowed	clean

The way in which we make sure we get good ____________ into our ______________ is to ____________ it first. To do this our ____________ has special cells which produce sticky ___________ which trap dust. There are also tiny hairs called ____________ to take the mixture back to the throat where it can be ____________.

Q2 The following diagram shows the *windpipe* and the parts which are present to clean the air in a *healthy* person. Match each boxed fact to the correct letter in the diagram.

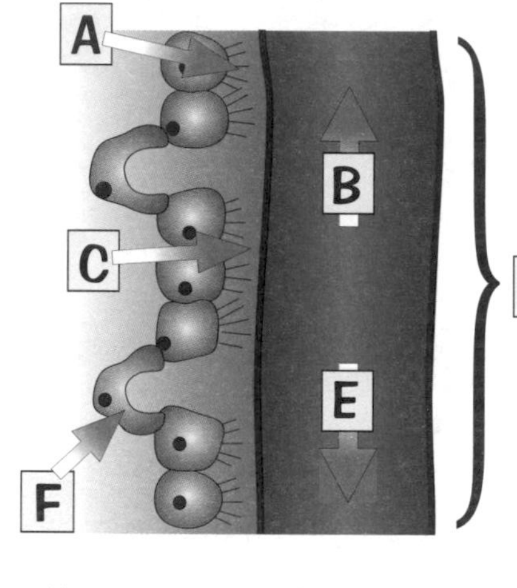

1) Thin layer of sticky mucus

2) Movement of mucus and dirt up to the throat

3) Cells with cilia move the mucus

4) Goblet cell to make mucus

5) Movement of clean air down to the lungs

6) The windpipe

1) .... 2) .... 3) .... 4) .... 5) .... 6) ....

Q3 The following diagram shows the windpipe of a *smoker*.

a) State two things which are different from those in a healthy person.

....

....

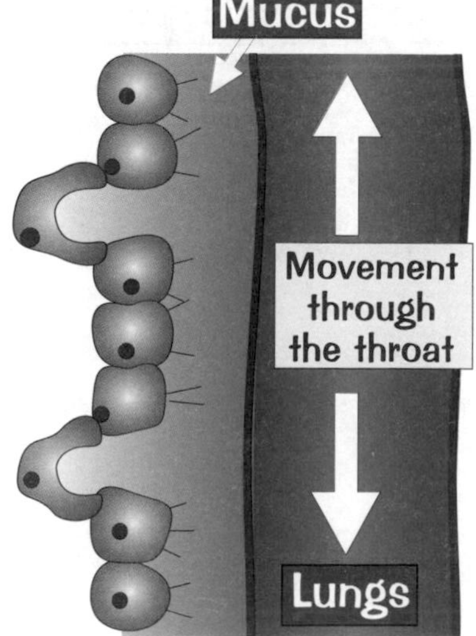

b) If *bacteria* are not trapped before air enters the lungs they can cause an infection. State the name of this disease.

....

c) When mucus collects in the tubes to the lungs it gives rise to an unpleasant action. Name this.

....

d) Give one reason why an unborn baby's development might be affected if the mother smokes during pregnancy.

....

....

Questions on Smoking

Q4 The normal process for cells in the body is to grow, then *divide*, and so replace cells which are too old.

a) Tobacco smoke contains chemicals which make cells divide too much and a serious disease may occur. Name this disease.

....

b) Apart from the serious disease in **a)** name two more diseases which have connections with smoking.

....

....

c) What is '*passive*' smoking?

....

....

d) Which poisonous gas that comes out of car exhausts is present in the smoke from smokers?

....

Q5 The following words are *key words* in this section. See if you can find them in the word search.

Bronchitis, inhaled, exhaled, alveoli, emphysema, nicotine, mucus, cilia, windpipe, tar, tumour, passive smoking, bronchioles, carbon monoxide, haemoglobin, bacteria.

F	B	A	C	T	E	R	I	A	S	I	E	Y	A	I	C
R	T	Z	B	C	N	Y	G	H	R	T	L	H	D	T	H
T	C	L	Q	E	I	C	E	M	P	H	Y	S	E	M	A
E	J	D	R	W	T	L	E	I	L	O	E	V	L	A	E
N	G	N	I	K	O	M	S	E	V	I	S	S	A	P	M
D	M	I	J	X	C	I	L	I	A	T	E	M	H	C	O
T	B	T	L	E	I	N	E	Z	N	B	I	Z	X	B	G
C	A	R	B	O	N	M	O	N	O	X	I	D	E	N	L
R	S	P	O	T	T	V	T	L	H	M	I	L	H	M	O
M	J	W	I	N	D	P	I	P	E	G	K	S	C	G	B
Q	N	J	D	R	C	L	A	R	Q	O	E	R	Q	O	I
I	B	R	O	N	C	H	I	O	L	E	S	F	T	Z	N
R	Y	P	E	T	T	V	I	N	H	A	L	E	D	M	A
M	J	V	R	U	O	M	U	T	E	G	K	S	R	G	K
Q	N	J	D	R	B	L	A	R	I	O	E	R	Q	O	E
F	M	R	F	W	T	M	U	C	U	S	C	F	T	Z	X

Questions on Respiration

Q1 Use the *word list* below to fill the blank spaces.

movement, respiration, energy, growth, glucose, carbon dioxide, reproduction.

In this section we show how ____________ is oxidised to produce ____________. This process is called ____________ and the glucose is broken down to make ____________, water and energy. All living things need energy for processes such as ____________, ____________, and ____________.

Q2 Respiration is a *chemical reaction*.

a) What are the *reactants* (the bits you start with)?

....

b) What are the *chemical products?*

....

....

c) What else is produced? Name three things it is used for.

....

....

....

....

d) Use the letters to fill in the boxes in the diagram describing respiration.

A=Air	D=Glucose	
B=Carbon Dioxide	E= Food	**Example:** G=Energy
C=Water	F=Oxygen	

[____] → [____] ↘

[____] → [____] ↗ [____] + [____] + [G]

Questions on Respiration

Q3 The following *experiment* was set up to show the breakdown of sugar by heat:

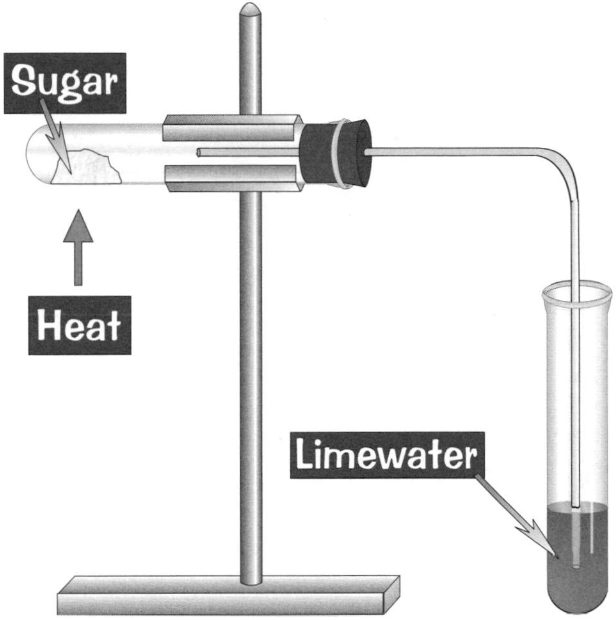

a) Why is *sugar* used in this experiment?

....

....

....

b) When the sugar is heated what happens to the *limewater*?

....

c) What does this prove?

....

d) Which process in the body does this experiment simulate?

....

e) Which gas must be used in this process and why?

....

f) If this process were taking place in our body cells what would be the most important product made? Explain why this is so.

....

....

....

....

Questions on Respiration

Q4 Glucose molecules have energy and some of this is released during respiration.

a) What in the body uses the energy released from glucose?

....

b) Does the energy have to be used up immediately? Explain your answer.

....

c) Write an equation for respiration using the following words:
(carbon dioxide, oxygen, water, energy, glucose.)

....

d) The glucose molecule contains carbon, hydrogen, and oxygen. In respiration it is oxidised (reacts with oxygen) to form three products. Name the products and state which are wastes and which are useful.

....

....

....

Q5 Plants get their energy from the *sun* and gases in the *atmosphere*, and we know that the atmosphere is not pure oxygen but a mixture of gases.

a) Name the two gases that are most common in the atmosphere.

....

....

Sometimes our muscles work very hard, especially if we are athletes.
This is when oxygen is used at an especially high rate to make vast amounts of energy.

b) Which cells in the body carry the oxygen around for respiration?

....

c) What happens if the body cannot work fast enough to supply as much oxygen as is needed for the breaking down of glucose?

....

....

....

....

Questions on Respiration

Q6 **a)** What type of *living organisms* does respiration take place in?

....

b) Which *cells* does respiration occur in?

....

c) What is the important and very useful product of respiration?

....

d) Explain why this product is so important.

....

....

....

Q7 The *key words* for this section are listed below:

aerobic respiration, glucose, carbon dioxide, energy, enzymes, water, oxygen, nitrogen, limewater, aerobics.

a) Fill the gaps in the puzzle below.

A) _ _ o _ _ c r _ _ p _ _ _ t _ _ _,

B) e _ _ _ m _ s,

C) _ n _ _ g _,

D) _ a _ _ o _ _ i _ _ i _ _,

E) _ _ t _ r,

F) o _ _ g _ _,

G) _ l _ c _ s _,

H) n _ _ r _ _ e _,

I) _ i _ _ w _ _ e _,

J) _ e _ o _ i _ _.

b) One word in the list above referred to a type of exercise where oxygen completely breaks down glucose and helps the body work hard. Which word is it?

....

Questions on Health

It's important to know about *drugs* because if they are not properly controlled they can damage our health. The *only people* we should trust to prescribe us with drugs are our doctors.

Q1 Complete the following table in the required places using the names and information boxes by matching the letters and numbers.

Name of drug	Facts about drug
(a)	Very expensive, addictive; leads to a sense of well-being; can cause death
Barbiturates	(b)
(c)	Causes hallucinations or 'trips' and dizzy actions
(d)	Causes a relaxed feeling or 'high'; makes driving or operating machinery hazardous; can cause mental problems
Cocaine	(e)

1) Can reduce anxiety but may cause death

2) LSD

3) Can speed up the brain and increase alertness but may cause depression or death

4) Heroin

5) Cannabis

a) .... **b)** .... **c)** .... **d)** .... **e)** ....

Q2 What do we mean when we say the following things about drugs:

a) they are *addictive?*

....

....

b) they have *side effects?*

....

....

Q3 Alcohol is easy to buy legally if you are over 18 years of age, but it can damage your health if taken without care, and it is a drug.

a) Circle the *group of drugs* that alcohol belongs to, given that it slows down the activity of the brain.

hallucinogen **stimulant** **depressant** **tranquiliser**

b) Which *two organs* of the body can be damaged by drinking too much alcohol?

....

c) Explain how the affects of alcohol make drink driving so dangerous.

....

....

....

Questions on Health

Q4 **a)** .... abuse refers to the practise of inhaling the fumes from a variety of substances.

b) Name three of these substances which are commonly found in households.

....

c) Circle **i)** In <u>pencil</u>, the effects 'glue sniffing' has and
ii) In <u>pen</u>, the damage it can do to the body.

i)	**Makes you sleepy**	**Makes you light headed**	**Gives hallucinations**	**Helps you to relax**
ii)	**Stops the process of digestion**	**Can damage brain and lungs**	**Can cause damage to the eyes**	**Can cause damage to the nervous system**

Q5 Match each diagram of a substance containing a drug with the diagram of the organ which it is most likely to damage.

1. ....

2. ....

3. ....

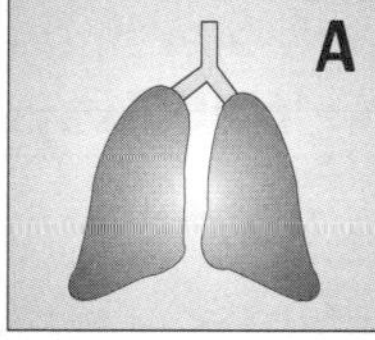

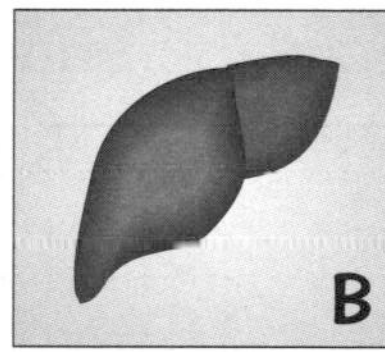

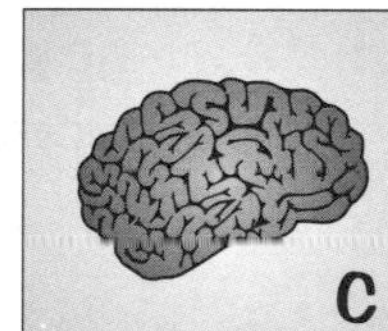

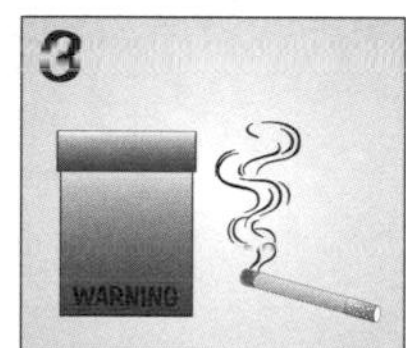

Q6 **a)** Fill the missing words below.

<u>B</u> _ _ _ _ _ _ _ and <u>V</u> _ _ _ _ _ _ are the two main <u>*micro–organisms*</u> which can cause disease.

b) Complete the table below, by putting the letters A-E in the appropriate column.

Bacteria	Viruses

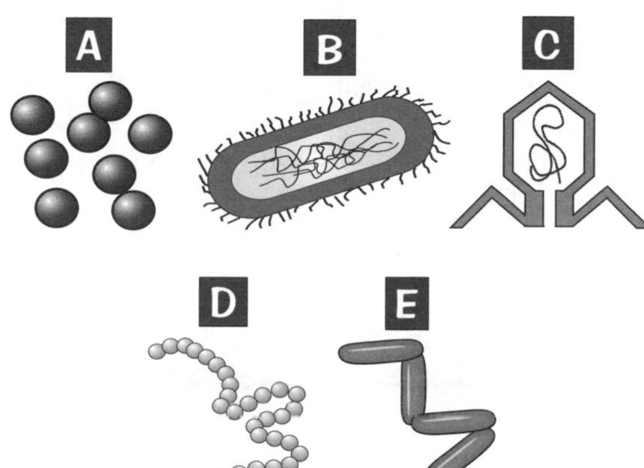

c) Which micro-organisms invade living cells?

....

Questions on Health

Q7 **a)** There are millions of *bacteria* everywhere - in your skin, air, water and soil. Some are important and do useful jobs (e.g. production of yoghurt), but others cause disease.

List three ways in which bacteria can enter the body.

....

....

b) Explain why it is important to cover your mouth or nose when you cough or sneeze.

....

....

....

....

c) When bacteria enter our body and start to multiply, what do we say we have?

....

d) Bacteria can get into drinking water and make you ill when you drink it.
Which disease can be spread in this way?

....

e) Why should we not eat food which is undercooked?

....

....

....

Q8 Put a tick or cross in the box at the end of each statement to indicate whether it is correct.

A *Addict* — a person who needs a drug to feel normal.	☐
B *Alcoholic* — a person who only drinks alcohol at breakfast.	☐
C Solvents do not damage the brain.	☐
D The side-effects of taking drugs can permanently damage your health.	☐
E A small amount of alcohol has no effect at all on the body.	☐
F Viruses are larger than bacteria.	☐
G A sneeze can travel as fast as a hurricane.	☐
H Micro-organisms can be seen with the naked eye.	☐

Questions on Fighting Disease

Q1 Fill in the gaps. All the words you need are in the word box, but so are some you don't.

immune disease red medicines natural defences germs immunisation skin white blood cells antibodies health

The body has its own ____________ ____________ against disease but it can be helped by _______________ and ______________________. The main armies of defence of the body are ____________ and ____________ ____________ ____________ which are part of the body's ____________ system.

Q2 Complete the sentences by ringing the correct word to show how a cut in the skin is *sealed* and the entry of bacteria is *prevented*.

When the skin is cut, (**dirt** / **bacteria**) can enter and cause disease, so (**platelets** / **healthy cells**) in the blood seal the wound. During this process (**red** / **white**) blood cells come to the site of damage and either (**eat** / **repel**) the bacteria or produce (**antibodies** / **safe germs**) to fight them.

Q3 **a)** What are the three ways that white blood cells fight microbes?

....

....

b) Complete the following sentence.

Once you have had a disease the a _ _ _ _ _ _ _ _ _ _ are produced much quicker the next time and your body has some i _ _ _ _ _ _ _ .

Q4 **a)** Which *process* (which is a good way to help the body defend against disease) does the diagram **A** show? ....

b) What is placed *into the body* during this process? ....

c) What is the *job* of the substance named in **b)**?

....

....

A

Arm

d) What is the name of the *liquid* which can protect you if you are given it before you have the disease?

....

e) Which group of medical chemicals *kill bacteria* and are very useful in treating diseases (but are not antibodies)?

....

Questions on Plant Nutrition

Q1 Plants make sugars in their leaves using *carbon dioxide*, *water* and *energy* from sunlight.

a) What name do we give to the process that plants use to make their own food?

....

b) Some insect pests eat plant leaves. What could happen to a plant infested by these insects?

....

The roots of some plants go far down into the soil, others spread just under the surface.

c) Name three functions (jobs) of the roots?

....

....

....

d) Some insect pests eat plant roots. What could happen to a plant infested by these insects?

....

Q2 Liz visited a garden centre. There were lots of bottles of *fertiliser* on display with a big sign saying "Feed your tomato plants! New Growall is all the food your plants need — buy it now!" Liz wasn't happy with the sign, and thought it wasn't accurate. Why was she unhappy — what is wrong with the idea that a fertiliser feeds your plants with all the food they need?

....

....

....

Q3 If you study a root using a microscope, you see tiny *root hair cells* like the one in the picture.

What substances are absorbed through the surface of the root hair cells and why do roots have root hairs and not just smooth surfaces?

....

....

....

....

Questions on Plant Nutrition

Q4 Scientists at the Pudsey Plant Research Centre wanted to find out what plants need to *grow* properly. They set up four beakers of water and put some small water plants in each. They then added some minerals to the beakers, and recorded the growth of the plants over the next few days. Their results are shown in the table below.

Beaker	Minerals	Appearance of plants
A	nitrate, phosphate, potassium	lots of healthy green leaves
B	nitrate and phosphate	leaves are yellow with dead spots
C	nitrate and potassium	leaves turning purple, roots not growing very well
D	phosphate and potassium	yellow leaves with weak stems

a) Which *mineral* is missing from beaker B compared to beaker A?
What happens to plants if this mineral is missing?

....

b) Which *mineral* is needed for roots to grow properly? Explain how you know this.

....

....

c) What happens to plants if *nitrate* is missing?

....

....

d) What would happen if you tried to grow plants in *pure water* with no minerals?

....

e) Nitrates provide nitrogen and phosphates provide phosphorus.
Explain why **i)** nitrogen and **ii)** phosphorus are important for plant growth.

i) ....

ii) ....

Q5 This is a list of the features of many leaves:

A) They are flat and wide; **B)** They are thin;

C) They have lots of veins; **D)** They have little holes (stomata) in the lower surface.

Explain how each feature lets the leaf make food for the plant efficiently.

A) ....

B) ....

C) ....

D) ....

Questions on Photosynthesis

Q1 In an experiment with two plants, one was put on the *windowsill*, and the other was shut in a *dark cupboard*. Both were watered regularly. After three days, the plant in the cupboard was taken out and compared with the other one. The plant from the windowsill looked green and healthy, but the other looked pale and some of its leaves had fallen off.

a) How do we know that *lack of water* was not to blame for the differences between the plants?

....

....

b) It was suggested that the plant in the cupboard was not as healthy as the one on the windowsill in the first place. What could you do to the experiment to show that this was not the cause of the difference?

....

....

c) Give a reason for the difference between the two plants after three days.

....

Two more plants were put on the windowsill. One was given water but the other one wasn't.

d) What do you expect to happen to the plant without water?

....

e) What do these two experiments tell you about plants — what things do they need to grow?

....

....

Q2 *Cress seeds* were sprinkled in two dishes lined with kitchen roll. The same amount of water was added to each dish to make the paper wet. After planting, the seeds were kept in different conditions. The pictures show how they grew. Explain what *conditions* each dish might have been put in.

Dish A

Dish B

....

....

....

Questions on Photosynthesis

Q3 A green leaf was boiled in water to soften it, and then boiled in ethanol. It was washed with water and some brown iodine solution was dropped onto it. The extra iodine solution was washed away.

a) The ethanol in the experiment turned green and the leaf went white. Why did this happen?

....

....

b) When the iodine was added to the leaf, it turned blue-black. What does this mean?

....

A plant with green leaves was put in the dark for two days, then a leaf was tested with iodine.

c) What result would you expect? Why would you expect this to happen?

....

....

Q4 The diagram to the right shows an experiment to study *photosynthesis* in pond weed. Bubbles made by the plant when a lamp was shone on it were collected in the test-tube. A glowing splint relit when put into the test-tube.

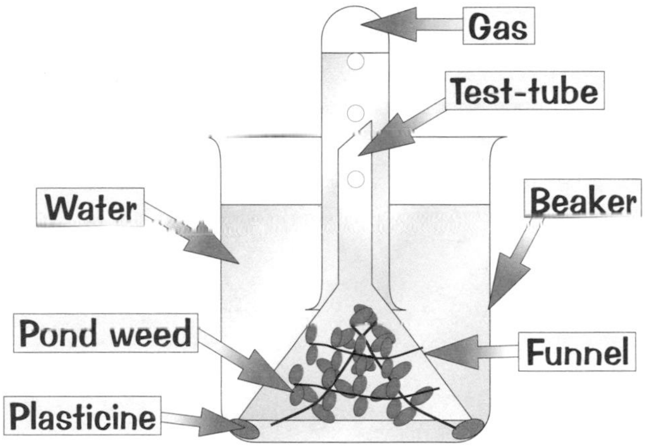

What *gas* is produced during photosynthesis? How do you know this?

....

....

....

....

Q5 Soda lime absorbs carbon dioxide. A plant sealed in a container with a dish of soda lime begins to turn yellow and dies, even if it gets lots of light, water and minerals.

What does this tell you about *photosynthesis?*

....

....

....

....

Questions on Photosynthesis

Q6 The list below shows substances involved in photosynthesis:

oxygen carbon dioxide water chlorophyll glucose

a) Which *gas* goes into the leaf for photosynthesis, and which gas comes out of the leaf?

....

b) What colour is *chlorophyll*, and what does it do?

....

....

c) Is water needed for *photosynthesis*, or is it made by photosynthesis?

....

d) What substances are *made* by photosynthesis?

....

e) Complete this *word equation* for photosynthesis using the words at the top of the page:

.... + ... $\xrightarrow{\text{light}}$ **Glucose** + ...

f) Light is shown in the equation. *Why* is light needed for photosynthesis?

....

....

Q7 Does photosynthesis happen at *night?* Explain your answer.

....

....

Q8 The picture below shows a tree growing in a field. The Sun is shining, so photosynthesis is taking place rapidly in the leaves.

a) What substance is *taken in* from the air by the tree? ....

b) What substance is *given out* into the air by the tree? ....

c) What substance needed for *photosynthesis* does the tree take from the soil?

....

....

Questions on Photosynthesis

Q9 Explain why *photosynthesis* is important to ourselves and other animals.

....

....

....

Q10 *Complete* the photosynthesis crossword:

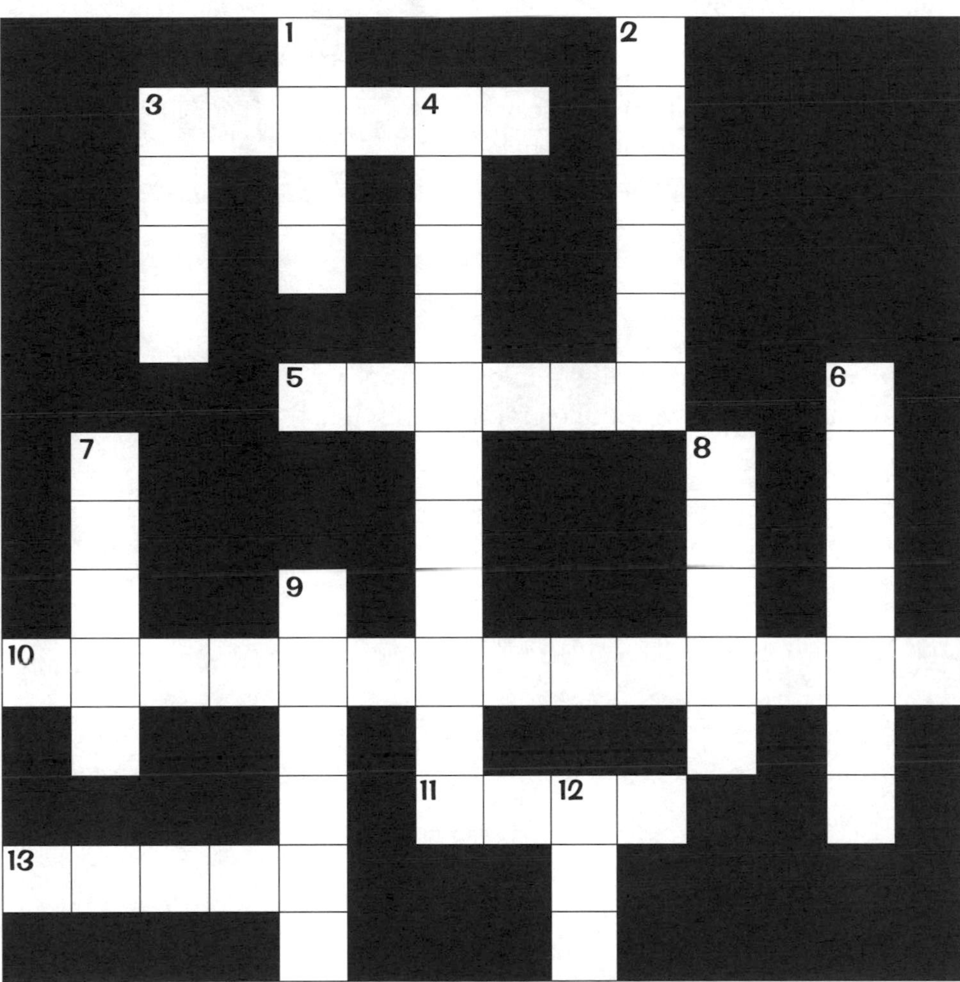

Across

3) Sugars are stored as this (6)

5) and **6)** down — gas needed for photosynthesis (6,7)

10) How plants make food (14)

11) Food is made here (4)

13) Chlorophyll looks like this (5)

Down

1) Plants can't photosynthesise in this (4)

2) We need it — plants make it in the light (6)

3) Roots get water from here (4)

4) Pigment that absorbs light (11)

6) see 5) across

7) Energy needed to make sugars (5)

8) Liquid needed for photosynthesis (5)

9) Test for starch with this solution (6)

12) Carbon dioxide comes from here (3)

Questions on Plant Growth

Q1 Complete these sentences about *plant growth*, by ringing the correct words from the pairs.

"Roots grow (**towards** / **away from**) the light, and (**with** / **against**) gravity."

"Shoots grow (**towards** / **away from**) the light, and (**towards** / **away from**) gravity."

Q2 Match the *beginning* of each sentence to the correct *ending* with an arrow:

Beginnings	Endings
nitrogen is needed for	glucose
phosphorus is needed for	healthy green leaves
photosynthesis is needed for	photosynthesis
potassium is needed for	glucose and oxygen production
starch is made from	strong stems and green leaves
water and carbon dioxide are needed for	healthy root growth

Q3 Farmer Palmer wanted to find the *best conditions* to grow his tomato plants. In the first experiment, the rate of photosynthesis was measured at different levels of light intensity. His results are shown on the graph on the right.

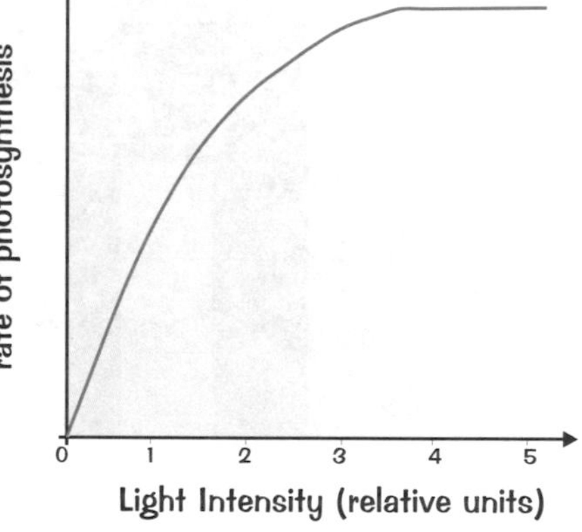

a) Why should he be interested in the rate of photosynthesis when he wanted to find out the *growth* of his plants?

....

....

b) What is the light intensity where the rate of photosynthesis reaches its maximum? Should Farmer Palmer use 10 units of light intensity to try to get his plants to grow faster?

....

In the next experiment, the tomato plants were grown at *different temperatures*. The second graph on the right shows the results.

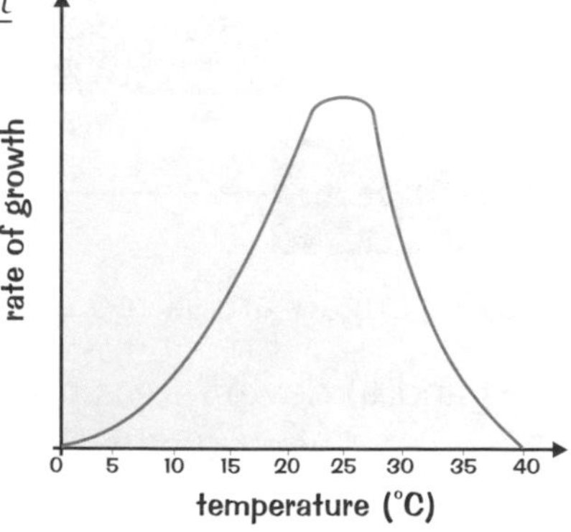

c) At what temperatures do the plants stop growing?

....

d) What temperature is needed to get the plants to grow at their fastest rate?

....

e) Heating and lighting cost money. Explain what Farmer Palmer should do to get his tomato plants to grow very quickly but without wasting money. (Clue: Why do you think tomatoes are often grown in greenhouses instead of outside?)

....

....

Questions on Plant Reproduction

Taken out of the curriculum but still important

Q1 Look at the diagram of a *flowering plant*.

a) Match the following parts to the labels W, X, Y and Z:

stem .... / roots .... / flower .... / leaf ....

b) Which part of the plant, W, X, Y or Z:

— absorbs water and minerals? ....

— absorbs light for photosynthesis? ....

— anchors the plant? ....

— contains the reproductive organs? ....

— makes food for the plant? ....

— supports the plant? ....

W

X

Y

Z

c) What are the functions (jobs) of the roots, stem, leaves, and flowers?

Roots: ....

Stem: ....

Leaves: ....

Flowers: ....

Q2 Complete this sentence about sexual reproduction in plants, by ringing the correct words:

The (**male** / **female**) sex cell is the pollen, and the (**male** / **female**) sex cell is the (**ovule** / **ovum**).

Q3 The diagram opposite is a cut-away diagram of a flower.

a) Add labels and labelling lines to the *anther* and the *filament* parts of the stamen (this is the male part of the flower — remember it as sta*men*). What is the job of the filament? What is the job of the anther?

....

....

....

b) Add labels and labelling lines to the *stigma*, the *style* and the *ovary*. What part of the flower do these three parts make?

....

c) What do you expect to find in the ovary? ....

d) Add labels and labelling lines to the *sepals* and the *petals*.

Questions on Plant Reproduction

Taken out of the curriculum but still important

Q4 **a)** What is the main difference in appearance between the sepals and the petals?

....

b) What is the function of the sepals?

....

c) What is the function of the petals?

....

Q5 Complete the sentences, by joining a beginning with an ending with an arrow:

Beginnings	Endings
the female sex cell in plants is called	the filament and anther
the female sex organ in plants is called	the stigma, style and ovary
the female sex organ is made up from	the carpel
the male sex cell in plants is called	the stamen
the male sex organ in plants is called	the pollen
the male sex organ is made up from	the ovule

Q6 Below are the names of plants. Three are pollinated by insects, and three are pollinated by the wind. Decide which are which and fill in the table below appropriately.

insect-pollinated	wind-pollinated

buttercup stinging nettle sunflower grass dandelion willow tree

Q7 Have a go at the flower wordsearch. The words to find are:

anther, filament, ovary, ovule, pollen, stigma, style.

There are two other words in the grid to do with flowers — can you find them both? Here's a clue.

S .... N
C L

W	P	A	O	V	U	L	E	R	A
C	Z	N	T	E	B	Z	E	M	O
A	E	T	N	I	H	E	G	V	G
R	Y	H	E	U	U	I	I	D	S
P	R	E	M	Z	T	K	E	X	P
E	A	R	A	S	Q	X	A	S	O
L	V	F	L	D	F	N	T	S	L
N	O	K	I	C	O	Y	O	L	L
H	P	A	F	Q	L	D	N	P	E
S	T	A	M	E	N	Y	Y	B	N

Questions on Plant Reproduction

Taken out of the curriculum but still important

Q8 The pictures on the right show two flowers cut away. One is a wind-pollinated flower, the other is an insect-pollinated flower.

A

B

a) What does *pollination* mean?

....

....

b) Which picture shows the *wind-pollinated flower?* Explain how the flower is adapted to pollination by the wind.

....

....

c) Which picture shows the *insect-pollinated flower?* Explain how the flower is adapted to pollination by insects.

....

....

d) Pollen from wind-pollinated flowers is often much lighter and smaller than the pollen from insect-pollinated flowers. Why do you think there is this difference between them?

....

....

Q9 Read the information below, then answer the questions.

> *Cross-pollination* is when the pollen of a flower lands on the stigma of another flower.
> *Self-pollination* is when the pollen of a flower lands on the stigma of the same flower.
>
> Cross-pollination allows more variety between plants, often producing better quality seeds and many plants have adaptations to make cross-pollination more likely than self-pollination.

a) What is the difference between self-pollination and cross-pollination?

....

....

b) The statements below give two adaptations. For each adaptation, suggest why it should make cross-pollination more likely than self-pollination.

— some plants only have male flowers, and others only have female flowers.

....

— the stamens and carpels mature at different times.

....

Questions on Fertilisation and Seed Formation

Q1 **a)** When a pollen grain lands on a stigma, a *pollen tube* grows down to the ovary and then into it. What is the name of the part of the flower that the pollen tube grows through?

....

b) The nucleus from the pollen grain passes through the pollen tube, meets the female sex cell, and joins with it. When a male sex cell joins with a female sex cell, what is this called?

....

c) The *fertilised ovule* grows into a seed. In which part of the flower does this happen?

....

Taken out of the curriculum but still important

d) Once the seeds have developed enough, they are dispersed from the parent plant. What does *dispersed* mean?

....

....

e) Some of the dispersed seeds will begin to grow into a new plant if the conditions are right. What name is given to the process of a *seed* starting to grow into a *seedling?*

....

Q2 The processes below are all to do with reproduction by flowering plants. Write them down in the correct order, starting with "release of pollen" and ending with "growth of seedling".

Dispersal | Fertilisation | Germination | Pollination

Growth of seedling | Growth of pollen tube | Release of pollen | Seed production

Release of Pollen → ....

....

....

....

....

Fertilisation and Seed Formation

Taken out of the curriculum but still important

Q3 Plants have developed various methods to carry their seeds far from the parent plant. Some plants, such as peas and lupins, are able to flick the seeds away from them. As with the transfer of pollen in pollination, plants can spread their seeds using the wind or animals.

a) The pictures show seeds from *dandelions* and *sycamore trees*. These plants rely on the wind to spread their seeds. For each seed, use the picture to explain how it is adapted to carry it far away from the parent.

Dandelion Sycamore

....

....

....

....

In many plants, the *ovary* develops into a fleshy fruit that contains the seeds. Fruits contain *sugars* and often have *bright colours*.

Bright red skin

Little hooks like "velcro"

Tomato Burdock

b) What is the advantage to an *animal* of eating a fruit?

....

....

c) What is the advantage to a *plant* of having its fruits eaten by animals?

....

....

d) The pictures show fruits from tomatoes and burdock. The plants rely on animals to spread their seeds. For each fruit, use the information in the picture to explain how it is adapted to carry the seeds far away from the parent.

....

....

....

....

e) Name a fruit eaten by animals. Suggest why it is attractive to animals.

....

....

Questions on The Carbon Cycle

Q1 In your answers to the questions below, choose from the following gases:

nitrogen oxygen argon carbon dioxide

a) Which gas in the air is needed for wood to burn?

....

b) When wood burns, water vapour is made. What else is made?

....

c) Use your answers to parts **a)** and **b)** to complete this *word equation* for *burning:*

wood + ... → water + ...

d) To stay alive we need to *respire*. Which gas in air do we need to breathe in to stay alive?

....

When we breathe out, our breath contains less of this gas, but a lot more of another gas. Which other gas?

....

e) Use your answers to part **d)** to complete this *word equation* for *respiration:*

glucose + ... → water + ...

f) Look at your answers to parts **c)** and **e)**. What do you notice about them?

....

....

g) The word equation for photosynthesis is:

carbon dioxide + water —(Sun's energy)→ glucose + oxygen.

What do you notice about burning, respiration and photosynthesis?

....

....

....

....

Questions on The Carbon Cycle

Q2 We can put burning, respiration and photosynthesis together to make the *carbon cycle*. The diagram below shows part of the carbon cycle.
Fill in the names for processes 1, 2 and 3.

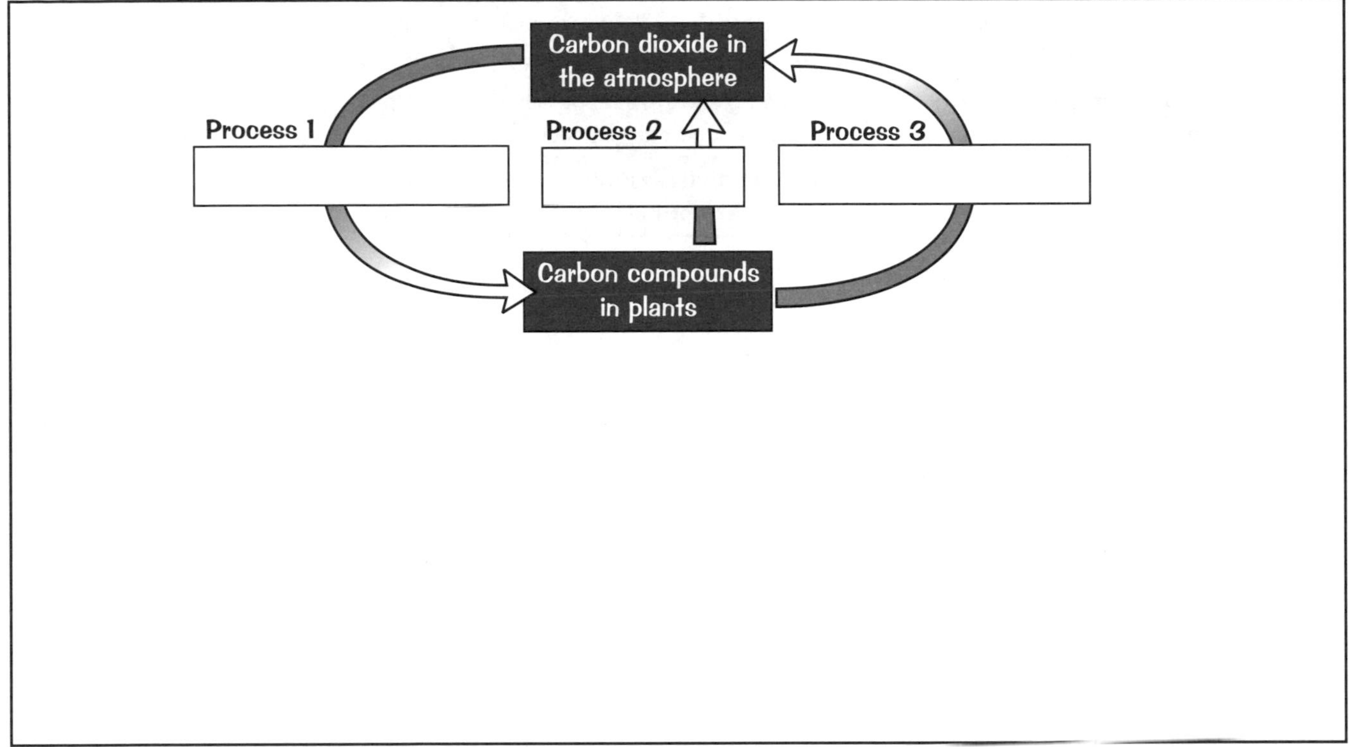

Q3 **a)** *Carbon compounds* such as glucose can get into animals, and carbon compounds in these animals can get into other animals. How does this happen?

....

b) Add labelled arrows and boxes to your diagram from question 2 to show carbon compounds getting into animals.

c) What happens to the carbon compounds in animals that are not needed?

....

d) Draw another labelled arrow to show what happens to these wastes.

Q4 Look at the following list. Which of these things *respire*?

bacterium, bird, dandelion, dead donkey, dog, fish, frog, human, seaweed, snake, soil, wooden table

....

....

Q5 Bacteria can feed on dead animals, plants and animal wastes. They respire as they do this.
Add a final labelled arrow to your diagram to complete your carbon cycle.

Questions on The Nitrogen Cycle

Q1 The sentences below explain all about *nitrogen fixation* (the change of nitrogen gas into a more reactive form, e.g. nitrates), but they are all in the wrong order. Read through them all, then answer the questions.

1) This acid makes nitrates in the soil.	3) The energy from lightning gets nitrogen to react with oxygen.	6) It takes a lot of enery to get nitrogen to react with oxygen.
2) Nitrogen is a very unreactive gas.	4) Nitrogen oxides are made when nitrogen and oxygen react.	7) When nitrogen oxides dissolve in rainwater, they make an acid.
	5) Plants can use nitrates to make proteins.	

a) Explain how you know that a lot of energy is needed to get nitrogen and oxygen to react.

....

....

b) What is made when oxygen and nitrogen react together?

....

c) Explain how the substance in your answer to part **b)** allows plants to make proteins.

....

....

d) Write down the sentences 1 — 7 in the correct order, and use them to help you explain how nitrogen fixation works.

....

....

....

....

....

....

....

....

....

....

....

....

....

Questions on The Nitrogen Cycle

Q2 There are bacteria in the soil called *denitrifying bacteria*. They convert nitrates in the soil back into nitrogen gas. The diagram below shows how nitrogen in the air can be converted into nitrates in the soil, and then back to nitrogen again.

a) Fill in the missing labels in the diagram below.

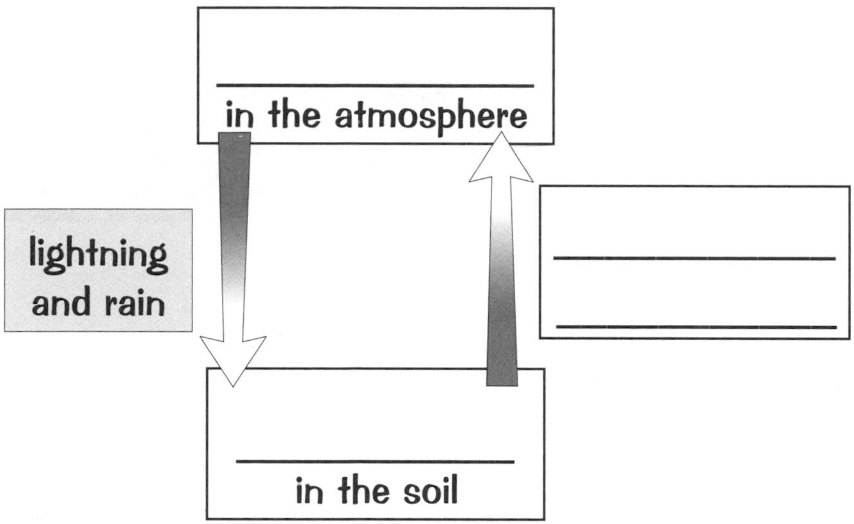

b) This diagram is part of the *nitrogen cycle*. Why do you think it is called a *cycle?*

....

Q3 When animals eat plants, the *protein* in the plants is used to make protein in the animals.

a) What substance do plants need from the soil to make proteins? ....

b) Give the names of two tissues or parts of an animal that are made of protein.

....

c) Add labelled arrows and boxes to your nitrogen cycle to show how the substance in the soil gets into animal proteins.

Q4 When animals and plants die, *decay bacteria* break the proteins down into nitrates in the soil. Add labelled arrows and boxes to your nitrogen cycle to show how proteins in plants and animals end up as nitrates in the soil.

Q5 Use your completed nitrogen cycle to answer these questions:

a) What processes produce nitrates in the soil? ....

b) What processes take nitrates out of the soil? ....

c) What jobs do the different bacteria do in the nitrogen cycle?

....

....

Questions on Variation

Q1 The tally chart below shows the eye colour of the children in a class at school. Eye colour is an example of *discontinuous variation* because there are a limited number of distinct options.

Eye Colour	Brown	Blue	Green	Hazel
Tally of Students	𝍸 ||||	𝍸 𝍸 ||	𝍸	𝍸 |

a) *Complete* the table on the right with the numbers of children with each eye colour.

b) On the graph paper below, draw a *bar chart* of number of children against eye colour. The vertical (side) axis should be the number of children (1 large square per child works well). The horizontal (bottom) axis should be divided into four equal parts, one for each eye colour. For each eye colour, plot the number of children as a bar on the chart. Make sure you label each axis with the headings from your table, and give your graph a title.

Colour of eyes	Number of children
Brown	
Blue	
Green	
Hazel	

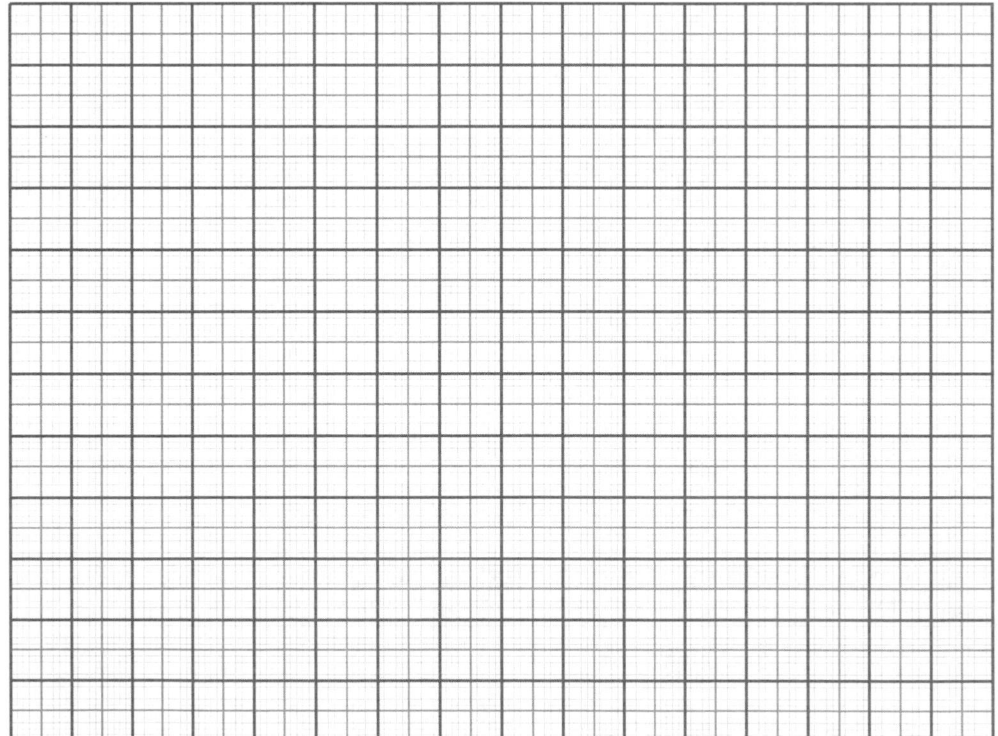

c) How many children altogether were included in the results? What percentage of the children had green eyes? Make sure you show your working out.

....

....

Questions on Variation

Q2 The heights of the girls in two Year 7 classes were measured. The results are shown on the right. You are going to draw a *graph* to show these results.

Height (cm)					
152	148	143	147	160	168
156	154	146	141	151	153
159	158	155	157	159	146
152	154	160	164	144	136
153	150	148	149	163	158

Height range (cm)	Number of girls
135-139	
140-144	
145-149	
150-154	
155-159	
160-164	
165-169	

a) Carefully work your way through the recorded heights, filling in the number of girls at each height range in the tally chart on the left. There are 30 girls altogether, so check that your tally count adds up to 30. If it doesn't, you have gone wrong somewhere.

b) On the graph paper below, draw a *bar chart* of the results. The vertical (side) axis should be the number of girls (1 large square per girl works well). The horizontal (bottom) axis should be divided into seven equal parts, one for each height range. Plot each number of girls from your tally chart as a bar. Make sure you label each axis and give your graph a title.

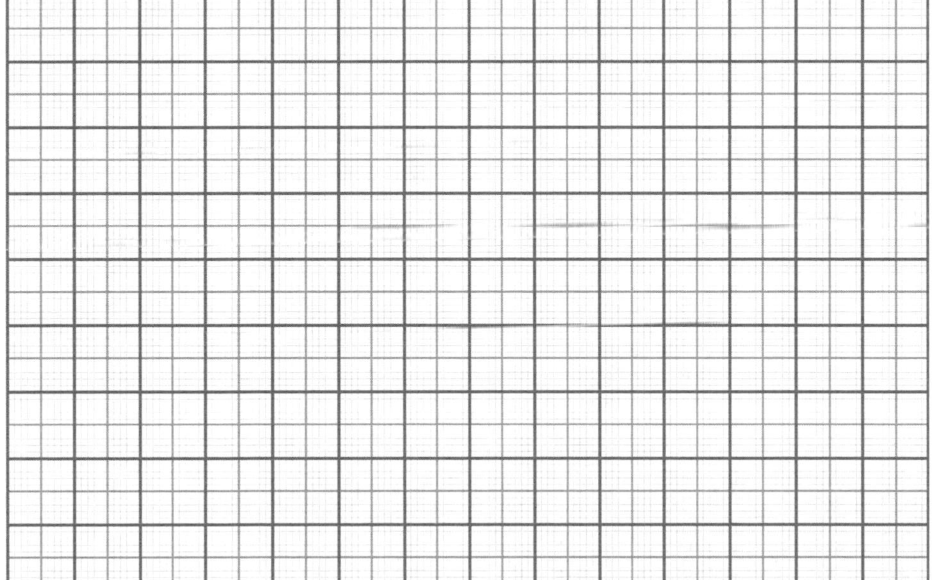

c) How tall would a girl have to be to be among the tallest five girls?
How tall would she have to be to be among the shortest ten girls?

Amongst Tallest .... Amongst Shortest ....

d) Although we measured the girls' heights to the nearest centimetre, and plotted their heights in ranges of 5cm, if we had a very precise ruler we could measure to tiny fractions of a centimetre. This is *continuous variation* because, for example, a girl could be any height between 150cm and 151cm, not just 150cm or 151cm. Give *two more examples* of continuous variation in people.

....

Questions on Environmental & Inherited Variation

Q1 Animals and plants do not all look the same, they vary. Some of this *variation* is *inherited* from their parents, and some is caused by the *environment* (where a plant grows, how you are brought up and what you eat, for example).

a) Compare the appearance of a *tree* with *yourself*. Give four ways in which you and the tree are different (hopefully there are plenty). Can you think of any ways in which your appearance is the same?

....

....

....

b) Compare the appearance of a *chimpanzee* with *yourself*. Give three ways in which you and the chimpanzee are different, and three ways in which you are similar.

....

....

....

c) *Compare* the appearance of one of your friends or family with yourself. Give three ways in which you are different from this person, and three ways in which you are similar.

....

....

....

d) Look back at your answers to parts a), b) and c). For each difference between you and the tree, chimpanzee or other person, write down whether you think the difference is *inherited* or due to the *environment*. Parts a) and b) should be fairly easy, but part c) might be harder – you might have difficulties deciding if a difference is due to environmental variation, inherited variation, or both. If you think it is due to both, say so and explain why.

....

....

....

....

....

....

....

Questions on Environmental & Inherited Variation

Q2 *Spider plants* are houseplants that produce lots of baby spider plants on *runners* from the parent plant (see the picture on the right). Every baby spider plant inherits the same information from the parent. Linda's spider plant has lots of baby spider plants. She plants several of them in separate pots, and lets them grow ready to sell at the school fair. Linda expected that all the new plants would grow the same because they came from the same parent plant, but some are bushier or taller than others.

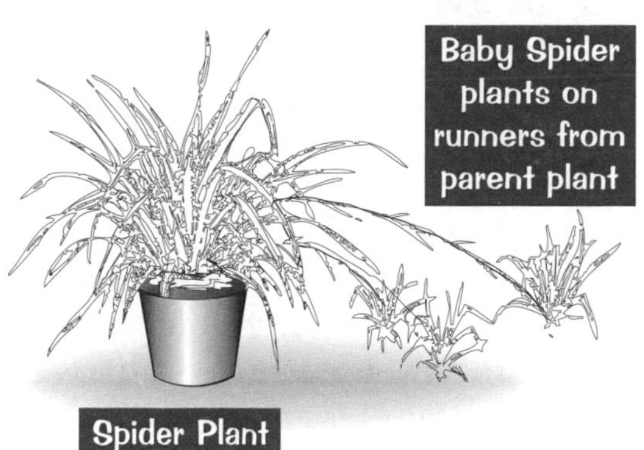

Name four *environmental factors* that could affect the growth of the plants. For each factor, explain what effect it would have on the growth of the plants.

1) ....

....

2) ....

....

3) ....

....

4) ....

....

Q3 *Identical twins* have exactly the same genes as each other. So they may both have brown eyes as this is an inherited feature. But one twin could weigh more than the other — this is an environmental feature because this twin might eat more than the other.

The list below gives some features of an old man called Bob. Decide which of Bob's features have been inherited from his parents, and which are due to his environment.

1) dark brown hair 2) blood group is O negative 3) short hair with a parting
4) scar under one eye 5) first name is Bob 6) speaks English 7) yellow fingers

....

....

....

....

....

Questions on Inheritance and Selective Breeding

Q1 Read this example of *selective breeding*, then answer the questions below.

> Panjit Jones, a budgerigar fancier, was having his birds beaten in shows because they were too small. He decided to change his *breeding program* to produce larger budgies. Some of his birds were bigger than the rest, so Panjit only allowed these birds to breed. When the baby birds had grown up, the smallest were sold to a pet shop, and the largest were allowed to breed. Panjit found that he had to keep doing this for several years until most of the birds he bred were large enough to win prizes at shows.

a) What did Panjit do to make sure that he was selecting for this feature?

....

....

....

b) Suggest why it took Panjit several years to produce a prize-winning flock.

....

....

....

c) Why is Panjit's breeding programme an example of *selective breeding*?

....

....

....

d) Panjit's birds did not all win prizes, even if they were large. Many of them did not have nice enough beaks to impress the judges. Describe how Panjit should change his breeding programme to produce large birds with lovely beaks.

....

....

....

....

Questions on Inheritance and Selective Breeding

Q2 *Dogs* are descended from *wolves*.
Pedigree dogs always produce puppies that show the features of the breed. Look at the pictures of the wolf, the golden retriever and the bulldog.

Golden Retriever
Bulldog
Wolf

a) What features have been selected to produce pedigree golden retrievers from wolves?

....

....

....

b) What features have been selected to produce pedigree bulldogs from wolves?

....

....

c) Suggest two problems you might find if you tried to breed bulldogs from pedigree golden retrievers.

....

....

....

Q3 Farmers often want to improve their crops or livestock. Study the pictures below. They show original *"wild type"* plant or animal, and the crop and livestock produced from them by *selective breeding*. For each one, write down which features have been selected for breeding, and suggest one other desirable feature not shown in the pictures.

Wild Wheat
Modern Wheat
Wild Boar
Modern Pig

....

....

....

....

....

Questions on Classification of Plants & Animals

Q1 Give three differences between *plants* and *animals*.

....

....

....

Q2 *Mammals* and *birds* are two groups of animals that have backbones.

a) What do we call animals with *backbones?*

....

b) Give three examples of a mammal, and three examples of a bird.

....

....

....

c) Give three differences between a mammal and a bird.

....

....

d) Give three features that mammals and birds have in common.

....

....

e) *Fish* are another group of animals with backbones.
Apart from living in water, give three differences between fish, and mammals and birds.

....

....

....

f) *Reptiles* and *amphibians* are two more groups of animals with backbones.
Give two examples of a reptile, and two examples of an amphibian.
How could you tell a reptile from an amphibian?

....

....

....

Questions on Classification of Plants & Animals

Q3 Animals without backbones are called *invertebrates*. Some have legs, others do not. Invertebrates with legs are called *arthropods*. There are four main groups.

a) Use the information below to decide which group each animal in the picture belongs to.

....

....

Group	Features
Arachnids (spiders)	Hard body divided into two main parts, eight legs
Crustaceans	Hard body divided into lots of segments, many legs
Insects	Hard body divided into three main parts, six legs, may have wings
Myriapods	Hard body divided into lots of segments, very many legs

A B C D

b) Give four features that the groups of organisms in the table have in common.

....

....

....

....

c) Give two ways to tell a wingless insect from a spider. ....

....

d) What is an *arthropod*? ....

....

Q4 There are many invertebrate groups without legs.
A *coelenterate* has a sack-like body with tentacles; *molluscs* have soft, slimy bodies, and may have a shell; *segmented worms* have soft, wet, long bodies divided into rings; *flatworms* and *roundworms* are long and thin but are not divided into rings.
The *word search* on the right contains eight words from the paragraph above. Can you find them all?

M _ _ _ _ _ _ _, F _ _ _ _ _ _ _ _ _,

R _ _ _ _ _ _ _ _ _ _ _, S _ _ _ _ _,

C _ _ _ _ _ _ _ _ _ _ _ _ _ _,

I _ _ _ _ _ _ _ _ _ _ _ _ _ _,

S _ _ _ _ _ _ _ _ _ _ _, S _ _ _ _ _,

E	M	O	L	L	U	S	C	Y	S	I	E
R	T	Z	B	C	D	Y	G	H	R	T	L
O	C	A	Q	E	C	C	E	E	A	O	S
U	J	D	R	W	D	L	V	R	K	E	E
N	Y	G	S	E	L	M	B	A	G	Q	A
D	M	I	J	X	T	E	I	M	I	C	E
W	I	Q	L	V	T	N	E	Z	N	B	I
O	L	P	N	R	R	N	E	Z	L	T	X
R	S	P	E	T	T	V	B	L	H	M	A
M	J	V	Z	E	T	O	D	S	E	G	K
Q	N	J	D	R	B	L	A	R	Q	O	E
I	M	R	O	W	T	A	L	F	T	Z	C

Questions on Keys

Taken out of the curriculum but still important

Q1 This *key* can be used to name these shapes:

A B C D

1) Does it have three sides?	Yes	triangle	No	go to question 2
2) Does it have five sides?	Yes	pentagon	No	go to question 3
3) Are the sides all the same?	Yes	square	No	rectangle

Use this key to identify the four shapes above.

....

Now alter the key so that it will also let you identify a circle and an ellipse (see box to the right).

circle

ellipse

....

....

....

....

....

Q2 The pictures on the right show some *common laboratory apparatus*.

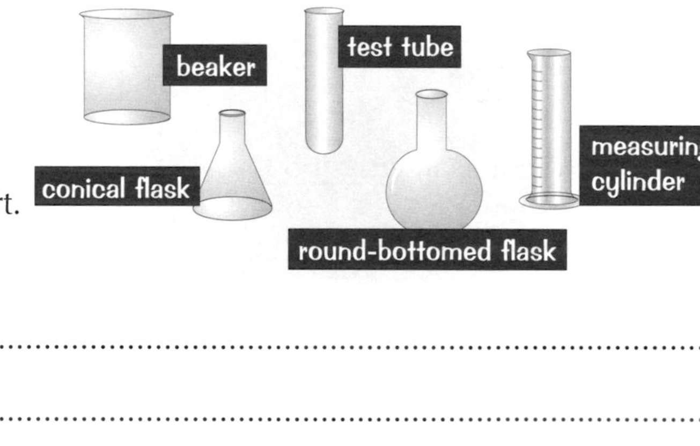

a) Work out your own key to tell them apart.

....

....

....

....

....

....

b) Explain how your key would be useful to someone who didn't know laboratory equipment.

....

....

Questions on Keys

Taken out of the curriculum but still important

Q3 The pictures show some *insects*. Use the key to identify each insect. Put your answers in a table below. You need to be able to recognise the *abdomen* (with the *tail* — which is the section on the left of the insects below), the *head* (here on the right) and the *thorax* (which is the section with the legs attached).

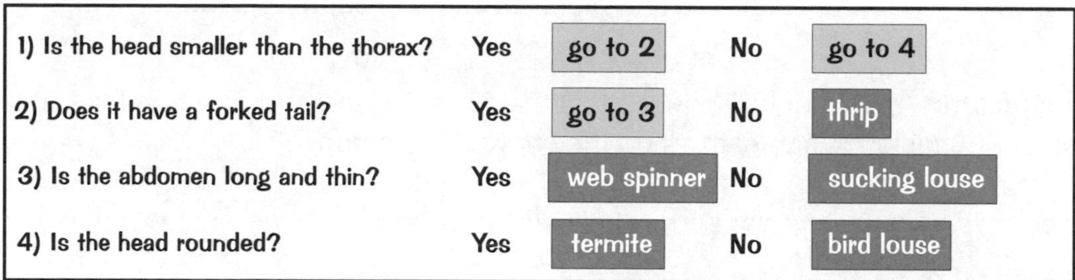

1) Is the head smaller than the thorax?	Yes	go to 2	No	go to 4
2) Does it have a forked tail?	Yes	go to 3	No	thrip
3) Is the abdomen long and thin?	Yes	web spinner	No	sucking louse
4) Is the head rounded?	Yes	termite	No	bird louse

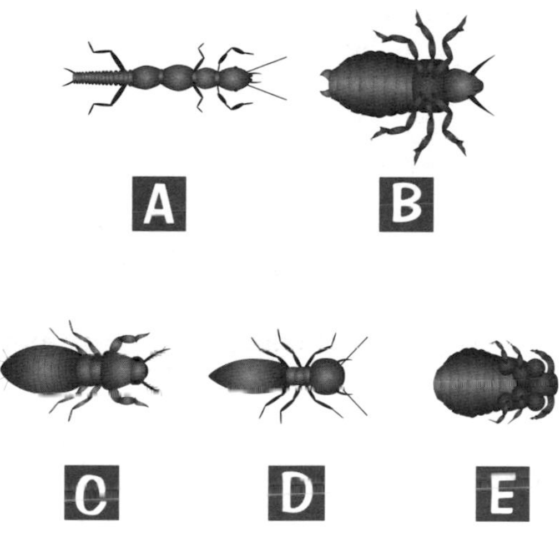

label	name
A	

Q4 Think of some people, animals, plants, objects or places that you might want to classify. Work out a key to identify them below. A good key will ask one less question than the number of objects. Does yours?

Questions on Adaptation

Q1 Complete these sentences by circling the correct words in the brackets:

The place where something lives is called its (**habitat** / **environment**).

The conditions in a habitat are the (**environment** / **situation**).

Over millions of years, animals and plants become (**adapted** / **similar**) to their environment.

Q2 **a)** The pictures (below right) show a plant that lives on land and one that lives in the sea (bladder wrack). What features do they have in common?

....

....

....

b) How do these features allow the plant to be adapted to its environment?

....

....

....

....

Plant that lives on land

Plant that lives in the sea

c) Land plants have sturdy stems that allow them to stay upright. Why should the plant need to stay upright?

....

....

d) If bladder wrack is uncovered by the tide, it flops onto the ground. Why does this happen?

....

....

....

e) It is called bladder wrack because of the little air bladders on its fronds. What are these for? — what do you think will happen when the tide comes in and the bladder wrack gets covered by water?

....

....

....

....

Questions on Adaptation

Q3 In the desert, it sometimes doesn't rain for years, although there can be a lot of water when it does rain. There can be very strong winds that whip up the sand and cause it to drift. Though the days are very hot, the nights are cold, and in the morning there is often dew on the ground. Some plants in the desert have shallow roots that spread just below the surface, whereas others have very long roots that reach deep underground.

a) Explain how the two different types of root are *adapted* to obtaining water in the desert. Are there any other *advantages* to having roots like these? Are there any *disadvantages?*

....

....

....

b) The list below shows some other *features* of desert plants. Suggest how they help the plants to be adapted to life in the desert.

1) The seeds can lie dormant in the soil for years until the rain comes.

2) Succulent plants store water in their leaves, stems, and roots.

3) They usually have small leaves, or modified leaves which form thorns.

1) ....

....

2) ....

....

3) ....

....

c) How are camels *adapted* to life in the desert? Think of as many adaptations as you can and, for each one, explain how it helps the camel to live in the desert.

....

....

....

....

....

....

....

....

Questions on Food Chains and Food Webs

Q1 Draw arrows to match the *words* to the *meanings*.

Words	Meanings
carnivores	animals that can eat both plants and animals
omnivores	animals that eat plants
herbivores	animals that eat other animals
consumers	organisms that can make their own food
producers	organisms that rely on other organisms for their food

Q2 In the food chain below, what do the arrows mean? ....

tiny plants → squid → whale

Write down the name of the *herbivore*, the *carnivore*, and the *producer*. Explain how you know this. ....

....

....

Q3 Food chains always begin with a certain type of living thing. What type of living thing is this? Write down two examples of this type of living thing. Why do they start off food chains?

....

....

Q4 The names below are all words to do with food chains, but with the letters muddled up. Unscramble the letters to find out what the words are and then find them in the word search:

Vince Roar, Mrs Oncue, Dina Choof, Ron Movie, Dr Prouce, Rover Hibe.

....

....

....

....

....

....

....

E	P	C	O	N	S	U	M	E	R
R	R	F	O	I	D	C	H	A	O
O	E	O	O	A	E	R	B	M	I
V	C	O	M	H	I	V	N	C	A
I	U	D	A	C	H	I	N	G	R
B	D	C	E	D	V	O	R	E	S
R	O	H	S	O	K	I	Z	X	L
E	R	A	R	O	A	R	N	I	V
H	P	E	R	F	V	I	B	R	A
X	E	R	O	V	I	N	R	A	C

Questions on Food Chains and Food Webs

Q5 Look at the woodland *food web*.

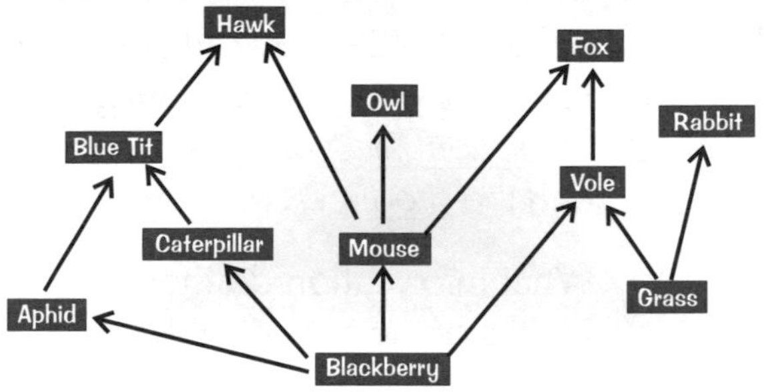

a) Circle the carnivores.
Which one is not a top carnivore?

....

b) Write down all the food chains that start with the blackberry and end with the hawk.

....

....

....

c) Write down all the food chains that end with the owl.

....

....

d) Explain what might happen to the number of voles and rabbits if the amount of grass increased.

....

....

e) Explain what might happen to the number of owls if the amount of grass increased.

....

....

f) Explain what might happen to the number of blue tits if the hawk dies.

....

....

g) Explain what might happen to the number of aphids if the hawk dies.

....

....

Q6 Decide whether each of the following sentences is true (T) or false (F) and then tick the appropriate box.

	T	F
"Primary consumers are always herbivores."	☐	☐
"Carnivores are always secondary consumers."	☐	☐
"In a food web, arrows can point in any direction."	☐	☐
"Top carnivores are always very large."	☐	☐

Questions on Number Pyramids

Q1 A *pyramid of numbers* is shown on the right.

a) Label the *primary consumer*, the *secondary consumer* and the *producer*.

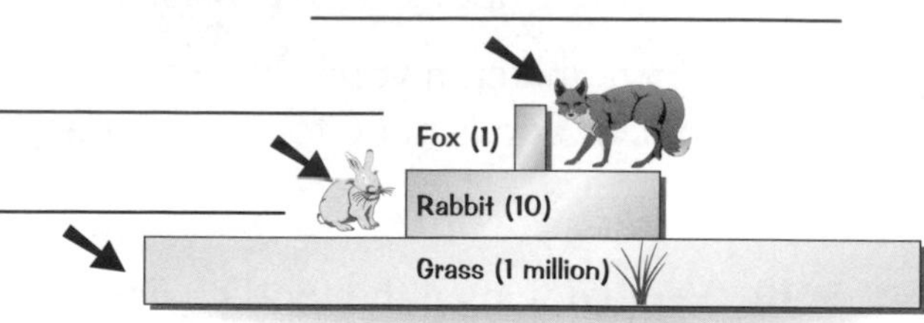

b) What information do the widths of the bars give us?

....

Q2 Here are two *food chains* with the numbers of each organism:

A) grass (50) → vole (10) → owl (1)

B) oak tree (1) → caterpillar (50) → blue tit (10)

Draw the pyramids of numbers for these food chains. Draw them to scale and label the bars with the name and number of each organism. One of the two pyramids doesn't look very pyramid-shaped. Explain why it looks like it does.

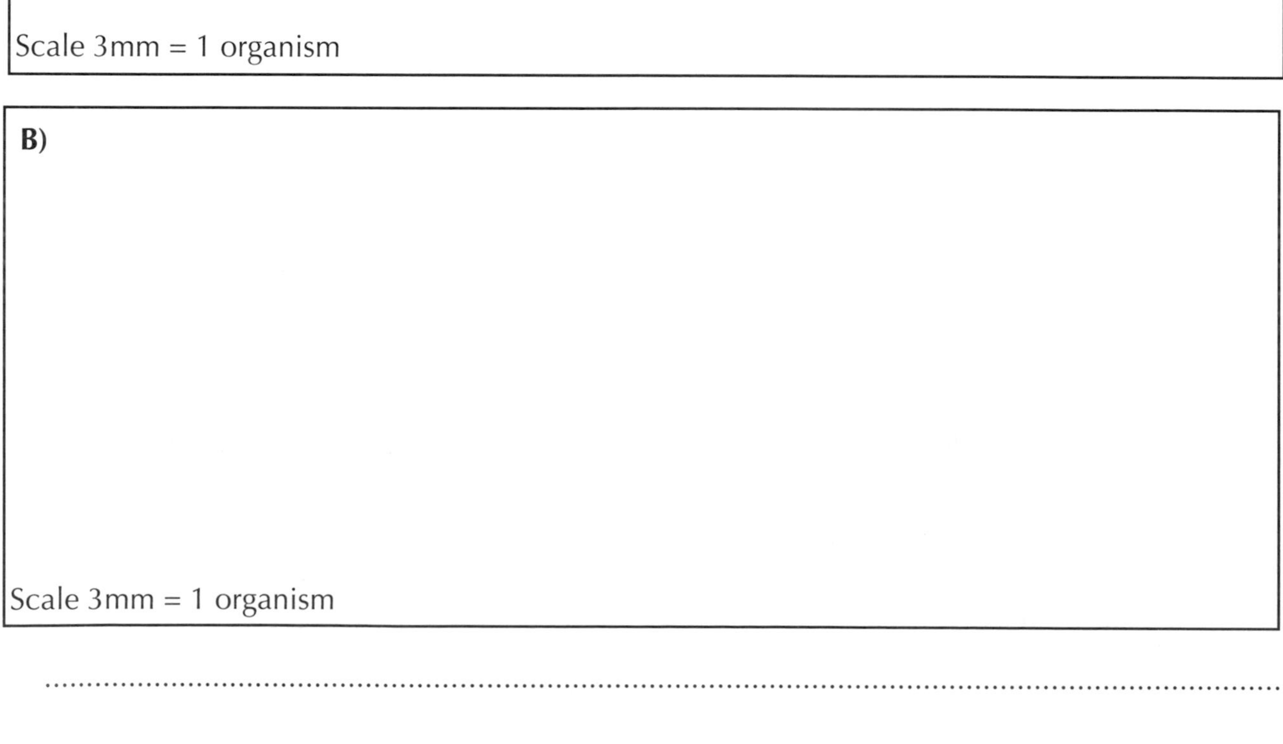

....

....

Questions on Number Pyramids

Q3 The following diagrams show four different pyramids of numbers.

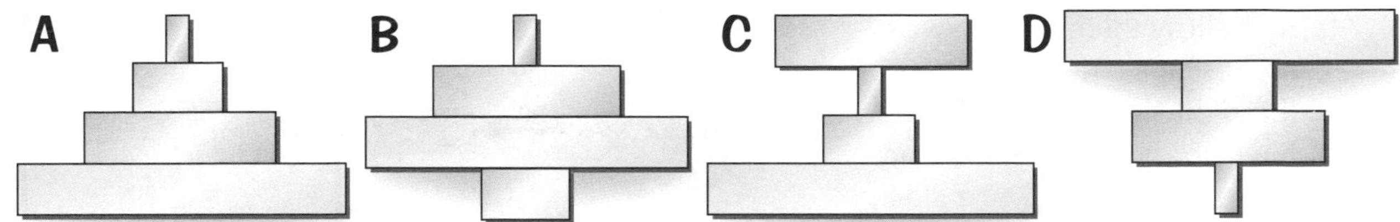

Match these food chains to the pyramids above, and explain why you think they match.

a) **blackberry → vole → fox → flea** is the food chain represented by pyramid ....

....

....

b) **grass → snail → bird → stoat** is the food chain represented by pyramid ....

....

....

c) **oak tree → caterpillars → bird → flea** is the food chain represented by pyramid ....

....

....

d) **rose bush → aphid → ladybird → bird** is the food chain represented by pyramid ....

....

....

Q4 a) In which *direction* does energy flow in a food chain? In which direction does it go in a pyramid of numbers?

....

....

b) There is a special name given to each step in the food chain – what is this name? (Hint: rearrange *Phil Coverlet* to find the two words). Energy is lost going from one organism to the next. Explain why this happens.

....

....

....

Questions on Survival

Q1 Foxes chase, catch and eat rabbits. Rabbits have features that allow them to run away and escape. The flow chart on the right shows how rabbits have *adapted* to run fast and escape foxes.

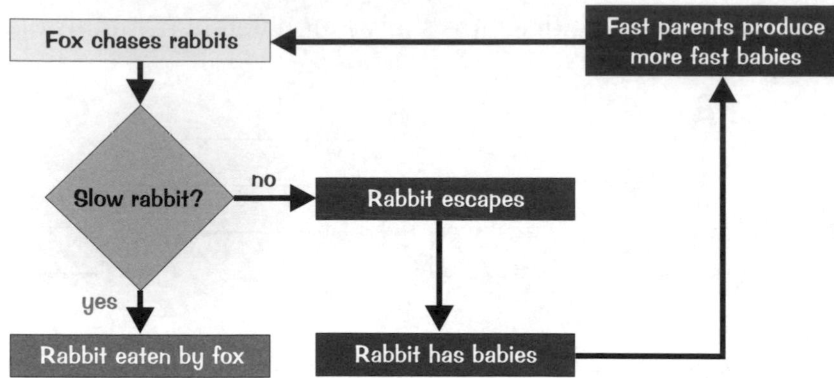

a) Why don't as many slow rabbits pass on their genes to the next generation?

....

....

....

....

b) Explain why more fast rabbits pass on their genes to the next generation than slow rabbits.

....

....

....

....

c) Explain why after a few generations rabbits become more able to escape the fox.

....

....

....

....

d) In a race between a rabbit from a field where there are foxes and a rabbit from a field without any foxes, which rabbit is more likely to win? Give a reason for your answer.

....

....

....

....

Questions on Survival

Q2 **a)** Design an *ultimate predator* that is good at surviving. Explain how it is adapted to be successful at catching its prey. It can have almost any features you like, but there is one rule – it cannot be invisible!

....

....

....

....

....

....

b) Design an *ultimate prey*. Not an animal that is really easy to catch, but one that is very difficult for a predator to catch and eat, and so is good at surviving. Explain how it is adapted to escape from predators. It can have almost any features you like, but again the same rule – it cannot be invisible!

....

....

....

....

....

....

c) Compare your ultimate predator with your ultimate prey. Do they have any features in common that make them good at surviving? If they do, make a list of these features.

....

....

....

....

....

....

....

Questions on Survival

Q3 You have been asked to write the screenplay for a film in which a terrible space alien has crash-landed on Earth. The army is trying to find the alien, but it can change itself to adapt to its surroundings. You need three thrilling scenes, one where the alien is in a forest, one where it is under the sea and one where it is in the desert. For each of these three places, make a list of the features you think the alien would give itself so that it could survive well there.

Features of the alien for the thrilling forest scenes...

....

....

....

....

....

....

Features of the alien for the rip-roaring undersea scenes...

....

....

....

....

....

....

Features of the alien for the scorching desert scenes...

....

....

....

....

....

....

Questions on Types of Materials

Q1 Complete the table below by listing products that can be made from _ceramic_, _glass_ and _plastic_.

Things made of ceramic	Things made of glass	Things made of plastic

Q2 List _two properties_ of each material (_glass_, _plastic_ and _ceramic_), _which make it useful_.

Glass: ....

Plastic: ....

Ceramic: ....

Q3 Choose an item from each column in Question 1, and say why you think those items were made from the material heading the column. (For example, _window panes_ are made of _glass_ because glass is _transparent_.)

Item 1) ....

Item 2) ....

Item 3) ....

Q4 You have been asked to design a jug suitable for carrying boiling water in. What material would you make it out of? Why would you use this particular material?

....

....

....

Q5 Classify the following objects as _ceramic_ (C), _plastic_ (P) or _glass_ (G).

China cup ☐
Brick ☐
Milk bottle ☐
Lead crystal tumbler ☐
Bin liner ☐
Kitchen tile ☐

Questions on Types of Materials

Q6 The nose cone of the *Space Shuttle* is covered with tiles made of a special type of *ceramic*.

What is the *reason* for covering the nose cone and why were *ceramic* tiles chosen?

....

....

Q7 What is a "*composite material*"? Give two examples of a composite material and suggest a use for each:

1) ....

2) ....

Q8 Fibre-glass is a *man-made material* made of *glass* and *plastic*.
It is often used to make boats.

GLASS + PLASTIC = FIBRE GLASS

What *advantage* does *fibre-glass* have over each of its two constituent materials for the construction of boats? ....

....

Q9 Many kitchens boast a "*ceramic hob* ". Why is *ceramic* a good material for making a cooker hob, and what, if any, are the *disadvantages* of using ceramic?

....

....

....

....

Questions on Raw Materials

Q1 *Crude oil* is a valuable *raw material*. Name five different things that we can make from crude oil.

1) ....

2) ....

3) ....

4) ....

5) ....

Q2 Bertha is a special machine made by Valtra (a friendly alien). It can make almost anything, provided it is supplied with the correct *raw materials*. Valtra and his amazing machine have been hired by a company to make saucepans.

What *raw materials* should Valtra consider feeding Bertha with? What are the *properties* of these particular raw materials that make them ideal for making saucepans?

....

....

....

....

....

Q3 Valtra (working at the mint now) decides he wants to make a stash load of *ten pound notes*. Name two raw materials he needs to supply Bertha with in order to make the money.

1) ....

2) ....

Questions on Raw Materials

Q4 *Raw materials* are those naturally occurring substances that we use to make other things. Link up the substance or item below with its corresponding *main* raw material:

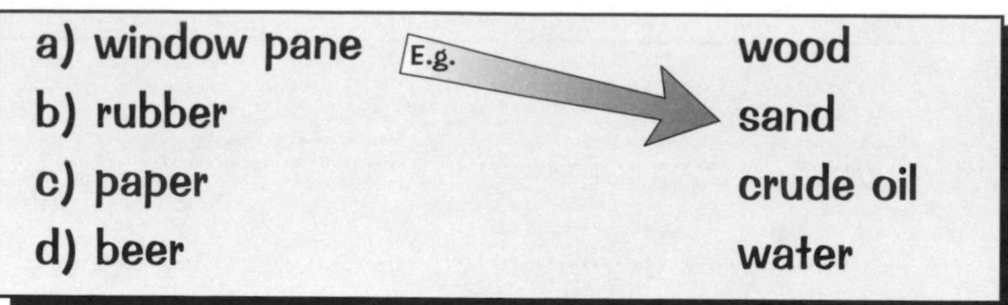

a) window pane
b) rubber
c) paper
d) beer
E.g.
wood
sand
crude oil
water

Q5 Which of these objects are *man-made* and which are natural substances (put M or N)? (Remember that man-made things are *chemically changed* during production. So an *oak* chair is still *natural*, even though it has been made into a new shape.)

An oak chair	N	A coffee cup		A book	
A biro		A washing-up bowl		A kitchen sink	
A T.V.		A mahogany chest		Paint	
A cricket bat		A beer mug		A brick wall	

Q6 *Coal* is a valuable *raw material*. Several *man-made substances* can be made either directly from it, or from the heat it produces when it burns. Name three different things that can be made, directly or indirectly, from coal.

1) ....

2) ....

3) ....

Q7 Another valuable raw material is air, which contains the gases shown in the diagram below:

Suggest a *use* for each of the gases shown: ....

....

Questions on Man-Made and Synthetic Materials

Q1 These pictures show some common items and the natural material they can be made from.

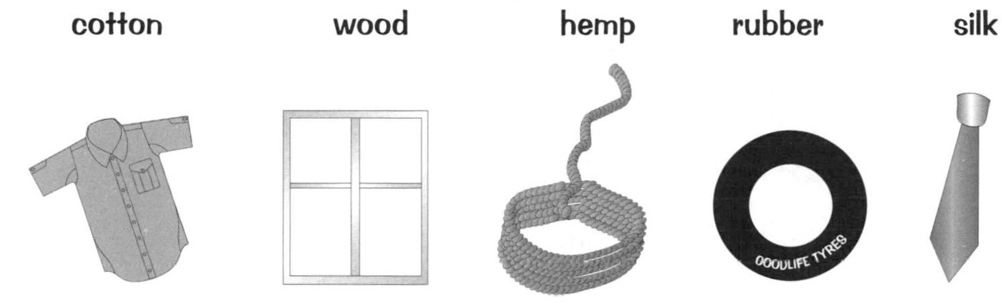

....

a) For each item above, write beneath it a *synthetic* (man-made) alternative material that could be used to make that item.

b) Complete the table, using the materials from section a).

Item	Material	Advantages	Disadvantages
Shirt	Cotton	Wears well, smooth	Expensive
	Nylon	Cheap, colourful	Scratchy, "sweaty"
Window			
Rope			
Tyre			
Tie			

Q2 On a visit to the local supermarket, George noticed several large bins used for *recycling* various bits and bobs. The bins were labelled "*Glass*", "*Paper*", "*Aluminium*", "*Other Metals*" and "*Clothing*".

a) What is *recycling*?..

b) What are the *benefits* of recycling?..

....

c) Why do you think that recycling glass is so worthwhile?
(Hint:— think about the raw materials involved in the making of glass).

....

....

....

Questions on Particle Theory

Q1 Answer the following *true* or *false* — put T or F in the space at the end of each question.

a) There are *strong* forces of *attraction* between particles in a solid. (___)

b) Particles in a *gas* are close together. (___)

c) *Liquids* are easy to compress. (___)

d) A *dense* material has lots of particles in a *small* volume. (___)

e) There are *no* forces of *attraction* between the particles in a *gas*. (___)

f) *Gases* can be *compressed* easily as there's lots of *free* space between the particles. (___)

g) In a *solid*, the particles are *further apart* than in a liquid or a gas. (___)

h) *Gases* have very *low* densities. (___)

Q2 In the following chart, tick the relevant boxes concerning particles in *solids*, *liquids* or *gases*.

	Particles are close together	Particles are held in fixed positions	Particles are moving
Solid			
Liquid			
Gas			

Q3 Match each of the pictures on the left (A, B and C) with the *correct arrangement* of particles on the right (X, Y and Z) by drawing a line between them.

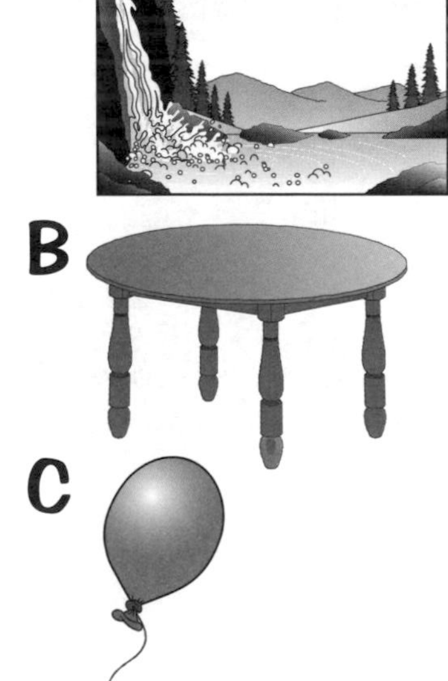

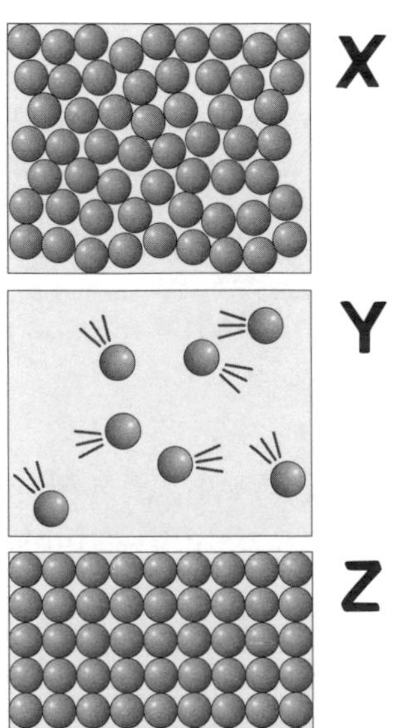

Questions on Particle Theory

Q4 It's important to know about the differences between the strengths of the forces *acting* in *solids*, *liquids* and *gases*. Use the key words below to write a few sentences about these differences. Mention how these forces affect the arrangement of particles in the three different states.

KEY WORDS: forces, attraction, particles, strong, weak

....

....

....

....

Q5 A liquid is poured into the first container, and then into each of the others, one at a time.

a) Does the liquid's *volume* remain the same each time? ....

b) Does the *height* of the liquid remain the same each time? ....

Q6 Describe the *arrangement* and *movement* of particles in a liquid, and list some *properties* of a liquid. You should be able to think of two things about the particles, and at least three properties of liquids.

....

....

....

....

Questions on Particle Theory

Q7 Fill in the missing words about particles in a solid. Words may be used once, more than once, or not at all.

fixed	closely	compact	dense	air	compressed
move	fast	vibrate	volume	flow	small

In a solid, the particles are held very ____________ together, in almost ______________ positions, although they do ______________ to and fro a little. The particles don't ____________ from their positions, so all solids keep a ______________ shape and ______________ and can't ______________ like liquids. Solids can't easily be ____________ because the particles are already packed very __________ together. Solids are usually ______________ , as there are lots of particles in a _____________ volume.

Q8 Explain why it is difficult to *alter* the *shape* of a solid. (Draw a simple diagram of particles in a solid to illustrate your argument.)

....

....

....

....

Diagram

Q9 This question concerns a *gas*, such as *steam*. Look at the diagram below and put a tick(✓) or a cross (×) through the phrases relevant to steam.

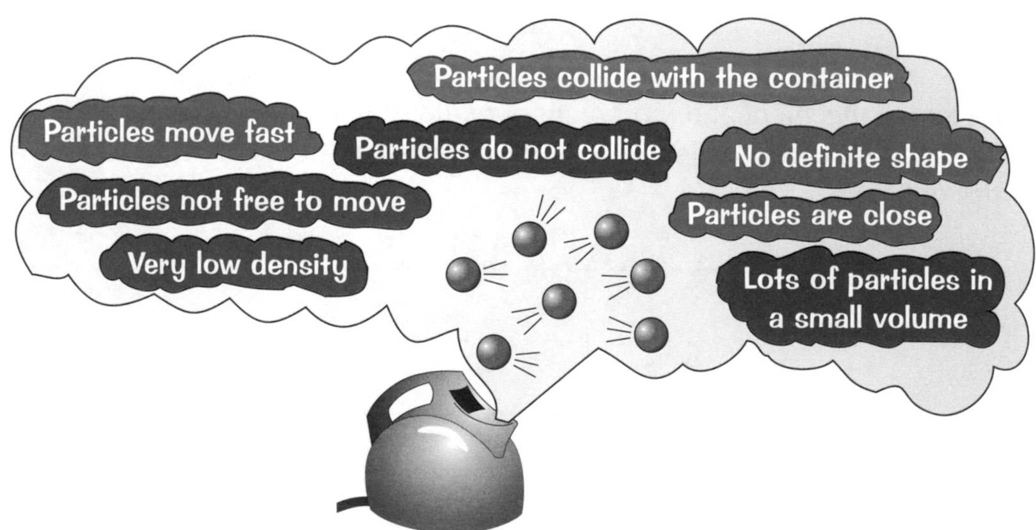
Particles collide with the container
Particles move fast
Particles do not collide
No definite shape
Particles not free to move
Particles are close
Very low density
Lots of particles in a small volume

Questions on Melting and Boiling Points

Q1 The "make-you-very-cross-word"!

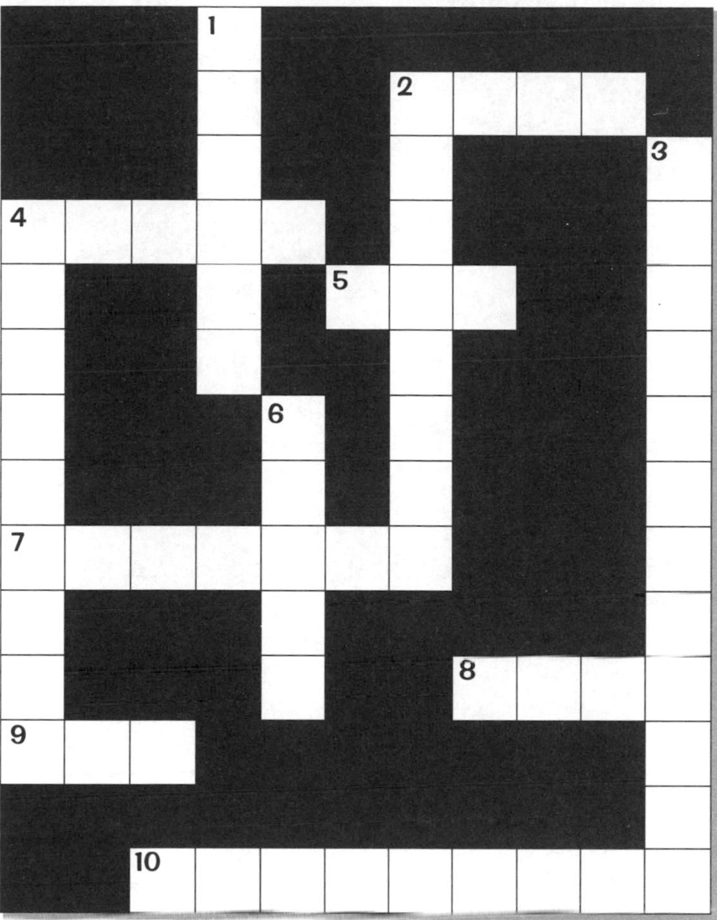

Across

2. The number of states of matter plus one (4)
4. State of matter in which the particles are held closely in fixed positions (5)
5. When a smell spreads, the particles move away from where they originated to where there are relatively ___ (3) of them.
7. Changing from a solid to a liquid (7)
8. When you do this to any substance, the particles gain energy (4)
9. Helium, hydrogen and air are in this state of matter (3)
10. Name for particles in a gas spreading out (9)

Down

1. To make sure there are no other chemicals contaminating a solid before you find its melting point (6)
2. Turning a liquid into a solid (8)
3. Formed as a liquid when steam meets a cold surface (12)
4. Solid changing to a gas (9)
6. Melting or boiling _____ (5)

Questions on Melting and Boiling Points

Q2 This question is about *changes of state* that a substance experiences, as displayed in the diagram opposite.

a) A, B, C, D and E represent changes from one state to another. *Name* each of these changes.

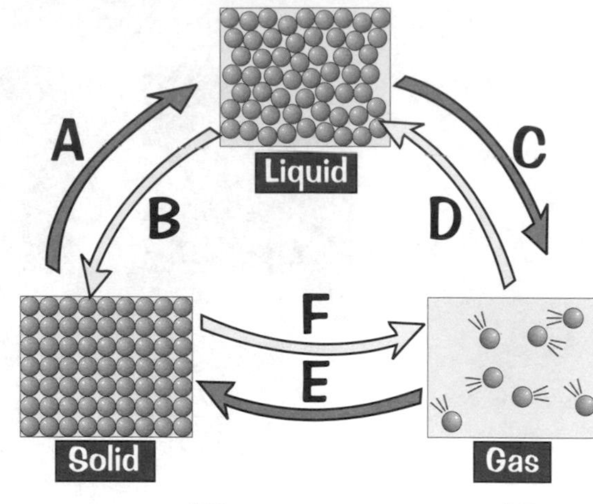

A	B	C	D	E

b) Describe the changes in *density* that the substance experiences as it melts.

....

....

Q3 Look at the diagrams below which show the compression of a gas (like in a cylinder in a piston). Gas particles collide with the container's sides — this is what causes pressure.

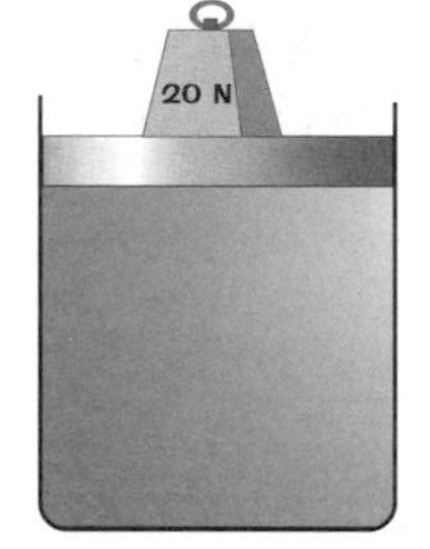

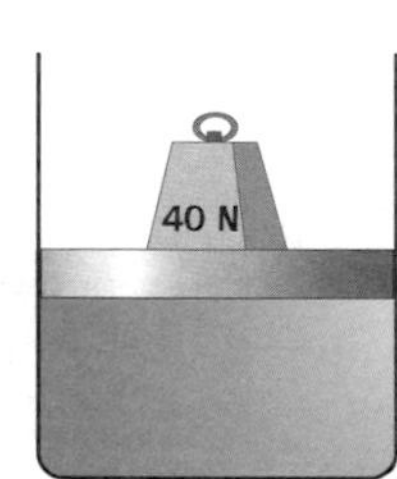

a) Describe why decreasing the volume makes the pressure increase.

....

....

....

....

b) Complete these sentences using the words in the box.

smaller	condensed	more often	boiling point	increases	100°C	squashed

If you reduce the volume of a gas, the pressure ______________ . This is because when the particles are ______________ up into a ______________ space they'll hit the walls __________ ______________ . A gas can be ______________ into a liquid by increasing the pressure. Water boils at a temperature of ____________ (which is called the ______________ ______________).

Questions on Melting and Boiling Points

Q4 Draw a labelled diagram in the box below to show how you would find and measure the *freezing point* of *water* (i.e. the melting point of ice). You should use a thermometer, filter funnel, conical flask/beaker and ice. What *reading* would the *thermometer* display?

Reading: °C

Q5 This diagram shows how to measure the boiling point of **i)** *pure water* and **ii)** *salty water*, by heating the flask from below.

a) What will be the *reading* on the thermometer if its bulb is placed at point X?

....

b) Which will have the *highest* boiling point, pure water or salty water?

....

Q6 Mixing *salt* with *water* causes the water to freeze at a *lower* temperature than normal. Explain why salt is put on roads when conditions become *very cold*.

....

....

....

....

....

Questions on Density

Density is how heavy something is for its size.
e.g. LEAD — is very dense (a small bit — weighs loads)
FEATHERS — are NOT dense (loads of them — weigh very little).

Density is all to do with MASS and VOLUME.

$$\text{Density} = \frac{\text{MASS}}{\text{VOLUME}}$$

or

$$\text{Density} = \text{MASS} \div \text{VOLUME}$$

The units are g/cm^3 or kg/m^3

Example 1: Cube B has the same volume as A, but B has a greater mass, so it's more dense.

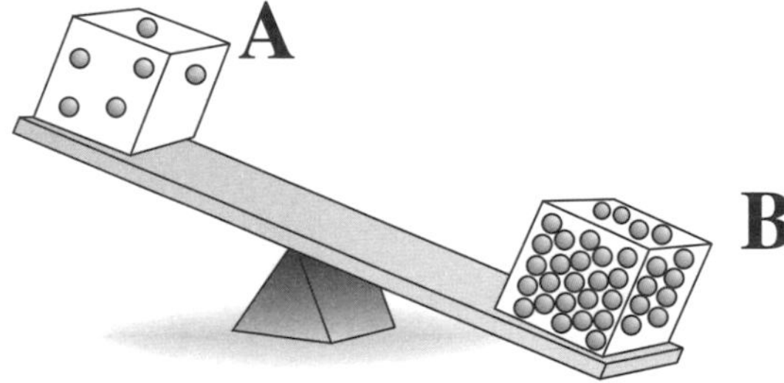

Example 2: A substance has a mass of 100g and a volume of $10cm^3$, what is its density?

Calculate this using the formula: Density = Mass ÷ Volume
Density = Mass ÷ volume = 100 ÷ 10 = $10g/cm^3$

Q1 **a)** Calculate the density of a substance whose mass = 200g and whose volume = $10cm^3$.

....

....

b) Calculate the density of a substance whose mass = 400g and whose volume = $10cm^3$.

....

....

Questions on Density

c) Calculate the density of a substance whose mass = 10,000g and whose volume = $50cm^3$.

....

....

Q2 a) Which is the most dense substance?

Substance	Density g/cm^3
Iron	7.9
Copper	8.9
Aluminium	2.7
Lead	11.3
Sodium	0.99
Water	1.0

Most dense = ...

b) Draw a bar chart below to show the density information above.

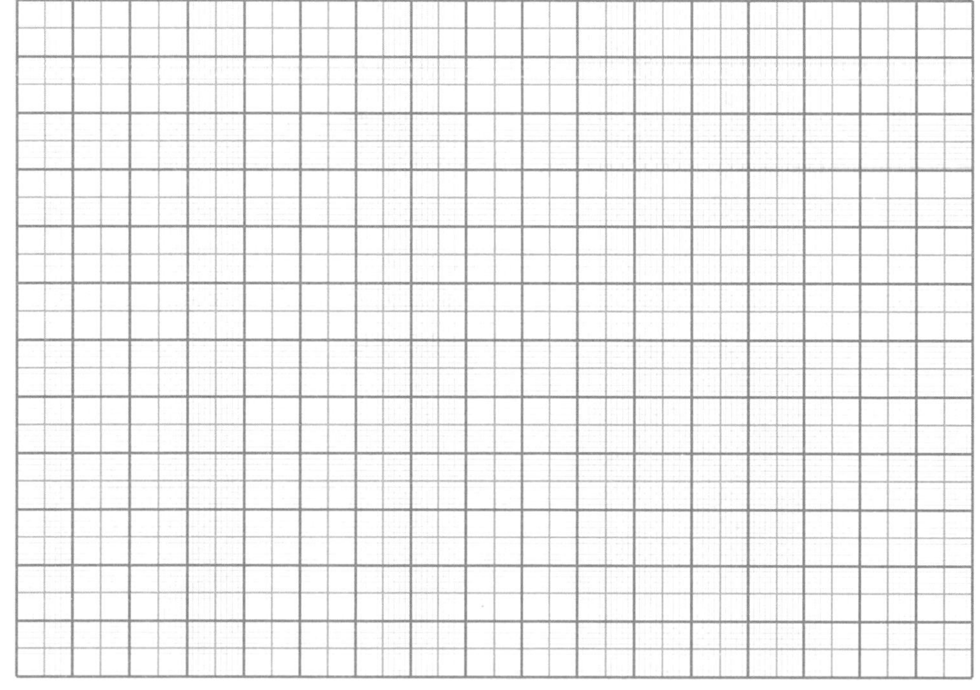

c) On the graph draw a horizontal line across on the $1.0g/cm^3$ line. Any material above this line will sink in water, and any below will float. Which elements would float and which would sink in water?

....

....

Questions on The Water Cycle

Q1 Look carefully at the diagram below which shows the *water cycle*.

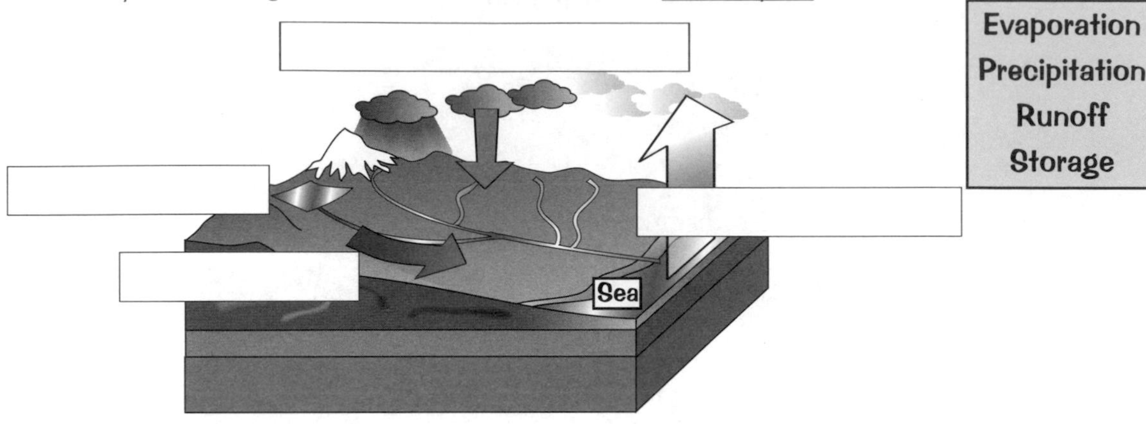

Evaporation
Precipitation
Runoff
Storage

a) *Fill in* the blank boxes using the words in the box.

b) What is *precipitation*? ....

....

c) What causes the water in the sea to *evaporate?*

....

d) What name do we give to a *large concentration* of tiny *water droplets*?

....

e) When these tiny droplets *cool* further, they form larger and larger droplets. What happens if the droplets become *too big?*

....

Q2 The water cycle can be considered to start at any of the four stages named in Question 1 (a). However, *evaporation* of the water from the sea, or any other large water mass, is often considered to be the *first stage*. Explain *evaporation* in terms of the *energy* and *movement of particles*.

....

....

....

Q3 *Rain* is obviously an important part of the water cycle. In some places it rains more often than others. Look at the land profile opposite, and suggest which place you think would have the most rain.

....

....

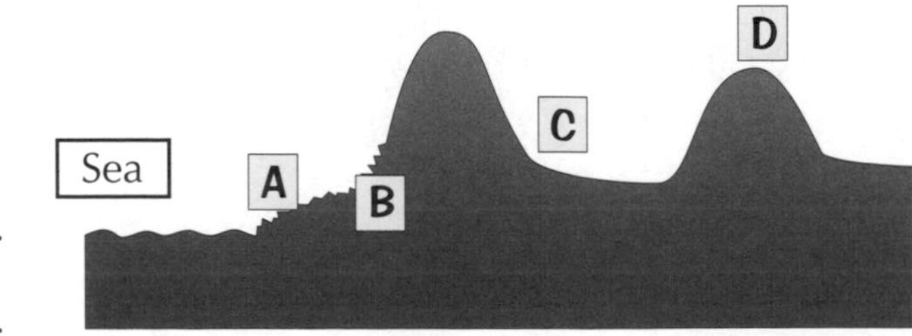

Questions on The Water Cycle

Q4 The water cycle may be represented as a "circular flow" diagram. Complete the missing parts of the diagram below.

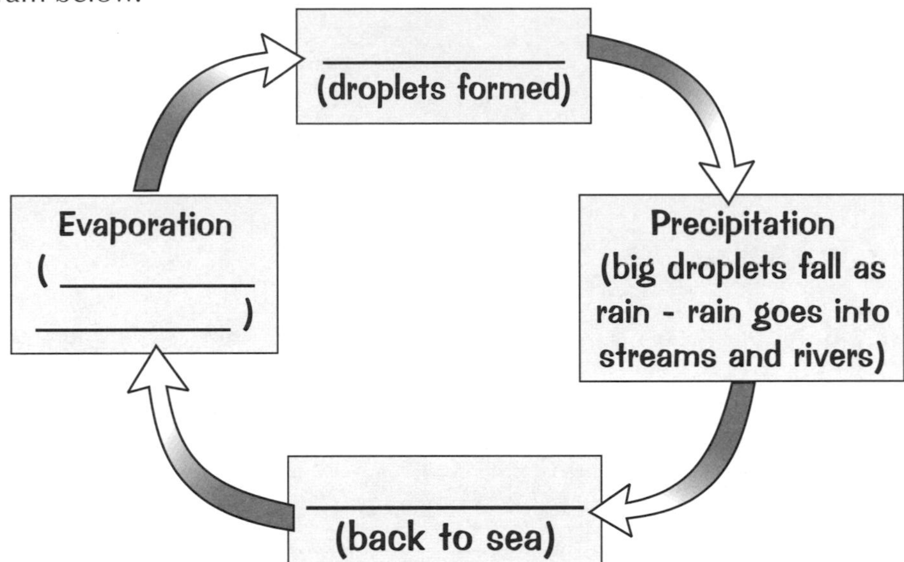

Q5 The passage below describes the water cycle. The start of each sentence is in the correct place, but unfortunately, the rest of each sentence has been *scrambled*. Unscramble the sentences by drawing *arrows* (→) between the boxes to reveal how the water cycle *works*.

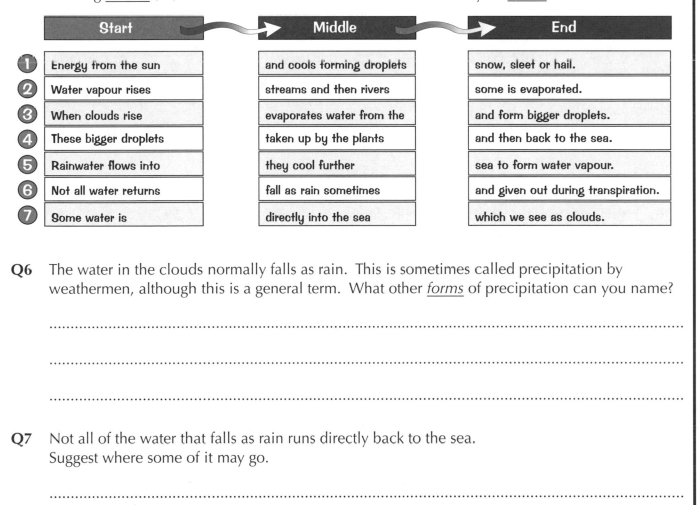

	Start	Middle	End
1	Energy from the sun	and cools forming droplets	snow, sleet or hail.
2	Water vapour rises	streams and then rivers	some is evaporated.
3	When clouds rise	evaporates water from the	and form bigger droplets.
4	These bigger droplets	taken up by the plants	and then back to the sea.
5	Rainwater flows into	they cool further	sea to form water vapour.
6	Not all water returns	fall as rain sometimes	and given out during transpiration.
7	Some water is	directly into the sea	which we see as clouds.

Q6 The water in the clouds normally falls as rain. This is sometimes called precipitation by weathermen, although this is a general term. What other *forms* of precipitation can you name?

....

....

....

Q7 Not all of the water that falls as rain runs directly back to the sea.
Suggest where some of it may go.

....

Atoms, Elements and Compounds

The diagram below represents the Periodic Table.

Q1 What is listed in the Periodic Table? ....

....

Q2 In the Periodic table, what is a group? ....

....

Q3 Groups have numbers to show where they are, but some also have names as well. Mark on the eight groups by putting the correct number above the correct column. Then name two groups of the Periodic Table.

....

Q4 What in the Periodic Table is a *period?* ....

....

Q5 Where are the metals and the non-metals? Left or right-hand-side? ....

....

Q6 Using a copy of the Periodic Table, pick the odd one out for each of the lists **a)** to **g)** and explain why it's different from all the others.

a) Magnesium, aluminium, lead, silicon:— ....

b) Ca, Cu, Cl, Cs:— ....

c) NaCl, KBr, MgO, LiI:— ....

d) CO, Co, Ca, Cu:— ....

e) Helium, argon, hydrogen, krypton:— ....

f) Li, Na, K, Fe:— ....

g) Lithium, nitrogen, oxygen, carbon:— ....

Atoms, Elements and Compounds

Q7 Write '*agree*' or '*disagree*' for each of the statements below.

a) An element can be *split up* into simpler parts by chemical methods. ....

b) All *matter* on Earth is made up of elements. ....

c) There are about *100* different elements. ....

d) There are *six* elements which are *non-metals*. ....

e) Each element has a *name* and a shorthand *symbol*. ....

f) Each element contains at least *two* atoms joined up. ....

Q8 Divide the following into two sets labelled *elements* and *compounds* by writing the name in the box below.

Sodium Chloride
Sulphur
Magnesium Oxide
Lead
Water
Methane
Propane
Carbon Dioxide
Oxygen
Helium
Calcium
Sulphuric Acid
Sulphur Dioxide
Carbon Monoxide
Chlorine

Elements: ....

....

Compounds: ....

....

Q9 Write down how many *atoms* are present in the molecules written below. (E.g. CO_2 contains 1 atom of carbon C and 2 atoms of oxygen O.)

a) Copper sulphate $CuSO_4$

....

b) Sodium chloride NaCl

....

c) Iron oxide Fe_2O_3

....

d) Ammonia NH_3

....

e) Water H_2O

....

f) Copper oxide CuO

....

Questions on Naming Substances

You need to remember the right way to name chemical compounds.

1) Two elements will combine to make a compound ending in *'ide'* (e.g. potassium chlor*ide*).
2) Two or more elements will combine with oxygen to make a compound ending in *'ate'* (e.g. copper sulph*ate*).
3) When two identical elements combine, the name of the substance *doesn't change*. (E.g. hydrogen).

Q1 This question concerns the *three rules* about *naming* compounds.

a) When two ________________ combine the ending is usually something _______.

b) When three or more different elements ___________, and one of them is ___________, the ending will normally be something ______________.

c) When two identical elements combine the name _________ change.

d) Give two examples of something ending in -ate. ....

Q2 Match the formula with the name of the compound:

water	Fe_2O_3
iron oxide	CO
carbon dioxide	HNO_3
nitric acid	CO_2
methane	H_2O
carbon monoxide	$NaCl$
sodium chloride	CH_4

Q3 Name the compound *sodium* makes with the following *elements:*

a) *Chlorine* .... **b)** *Bromine* .... **c)** *Oxygen* ....

Q4 *Name* and give the chemical symbols for the *elements* in the following compounds:

a) Calcium carbonate. ....

b) Calcium oxide. ....

c) Potassium hydroxide. ....

d) Copper sulphate. ....

Questions on Elements

Q1 Give the names of the elements represented by the following symbols:

a) C .... **d)** Cu ....

b) Cl .... **e)** Na ....

c) Ca .... **f)** F ....

Q2 Which of the elements in Question 1 are non-metals?

....

Q3 Give the names of those elements whose symbols appear in this shop sign.

C.HOPKINS CaFe

....

....

....

Q4 Look at the pictures below. Write the formula of the substance shown next to each picture. Then give the names of the substances in the space below.

A (H)(H) H_2	**B** (He)	**C** (Cl)(Cl)
D (Ar)	**E** (O)(O)	**F** (I)(I)

A) Hydrogen..

B) ....

C) ....

D) ....

E) ....

F) ....

Questions on Elements

Q5 In this mammoth word search there are the names of the first twenty elements from the Periodic Table. There are also ten extra elements or compounds — find 'em fast...

I	O	D	I	N	E	N	N	V	M	U	I	S	S	A	T	O	P
R	C	F	Z	S	A	L	T	P	S	B	R	E	V	L	I	S	E
O	U	Q	M	L	I	C	N	I	Z	Y	F	A	X	U	V	W	D
N	U	S	A	M	L	L	U	E	C	H	L	O	R	I	N	E	I
S	M	R	T	U	L	L	I	T	P	N	U	G	O	K	L	L	X
U	U	M	U	I	C	L	A	C	I	H	O	F	F	L	M	T	O
L	I	L	O	I	J	E	H	R	O	J	R	S	E	E	R	I	R
P	L	D	P	A	L	K	G	J	S	N	I	D	D	A	S	N	E
H	E	I	H	H	Y	D	R	O	G	E	N	C	C	D	T	E	P
I	H	C	O	Y	U	R	M	M	N	O	E	Z	A	U	P	G	P
D	E	A	S	D	A	R	G	J	K	N	B	B	W	R	C	Y	O
E	Y	C	P	R	N	L	I	T	H	I	U	M	V	T	B	X	C
A	R	I	H	O	O	I	K	C	H	I	U	M	B	B	B	O	A
G	U	R	O	X	G	M	E	F	A	N	E	G	O	R	T	I	N
O	C	T	R	Y	R	E	E	G	U	C	R	I	H	O	O	P	O
L	R	I	U	P	A	L	U	M	I	N	I	U	M	D	K	F	R
D	E	N	S	O	D	I	U	M	N	N	M	D	L	Y	V	A	O
A	M	U	I	S	E	N	G	A	M	U	I	L	L	Y	R	E	B

Q6 The table below gives information about the elements: copper, oxygen, mercury, sodium, and sulphur. Use the table to identify the elements A, B, C, D and E.

Element	Melting Point(°C)	Does it conduct electricity?	Does it catch fire when heated?
A	1083	YES	NOPE
B	-219	NOPE	NOPE
C	-39	YES	NOPE
D	98	YES	YES
E	113	NOPE	YES

A: ....

B: ....

C: ....

D: ....

E: ....

Having Fun with Symbols

Q1 Look at the secret message below, then use the symbols you have learnt and the symbols listed below to decipher the message.

> **Phosphorus, uranium, phosphorus, iodine, (lithium-iodine), sulphur/ Tungsten, hydrogen, oxygen/Tungsten oxygen, (rhodium-hydrogen), potassium/ Hydrogen, argon, (dysprosium-yttrium)/ Tungsten iodine (lithium-iodine), (Lithium-iodine),/ (dysporsium-yttrium) oxygen / Tungsten, (Einsteinium-sulphur), (lithium-iodine), (lithium-iodine) / indium / suphur, astatine, sulphur.**

....

....

....

....

Actinium	Ac	Gold	Au	Preseodymium	Pr
Aluminium	Al	Hafnium	Hf	Promethium	Pm
Americium	Am	Helium	He	Protoactinium	Pa
Antimony	Sb	Holmium	Ho	Radium	Ra
Argon	Ar	Hydrogen	H	Radon	Rn
Arsenic	As	Indium	In	Rhenium	Re
Astatine	At	Iodine	I	Rhodium	Rh
Barium	Ba	Iridium	Ir	Rubidium	Rb
Berkelium	Bk	Iron	Fe	Ruthenium	Ru
Beryllium	Be	Krypton	Kr	Samarium	Sm
Bismuth	Bi	Lanthanum	La	Scandium	Sc
Boron	B	Lead	Pb	Selenium	Se
Bromine	Br	Lithium	Li	Silicon	Si
Cadmium	Cd	Lutetium	Lu	Silver	Ag
Caesium	Cs	Magnesium	Mg	Sodium	Na
Calcium	Ca	Manganese	Mn	Strontium	Sr
Californium	Cf	Mendelevium	Md	Sulphur	S
Carbon	C	Mercury	Hg	Tantalum	Ta
Cerium	Ce	Molybdenum	Mo	Technetium	Tc
Chlorine	Cl	Neodymium	Nd	Tellurium	Te
Chromium	Cr	Neon	Ne	Terbium	Tb
Cobalt	Co	Neptunium	Np	Thallium	Tl
Copper	Cu	Nickel	Ni	Thorium	Th
Curium	Cm	Niobium	Nb	Tin	Sn
Dysprosium	Dy	Nitrogen	N	Titanium	Ti
Einsteinium	Es	Nobelium	No	Tungsten	W
Erbium	Er	Osmium	Os	Uranium	U
Europium	Eu	Oxygen	O	Vanadium	V
Fermium	Fm	Palladium	Pd	Xenon	Xe
Fluorine	F	Phosphorus	P	Ytterbium	Yb
Francium	Fr	Platinum	Pt	Yttrium	Y
Gadolinium	Gd	Plutonium	Pu	Zinc	Zn
Gallium	Ga	Polonium	Po	Zirconium	Zr
Germanium	Ge	Potassium	K		

Having Fun with Symbols

Q2 *Translate* the message below in the same way as you did for Question 1 on Page 97.

Iodine / (Lutetium-uranium), oxygen vanadium, (europium-uranium) / Holmium, (manganese-nitrogen), (europium-uranium) Tungsten, oxygen, (rubidium-boron) potassium. Molybdenum rhenium / fluorine, oxygen, (rubidium-boron) / (manganese-nitrogen) (europium-uranium).

....

....

....

....

Q3 Now *translate* the message below into symbol code:

Best do some work matey!

....

....

....

....

Q4 Think of a message to *send* to a friend.

....

....

....

More Questions on Naming Substances

Q1 *Circle* the correct formula for each of the following compounds:

a) Water — H_2O / H_2O_2

b) Sulphur dioxide — SO_3 / SO_2

c) Copper oxide — CuO / CuO_2

d) Magnesium oxide — MgO_2 / MgO

e) Sodium chloride (table salt) — $NaCl$ / $NaCl_2$

f) Copper sulphate — $CuSO_3$ / $CuSO_4$

g) Calcium carbonate — $CaCO_2$ / $CaCO_3$

h) Ammonia — NH_2 / NH_3

i) Chlorine — Cl / Cl_2

j) Sulphuric acid — H_2SO_4 / HNO_3

k) Carbon dioxide — CO / CO_2

l) Methane — CH_4 / CHO_4

Q2 Match the names and formulae with the pictures below. Some have been done for you. (Words to use: **water**, **nitrogen**, **carbon dioxide**, **NH_3**, **H_2O**, **N_2**, **HCl**)

a)

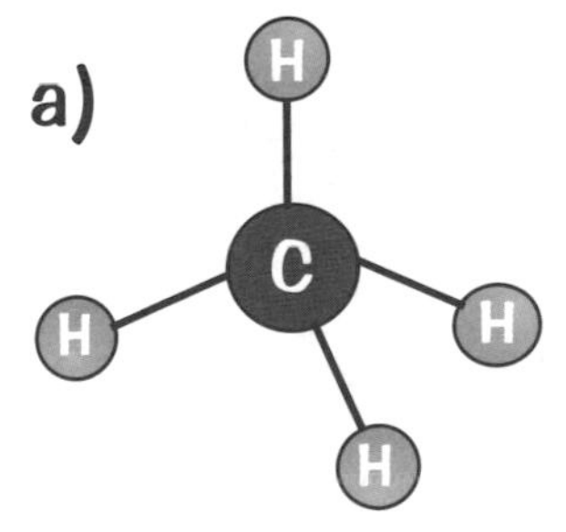

CH_4 Methane

b)

N H H H

.... Ammonia

c)

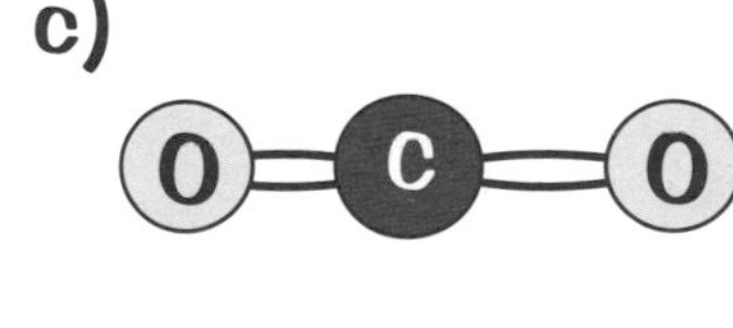

CO_2 ....

d)

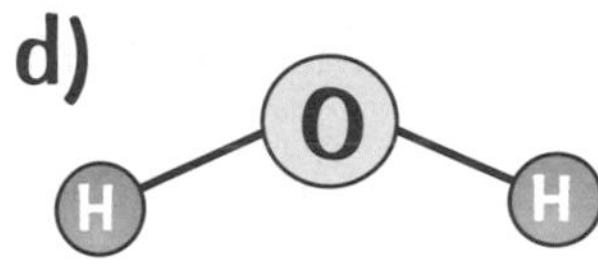

....

e)

N N

....

f)

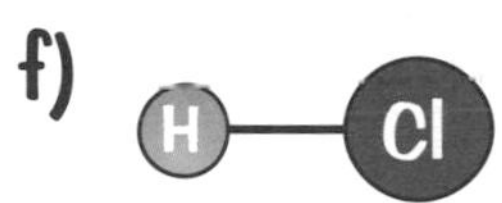

.... Hydrogen chloride

Q3 *Copper can be obtained from its ore, copper sulphide, in two stages.*

1st stage: Copper sulphide reacts with oxygen from the air to form copper oxide and sulphur dioxide gas.
2nd stage: Copper oxide reacts with carbon to form copper and carbon dioxide gas.

a) What are the *compounds* mentioned in the text above? ....

b) Say which *elements* the compounds in your previous answer contain. ....

c) Which of the two sentences below are true and concern the above passage:

i) Carbon reacts with an element to form carbon dioxide gas. ....

ii) Oxygen reacts with a compound to form copper oxide and sulphur dioxide. ....

Questions on Separating Substances

Q1 From the following list of substances, identify which are *elements* *(e)*, which are *compounds* *(c)* and which are *mixtures* *(m)*. Write the appropriate letter (e, c, or m) next to the substance.

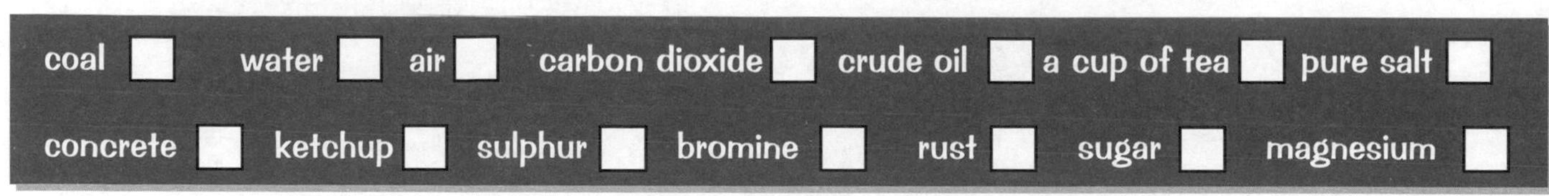

coal
water
air
carbon dioxide
crude oil
a cup of tea
pure salt
concrete
ketchup
sulphur
bromine
rust
sugar
magnesium

Q2 Mixtures can be separated by different methods. For each of the mixtures below say which method you would use to separate them. (Write F for *filtration*, D for *distillation*, E for *evaporation* and C for *chromatography* below the relevant diagram).

....

Q3 The local garden centre sells lawn sand, which is a *mixture* of *sharp sand* and *fertiliser* (ammonium nitrate). It should be made up from a *50/50* mix of each, measured by weight. Your neighbour has bought some but believes that the garden centre has cheated her by adding more of the sand (which is not as valuable as the fertiliser). Your neighbour has asked you to help her prove that she has been cheated. Outline briefly the steps you would take to test her idea and explain briefly *why* you are doing each step.
(Hint — remember fertilisers are soluble in water).

....

....

....

....

....

....

....

Questions on Separating Substances

Q4 Chromatography is the name given to the process of separating dyes and inks. Black ink consists of several different colours mixed together. If a spot of ink is put on some filter paper and the paper is left to stand in ethanol, the ink will separate out into its different components. The more soluble the dye is in ethanol, the further it travels along the paper. Look at the diagram.

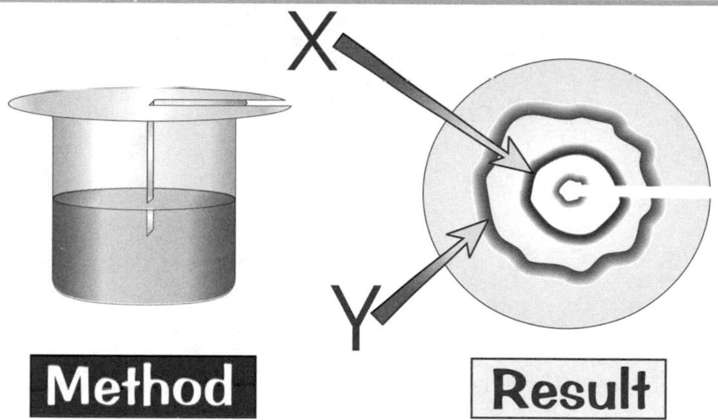

a) Which of the colours, X or Y is most *soluble?* ....

b) How can you tell? ....

Q5 The Headmaster received an anonymous note from a Year 9 pupil demanding more chips at lunch time. He passed the letter to Mr D. Orbital, Head of Chemistry, to be analysed.

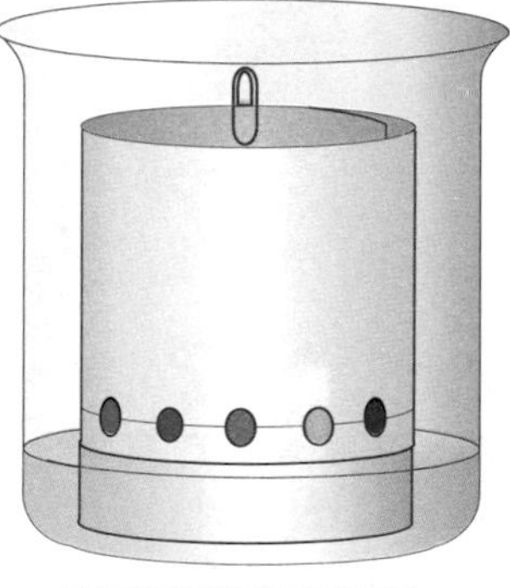

Ink samples from several pupils were also examined.

The picture on the right shows the results.

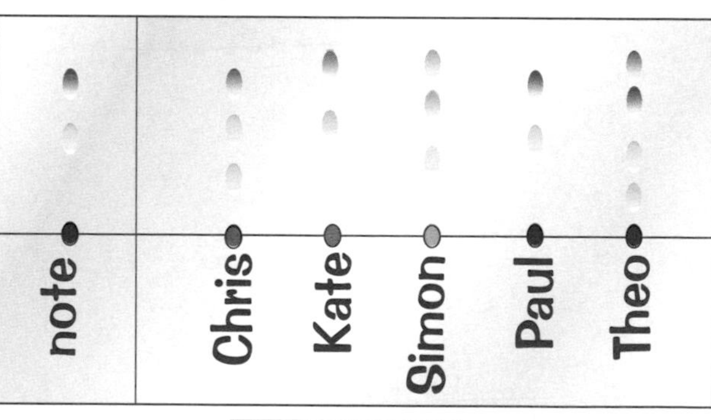

a) How *many* colours were in the suspect's ink? ....

b) Which pupils could *not* have written the note? ....

c) Who is likely to be the *guilty* pupil? ....

d) Give a clear *explanation* of the reason for your decision: ....

....

Questions on the Properties of Metals

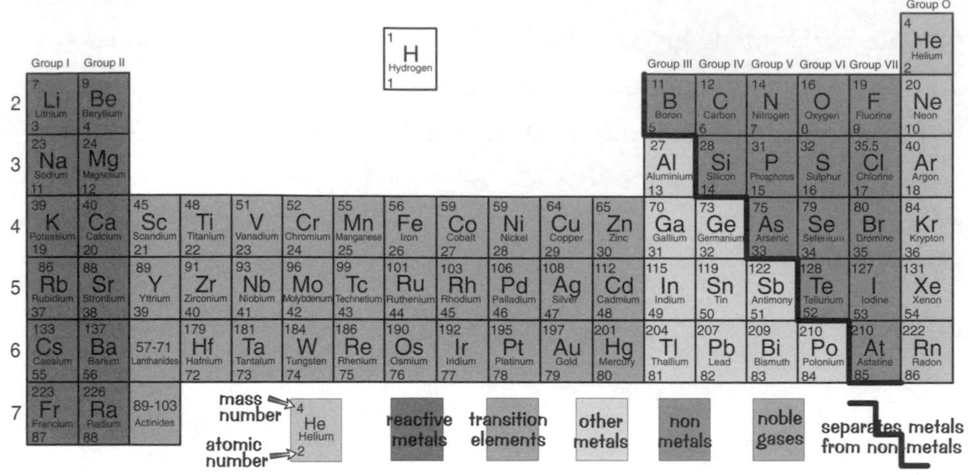

The metals in the Periodic Table have many properties that make them useful.

Q1 Which two properties of metals means copper is a suitable material for saucepans?

1) ....

2) ....

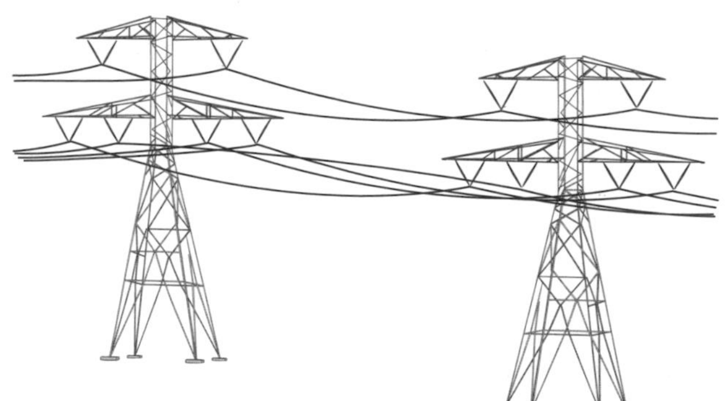

Q2 What property of metals makes them useful for overhead power cables? Why is _aluminium_ used instead of _copper?_

....

....

Q3 What _two_ metals are commonly used to make _cans?_ Suggest how this machine could sort out the different types of can for recycling and state what _property_ of the metal is used.

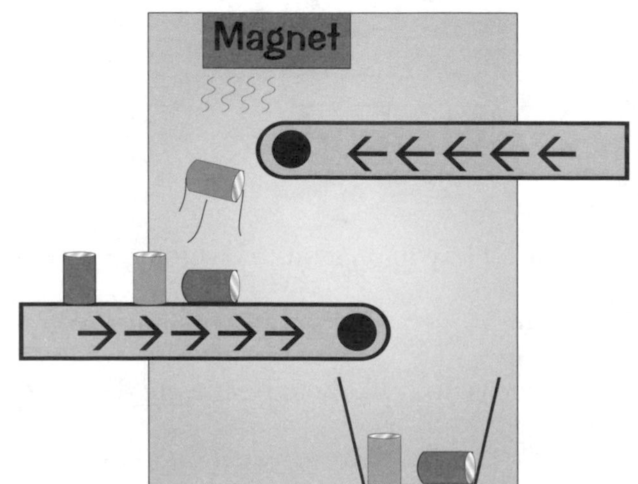

....

....

....

Questions on the Properties of Metals

Q4 An *alloy* is a mixture of two (or more) *metals*. Often, the resulting product has different, hopefully better, properties than the metals it contains (when used on their own). Some alloys are listed below. Suggest which *benefits* of each metal are being used in the alloy. (For example, *solder* contains *tin*, which is a good conductor of electricity, and *lead*, which has a low melting point (for a metal)).

Find out the metals present in the following alloys:

BRASS	STAINLESS STEEL	TITANIUM ALUM	COINAGE SILVER

....

....

....

Q5 Rust (iron oxide) is a complicated *oxide* of iron. When iron reacts with oxygen in the air it goes *rusty*.

a) What compounds are formed when these metals react with *oxygen*?

i) magnesium ....   **ii)** lead ....

iii) copper ....   **iv)** calcium ....

b) If you could *dissolve* the products in *water* and test them with *Universal Indicator*, what *colour* would you see and what would this *mean*?

....

....

Q6 Metals have many properties which make them extremely useful to us. The examples below show some of the uses of metals. For each one, write underneath it which property, or properties, are being *utilised*.

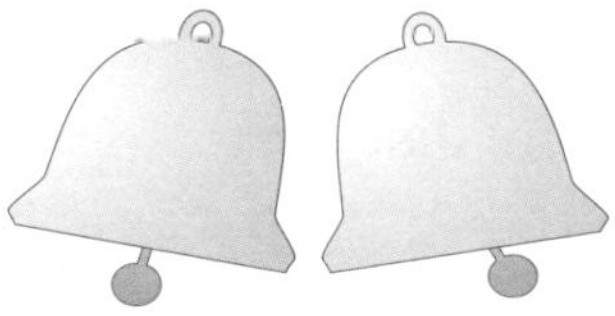

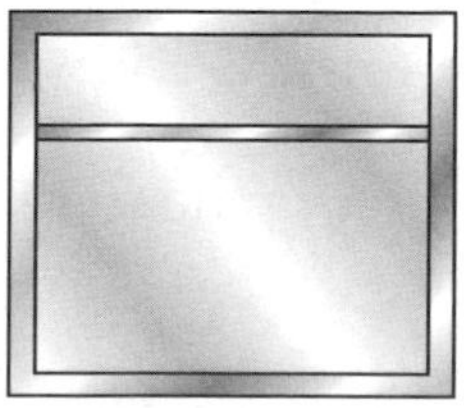

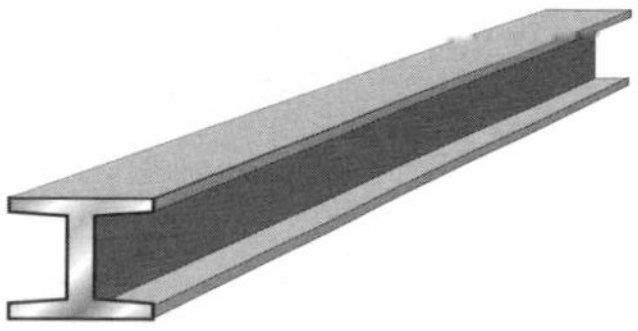

....

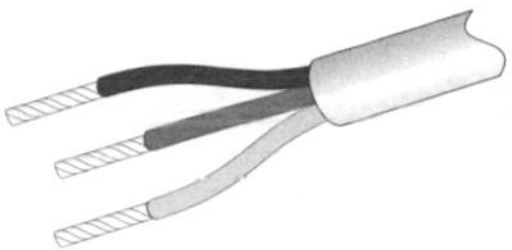

....

Questions on the Properties of Metals

Q7 Read carefully the descriptions given below that describe three different balls. The balls are made of either *metallic* or *non-metallic* elements. For each, write down whether it's made of a metal or a non-metal.

> Ball 1 is a dull blue colour. It feels *slightly warm* when you pick it up and is *fairly light*. When it was dropped on a wooden floor there was a *dull thud* and the ball *crumbled* slightly.
>
> Ball 2 is a shiny brownish orange colour. It feels *cold* when touched and is surprisingly *heavy*. Although there was no *obvious sound* when dropped on the floor, it did leave a *mark* in the wood.
>
> Ball 3 is grey in colour. It is *light* but *hard*, and when dropped on the floor it makes a sharp bang of a noise.

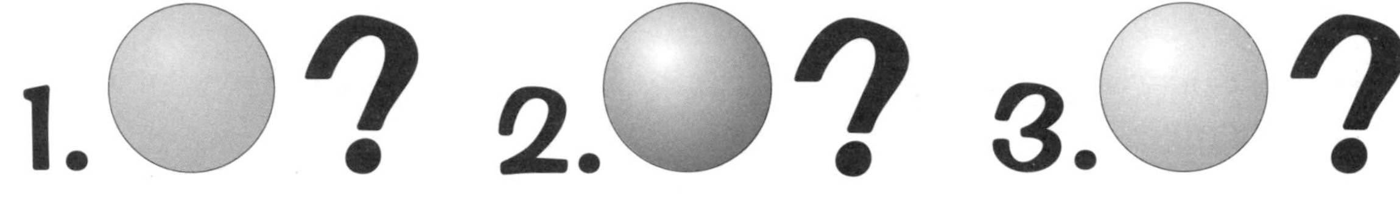

....

Q8 Which of the objects in the fish pond could be lifted out using the *magnetic* fishing rod?

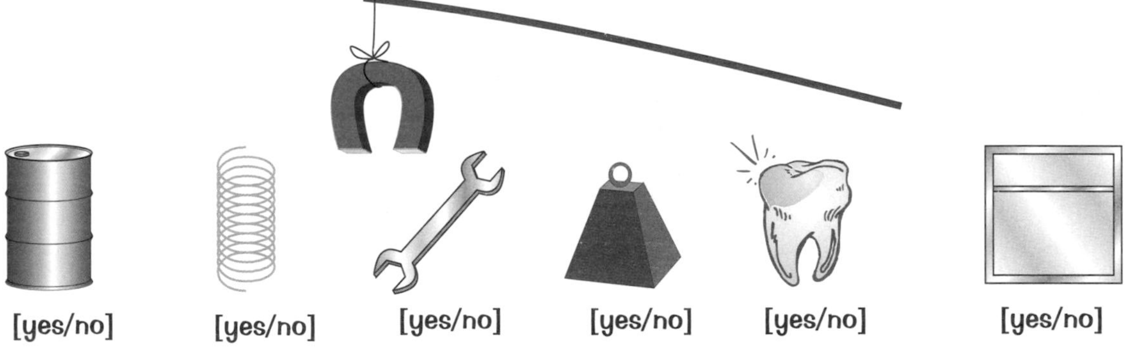

Q9 George and Colin were experimenting with materials. They were trying to break them (as usual!!). Here is a picture of the method they used (i.e. bending them).

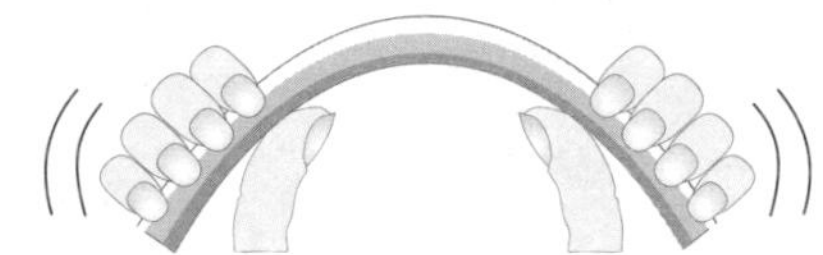

And here is a list of the materials they tested. Each was in the form of a 1cm diameter rod of length 15cm...

glass	sulphur	iron	copper	polystyrene	graphite	lead

Use your knowledge of metals and non-metals to suggest what would happen to each substance under test.

....

....

Questions on the Properties of Non-Metals

Q1 Look at this part-diagram of the Periodic Table.
Use a coloured pencil to shade in all the *non-metals*.

a) Mark the group which consists totally of *gases* with a large red "G".

b) Mark an example of a *liquid* with a large blue "L".

c) Mark the *solids* with a large brown "S".

B	C	N	O	F	Ne
Al	Si	P	S	Cl	Ar
Ga	Ge	As	Se	Br	Kr
In	Sn	Sb	Te	I	Xe
Tl	Pb	Bi	Po	At	Rn

Given that a large number of the *non-metals* are gases, what does this tell you about the *densities* of non-metals in general?

....

....

....

Q2 The "lead" in pencils is really a non-metal called *graphite*.

a) What *element* is graphite?

....

b) What happens if you try to *bend* the pencil?

....

c) What property of *non-metals* in general does this show?

....

....

This element found in part **a)** is different to most other non-metals in one particular way. Use the diagram of graphite on the right to explain what this *unique property* is and the *reason* it occurs.

....

....

....

....

Questions on the Properties of Non-Metals

Q3 Which of these non-metals are attracted to the *magnet*?
Circle Y for Yes or N for No.

Sulphur [Y/N]	Carbon [Y/N]	Bromine [Y/N]
Chlorine [Y/N]	Silicon [Y/N]	Iodine [Y/N]

Q4 *Diamond* is another form of *carbon*, so it's a *non-metal*. However, it is very unusual for a non-metal in *two* ways. What are the two factors that make diamond an *unusual* non-metal?

1) ....

2) ....

Q5 *Sulphur* is a non-metal, yellow-coloured solid, often bought in the form of a stick called *roll sulphur*. It is easy to grind into a powder, as shown below.

If sulphur is similar to most other non-metals, what does this tell you about the *strength* of non-metals?

....

....

Q6 Both sulphur dioxide and carbon dioxide dissolve in *water*. What *colour* would their solution change the Universal Indicator to and what does this tell you about the *oxides* of sulphur and carbon?

....

....

....

....

Indicator

Questions on the Properties of Non-Metals

Q7 John and Linda were asked to investigate the properties of metals and non-metals. They tested sulphur, graphite, iron, lead and a mystery substance called "Q". Here are the results for "Q":

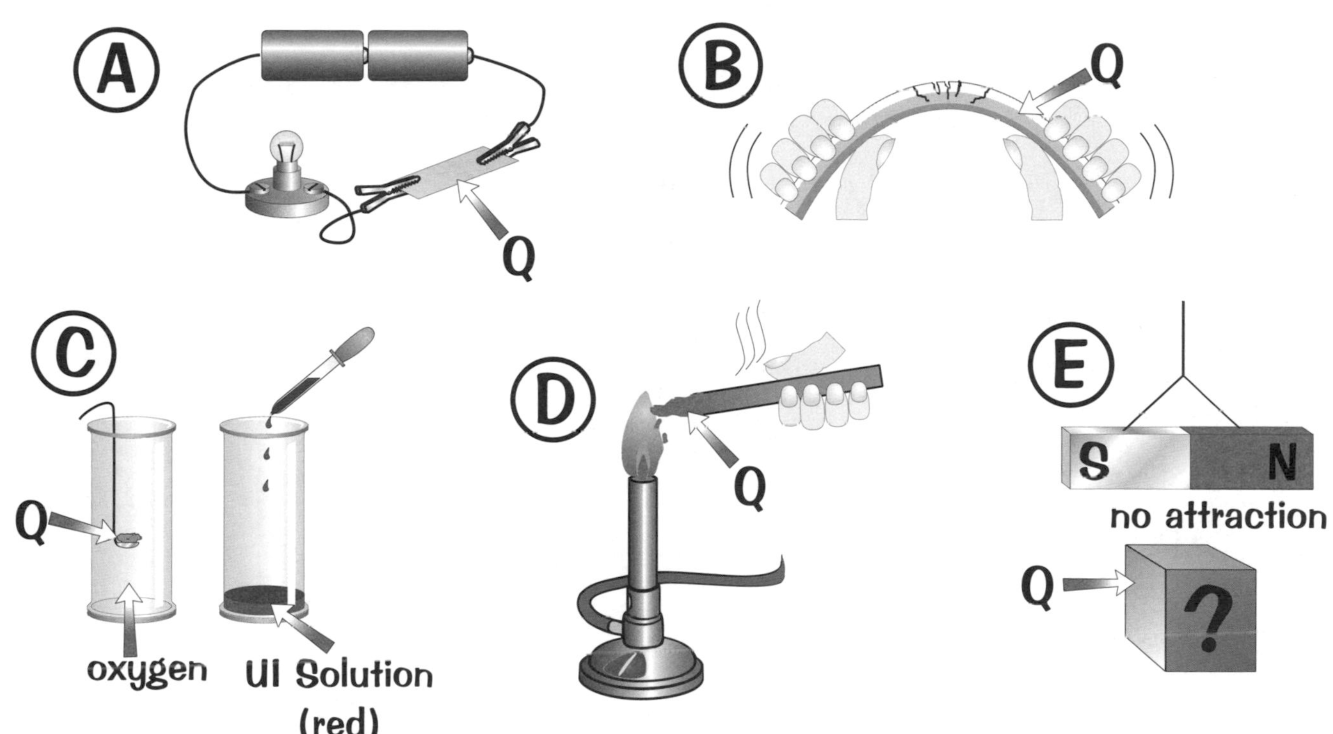

a) First of all, say whether Q is a <u>*metal*</u> or a <u>*non-metal*</u>. Give <u>*reasons*</u> for your choice.

....

....

b) What results would you expect for each individual test when performed on samples of <u>*sulphur*</u> and <u>*iron*</u>?

....

....

....

....

....

....

Questions on Chemical Change

Q1 Use the clues to fill in the puzzle below. What is the special phrase that reads downwards in the first column?

	1	2	3	4	5	6	7	8	9	10	11	12	13	14
a			M				T							
b			A											
c			D								C			
d		A												
e		C												
f				A		Y								
g				A										
h				E					E					
i			P								H			
j				T										
k				M				U						
l		E								E				
m			U											
n										T				

a) Another name for burning.

b) Given out in exothermic reactions.

c) Opposite of exothermic.

d) This is not lost in a chemical reaction.

e) When water becomes a solid, it becomes ____.

f) A chemical change can be speeded up by this.

g) Opposite of acid.

h) Another name for calcium carbonate.

i) This forms a blue solution.

j) Another word for thermal energy.

k) A very useful, light metal.

l) An acid and an alkali together do this.

m) A product of photosynthesis.

n) This splits up compounds in electrolysis.

AND THE PHRASE IS: ....

Q2 Jane says that *melting ice* is a *chemical change*. Steve says that she is wrong. Who do you agree with? Explain your answer.

....

....

....

....

....

Questions on Chemical Change

Q3 Kim decided to carry out an experiment to see if heating *calcium carbonate* changes it in any way. She set up the apparatus below and recorded the *weight* of the calcium carbonate and the test-tube *before* and *after* the experiment (after they'd cooled down). She found that the *calcium carbonate* changed to *calcium oxide* on heating. The results were: Mass before — 25.00g, mass after — 24.65g.

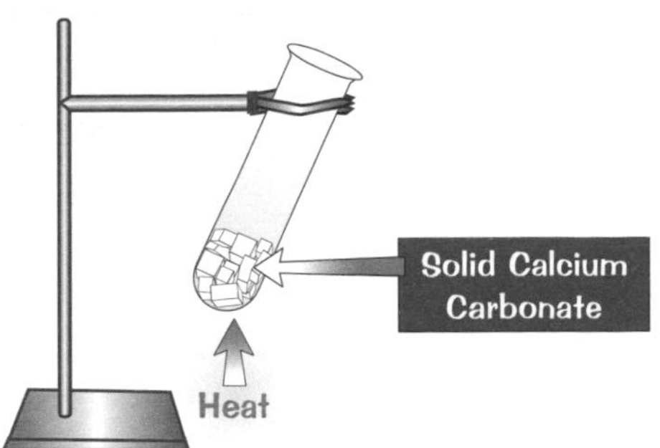

a) What was the *difference* in weight?

b) Had the *calcium carbonate* lost or gained weight?

c) Explain why this happened.

d) Kim also noticed that carbon dioxide was given off during the heating process. Write an *equation* in words to show what has happened.

e) What *type* of reaction is this?

f) Why was it important that Kim left the test-tube to *cool* before weighing it again?

Q4 Adam put a piece of *magnesium* into some *acid*. He noted the temperature at the beginning and at the end of the reaction.

a) Using a thermometer he found that the test-tube was hot. What does this tell you about the reaction that took place?

b) Is there any way Adam could get the piece of *magnesium* back to the way it was before?

Questions on Reduction of Metal Ores

Taken out of the curriculum but still important

Q1 Sometimes, the pure materials we want are found in nature mixed with other things. An example of this is iron. It is found in the ground as iron ore, which is made up of iron, oxygen and a few other things. Iron is extracted from its ore in a large piece of industrial apparatus called a *Blast Furnace*.

a) What is the main element in *coke?*

....

b) Complete the equation below showing how the coke and iron ore react. (Words to use: carbon, iron, dioxide, carbon.)

.... + Iron oxide → .... + ...

c) Why do you think the temperatures need to be so high?

....

Iron ore, coke and limestone

1500°C

Hot air

Molten iron

A Blast Furnace

d) The *limestone* removes impurities from the iron. Why is this done?

....

....

Q2 *Lead oxide* can also be changed into lead in a similar way — using carbon. Draw a diagram to show how you could do this in the laboratory. Explain what would happen. (Apparatus to use: crucible, tripod, clay pipe triangle, Bunsen burner, heat mat, carbon, lead oxide).

....

....

....

....

....

....

....

....

Questions on Combustion

Taken out of the curriculum but still important

Q1 Joshua's teacher set up the apparatus below to demonstrate another useful reaction involving burning.

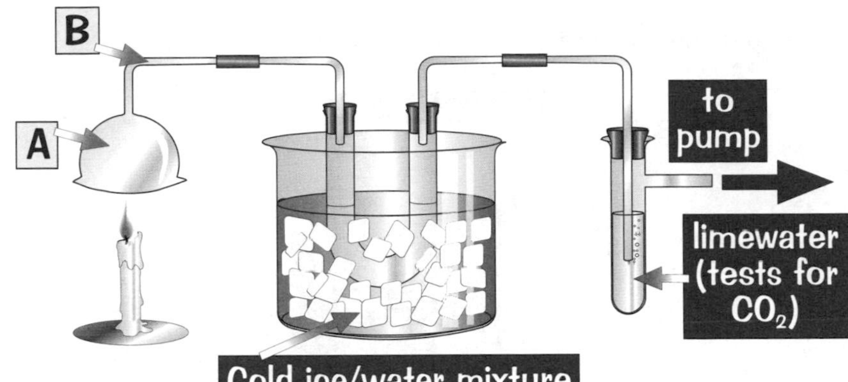

a) Name parts A and B.

A = ... B = ...

b) For what reason does the apparatus have:

i) ice? ....

ii) limewater? ....

c) i) What will be seen in the *U-tube?* ....

....

ii) What will happen to the *limewater?* ....

....

d) What does this experiment show about the things that are made when the candle *burns?*

....

....

e) The teacher then put a piece of rocksil wool soaked in meths under A and carefully lit it. What would you expect to see this time?

....

f) These reactions change one type of energy to another. What is the *chemical energy* from the fuel *changed* into?

....

Questions on Useful Chemical Reactions

Taken out of the curriculum but still important

Q1 *Yeast* is very important. One of its main uses is in the making of bread — it makes bread rise by converting *sugar* into *carbon dioxide* and *alcohol*. Yeast works best at around 40°C.

These three experiments were set up as below, with the same volume of dough.

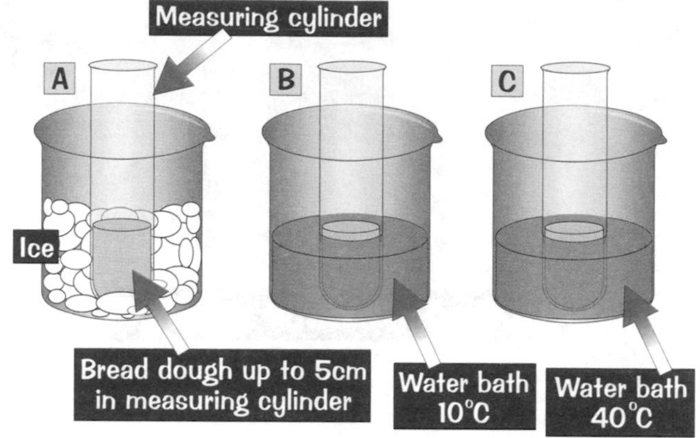

The experiments were left for 45 minutes. After that, the volume of the dough was measured.

a) Why is it important that all test-tubes started with the *same amount* of dough?

....

....

b) In this experiment the volume of dough was measured and compared.
Why would it be a bad idea to measure and compare the weights of the doughs?

....

....

c) In which cylinder do you think the dough would rise the *most*, and the *least?*

....

....

d) What happens to the *alcohol* during baking?

....

e) What is the *name* given to this reaction?

....

f) Which *by-products* of this reaction are useful?

....

....

Questions on Useful Chemical Reactions

Taken out of the curriculum but still important

Q2 Use the clues to find the mystery word in the shaded box. Some letters have been done for you. All the clues have something to do with *neutralisation reactions* and their units.

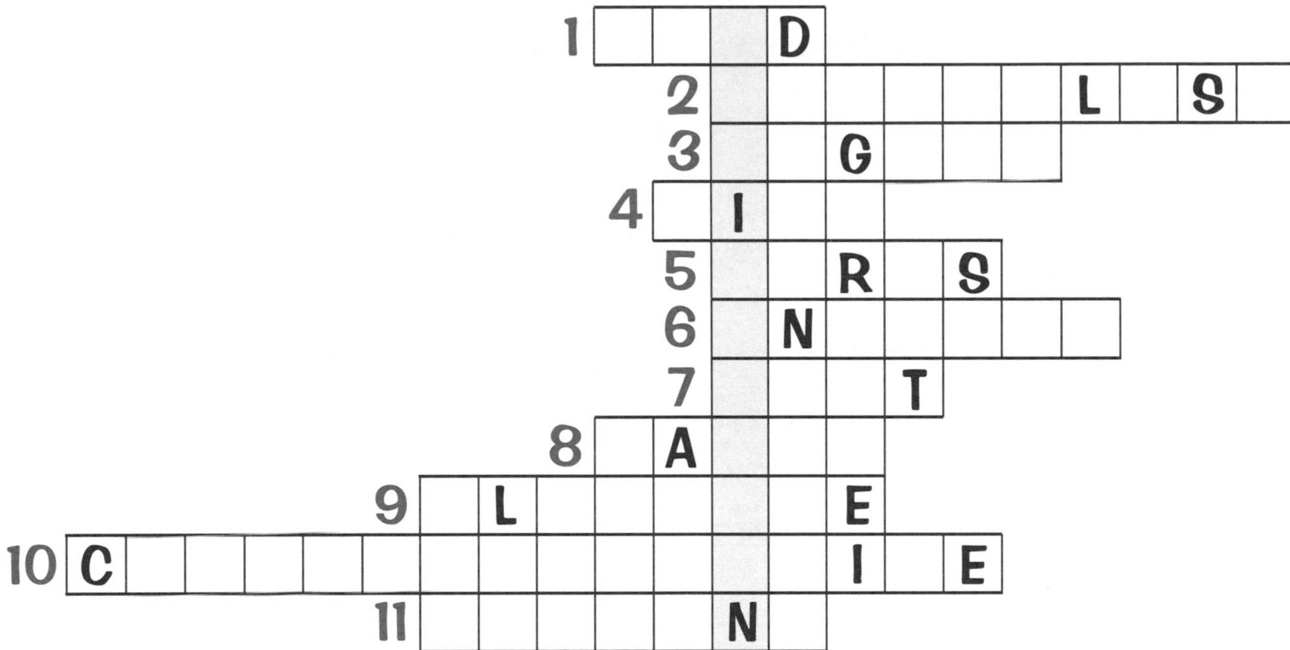

The mystery word is ....

Clues:

1) Too much of this causes indigestion.

2) An acid will do this to an alkali.

3) Acid helps the stomach to do this with food.

4) and **5)** Acid in our stomachs does this as well, which helps to prevent disease.

6) These can be damaged by the wrong pH, and are very important for digestion.

7) and **8)** An acid and an alkali together form these two things.

9) Potatoes grow best in this type of soil.

10) Another name for "slaked lime". (Two words, 7,9)

11) Another word for combustion.

Questions on Equations

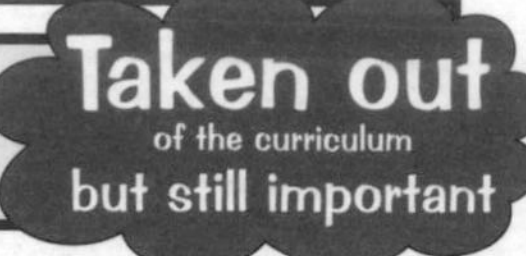

In all chemical equations the reactants turn into products, and we have an arrow between the two as shown below.

Reactants —go to→ **Products**

For example:

Cake ingredients may go to produce a tasty cake.

Cake ingredients —go to→ **Tasty cake**

Q1 Write down the names of the *reactants* and *products* in each of the equations in the table below.

A) Magnesium + oxygen → magnesium oxide.

B) Carbon + oxygen → carbon dioxide.

C) Lead oxide + carbon → lead + carbon dioxide.

D) Sodium hydroxide + hydrochloric acid → sodium chloride + water.

E) Calcium carbonate → calcium oxide + carbon dioxide.

Equation	Reactants	Products
A		magnesium oxide
B	oxygen & carbon	
C		
D		
E		

Taken out of the curriculum but still important

Questions on Equations

Q2 Complete the following equations by writing in the correct product after the arrow.

a) Iron	+	sulphur	→	....	....
b) Iron	+	oxygen	→	....	....
c) Magnesium	+	oxygen	→	....	....
d) Sulphur	+	oxygen	→	....	....
e) Hydrogen	+	oxygen	→	....	....
f) Magnesium	+	sulphur	→	....	....
g) Aluminium	+	chlorine	→	....	....
h) Hydrogen	+	iodine	→	....	....
i) Carbon	+	oxygen	→	....	....
j) Iron	+	bromine	→	....	....

Q3 Complete the following equations by filling in the spaces.

a) Potassium	+	....	→	potassium chloride
b) Iron	+	....	→	iron sulphide
c)	+	oxygen	→	lead oxide
d)	+	oxygen	→	calcium oxide

Q4 Complete the following equations by filling in the spaces.

a)	+	....	→	sodium chloride
b)	+	....	→	sodium sulphide
c)	+	oxygen	→	magnesium ....
d) Calcium	+	....	→	.... oxide

Questions on Reactivity of Metals

Before you can tackle questions on *displacement reactions*, you need to know about the reactivity series. The important fact you must learn is:

"A *more reactive* metal will *displace* a *less reactive* metal from its compound."

Metals that are higher in the reactivity series will *displace* or *replace* metals that are lower in the reactivity series. The reactivity series is simply a *list of metals* in order of reactivity. So if you don't know the reactivity series you don't stand a chance!

Q1 Put the following metals in the order of the reactivity series, starting with the *most* reactive.

Magnesium, Iron, Potassium, Copper, Aluminium, Zinc.

....

....

....

Q2 To find out how reactive some metals were, David and Emma put four particular metals in a solution of *copper sulphate*.

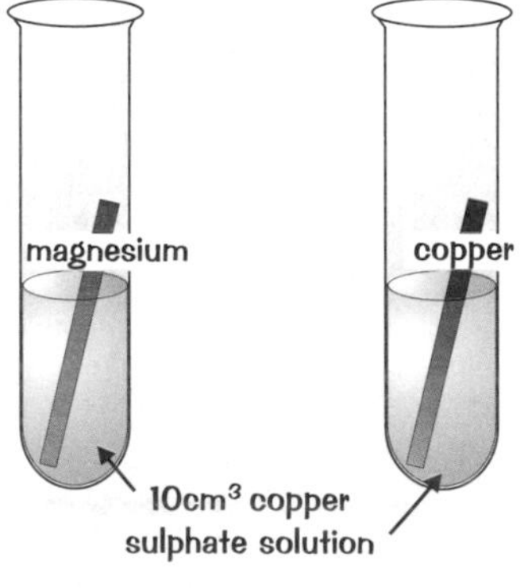

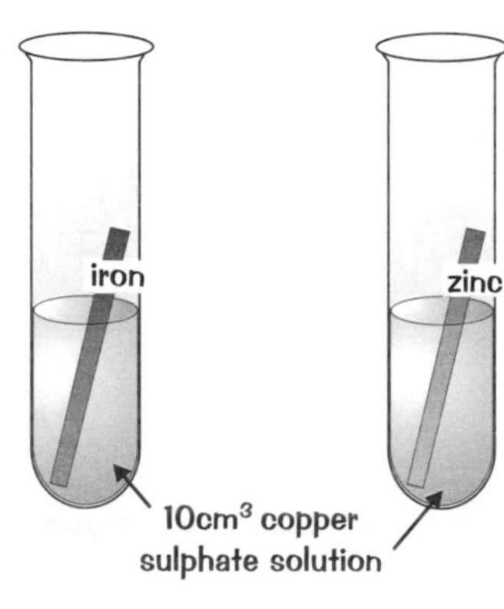

a) They made sure that the *same volume* of copper sulphate of the *same strength* was in each test tube and that the metal strips were of the *same length*. Why is this so important?

....

....

....

....

Questions on Reactivity of Metals

b) Complete the table to show what happened in each test tube after half an hour. Was anything *deposited?*

Metal in copper sulphate solution	Observation after half an hour
magnesium	
copper	
iron	
zinc	

c) Write an equation, *in words*, to show what has happened in the test tube to the *zinc* and *copper sulphate?* (Words to use: **copper** / **zinc** / **sulphate** / **copper** / **zinc** / **sulphate**).

....

d) Which is the *most reactive* (most strongly reacting) metal in this experiment?

....

e) If David and Emma were to put a piece of *silver* into another test tube of *copper sulphate*, what would you expect them to see? Explain your answer.

....

....

Q3 a) Some metals were placed in an *iron sulphate* solution. Fill in the table with a *tick* to show which metals reacted.

Metal	Reaction with iron sulphate
(i) Magnesium	
(ii) Aluminium	
(iii) Iron	
(iv) Lead	
(v) Copper	

Stick your tick in here

b) What would be *deposited* in the tubes that showed a reaction had taken place?

....

c) *Aluminium* is a fairly reactive metal that often has a protective layer on due to oxidation with air. This means it sometimes seems reluctant to react. Name the *protective layer*.

....

Questions on Displacement Reactions

Q1 Fill in the missing words using the clues below and find the mystery metal in the coloured band.

	1	2	3	4	5	6	7	8	9	10	11
		a	·	·	·	·	·	·	·	U	·
							b	·	·	·	N
							c	·	E	·	·
d	·	E	·	·	·	·	·	·			
e	·	·	·	·	R	·	·	S	·		
					f	·	·	O	·		

The mystery metal is:

....

a) A reactive metal that would *displace* zinc from zinc sulphate, and reacts with *steam*.

b) This is more reactive than *copper*.

c) A metal less reactive than *iron* — but only just.

d) Copper cannot displace zinc from zinc sulphate because it is not _______ enough.

e) When magnesium is added to copper sulphate the liquid turns ______.

f) This would be seen coating the zinc strip in the reaction between *zinc* and *iron sulphate*.

Q2 a) Complete the table below, putting a tick where a reaction occurs.

Salt solution → / Metal ↓	magnesium sulphate	aluminium sulphate	zinc sulphate	iron sulphate	copper sulphate
magnesium					
aluminium					
zinc					
iron					
copper					

b) Write down the *salt solutions* you would expect *lead* to react with.

....

....

c) Which metal would you expect to react the fastest with *copper sulphate* solution? Explain your answer.

....

....

....

Questions on Displacement Reactions

Q3 Hannah and Mark were given a solution of *iron sulphate* and four metals; *iron*, *magnesium*, *copper* and a mystery *metal X*. They were asked to investigate the reactivity of metal X compared to the other metals. They put each piece of a metal into a test tube of iron sulphate and left them for half an hour.

a) Draw a diagram to show how they might have set up the apparatus.

The results are shown opposite:

Metal	Reaction with iron sulphate
iron	no reaction
magnesium	iron deposited
copper	no reaction
metal X	no reaction

b) They then tested *metal X* and *iron* in copper sulphate solution. Both deposited *copper*. Why did they test these two with *copper sulphate* solution?

....

....

c) What could *metal X* be?

....

d) How do you know metal X is more *reactive* than copper?

....

....

e) Put all the metals listed in the table in order of *reactivity* (most reactive first).

....

Questions on Metal Extraction

Q1 How easy or how hard it is to *extract* a metal from its ore depends on how *reactive* it is. Match up the following metals to their method of extraction, by drawing a line to the correct method from each element.

Metal	Method of extraction
iron	very unreactive, found on its own
copper	electrolysis
potassium	unreactive but purified by electrolysis
gold	reduced by coke
magnesium	electrolysis

Q2 Explain why *silver* is found in the ground on its own but *calcium* is combined with other substances by selecting the correct answer A → D.

A) Silver is very reactive and so is calcium.

B) Silver is very unreactive and so is calcium.

C) Silver is very unreactive and calcium is quite reactive.

D) Silver is very reactive and calcium is quite unreactive.

Answer = ☐

Q3 *Gold* is a very expensive metal and yet compared to other metals it is easy to extract. Can you think why this may be?

....

....

....

Q4 The ease with which metals are extracted from their ores depends upon their position in the reactivity series. Patricia says that those higher in the reactivity series are harder to extract than those lower down. Fiona says she is wrong and that those lower are harder to extract. Who do you agree with? Explain your reasons.

....

....

....

....

Questions on Metal Extraction

Q5 *Copper* can be purified by *electrolysis*. *Copper* can be found in the ground on its own or with something else.

a) When an element is combined with another element, the substance is known as a what?

....

b) The diagrams below show how *copper* can be extracted in a lab from *copper carbonate*. The diagrams are not in order. Put them in their correct order and fill in the labels.

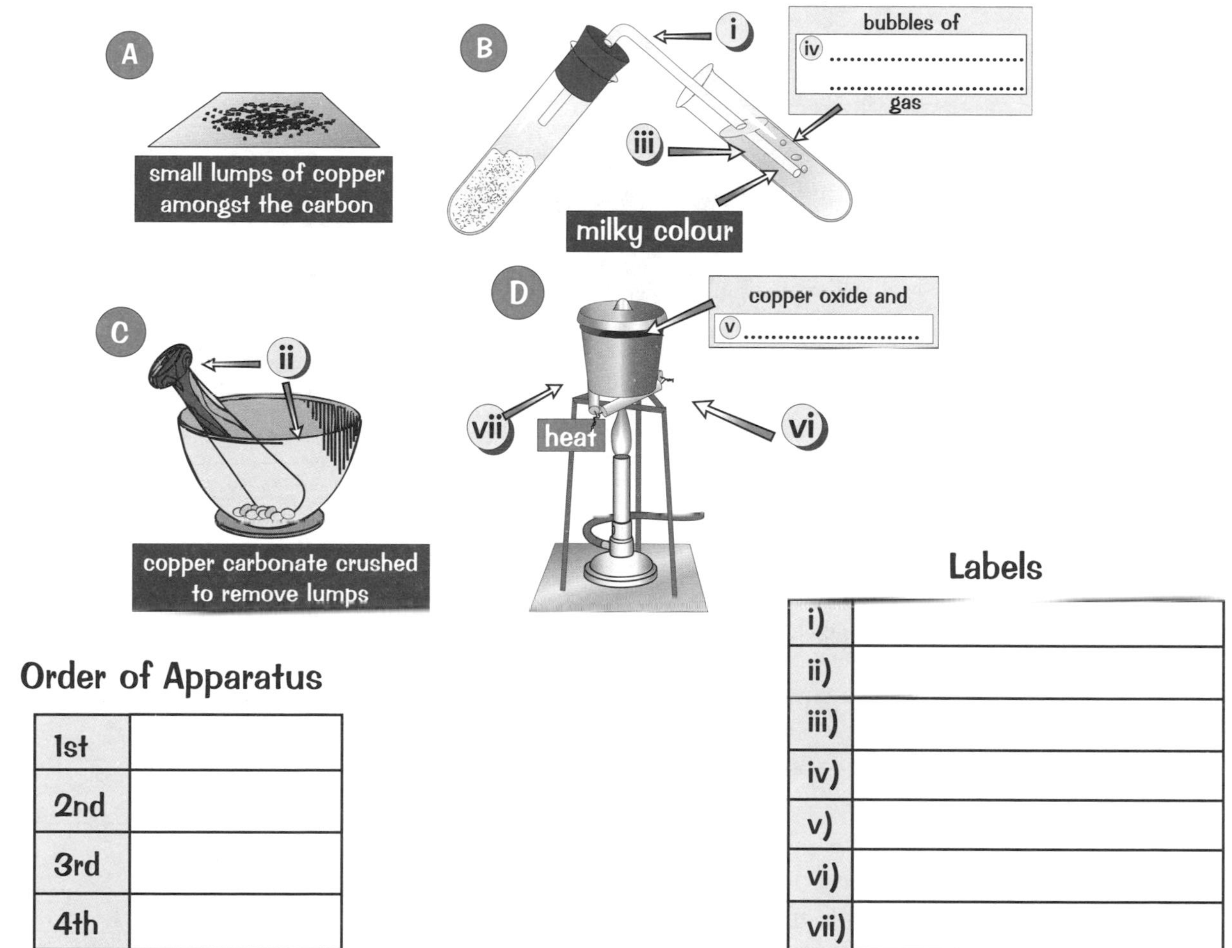

Order of Apparatus

1st	
2nd	
3rd	
4th	

Labels

i)	
ii)	
iii)	
iv)	
v)	
vi)	
vii)	

c) Copper carbonate is changed into copper oxide by heating. This then reacts with v) to make copper. What is the name of this process? Circle your choice from the list below:-

Combustion	Oxidation	Reduction	Electrolysis

d) The copper carbonate was weighed before it was heated the first time, then allowed to cool before being weighed again. 1st weight: 25.00g. 2nd weight: 24.36g.

What is the name given to a reaction where heat breaks up a substance?

....

Questions on Metal Extraction

Q6 *Sodium* is a *reactive* metal. It can be found as brine, which is *sodium chloride* dissolved in water. It is also often found in a rock called *rock salt*, which is impure solid sodium chloride.

a) One way to get *pure* sodium chloride is to purify rock salt. Below are some diagrams completely unlabelled and muddled up. Put them in order and explain, using them to help you, how we get solid (*pure*) sodium chloride from rock salt.

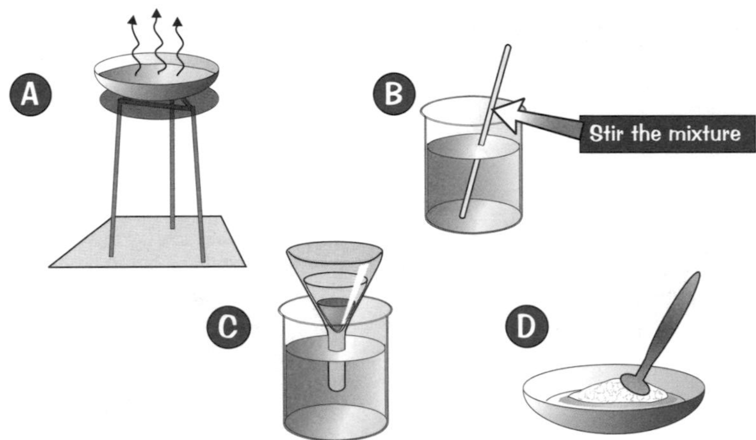

Correct order:

b) Name two separation techniques used in the diagrams.

Once we have solid sodium chloride we can extract the sodium from it by electrolysis. For this to happen the sodium chloride has to be heated to a very high temperature (about 800°C) so that it melts.

+ -
Positive electrode (anode)
Negative electrode (cathode)
HEAT

c) What is the name given to the positive and negative electrodes?

d) What two elements will sodium chloride split up into using this apparatus?

Questions on Rusting

Q1 David left an *iron nail* in the garden for a week. When he went to use it he found that it had changed colour.

a) What colour had it changed to?

....

b) What had happened to the nail?

....

....

c) He carried out an experiment. This time he carefully weighed another nail and left it for one week in the garden before carefully re-weighing it.

50.10
Before

50.47
After

i) What was the *difference* in weight?

....

Was it an *increase* or a *decrease?*

....

ii) What do you think caused this difference?

....

....

d) Write an equation in words to explain this reaction.

Iron + Oxygen $\xrightarrow{\text{Water}}$ ....

e) What *type* of reaction do we call this?

....

....

Questions on Rusting

Q2 Sally found a nail in the bottom of her deep fish pond. She was amazed to find it hadn't rusted as much as the nails in her dad's shed. Explain why the nail in the pond had rusted less.

....

....

....

Q3 *Rust* is the name we give to the *corrosion* of iron. Iron is used for many things and if we want it to last we have to *protect* if from the oxygen and water.

We can protect iron by:

i)	**Painting** —	a thin layer of paint stops contact with oxygen and water.
ii)	**Oiling** —	a thin layer of oil stops oxygen and water touching the iron.
iii)	**Alloying** —	mixing the iron with other things can stop the rusting process.
iv)	**Plating** —	cover with a thin layer of another metal stops the rusting process.
v)	**Plastic coating** —	a layer of inert plastic stops oxygen and water touching the iron.

For each of **a)** → **g)**, pick the best way (from **i)** → **iv)**) of protecting the metal object.

a) Gate ....

b) Hull of a boat ....

c) Dustbin ....

d) Bike chain ....

e) Tin of beans ....

f) Car body ....

g) Coins ....

Q4 Drain pipes and gutters were once made from iron. New houses have plastic drain pipes and gutters. Explain why this is.

....

....

....

....

Questions on Rusting

Q5 Answer the questions and then use the first letter of each answer to find the name of a metal that definitely doesn't rust!

a) Some metals do this when oxygen and water are around. ....

b) This is needed with water for iron to rust. ....

c) This helps prevent rust (if only for a while). ....

d) A very inert material that can be used to protect iron — it can also be used to make bags.

....

e) Iron has to be .... from its ore (iron oxide).

f) We put metals into this depending on how lively they are! (2 words).

....

And the word is ....

Q6 Iron can be protected by *sacrificial protection*. This means wrapping a piece of metal (which is higher in the reactivity series) around the iron nail. The metal wrapped around the iron will corrode instead of the iron. In other words it's being sacrificed.

The diagram below shows which metals are wrapped around the nail.

a) How would you ensure that this was a fair test? ....

....

b) Which tubes would you have seen rust in? ....

....

c) Normally the more reactive metal will corrode instead of the iron. Potassium and sodium are much higher in the reactivity series than iron and would corrode instead. Explain why it would not have been sensible to use these metals.

....

....

Questions on Reactions of Metals with Acids

Q1 Two cans for orange segments in orange juice were made of two different types of metal. Can A was made of *copper* and Can B was made of *zinc*.

a) Which can is the most likely to last the longest if the segments were to be kept in the can?

....

b) Give an account of what may happen in can B after a while. ....

....

c) Why does nothing happen in can A, even after a few months? ....

....

d) Would the orange segments in can B be safe to eat after a few months?

....

e) Suppose a new orange segment canning company had started up. Which of the above metals would you suggest they used for their cans?

....

Q2 A student set up four test tubes as in the diagram below. The student returned every two minutes for a total of six minutes, and recorded what he saw in the table on the next page.

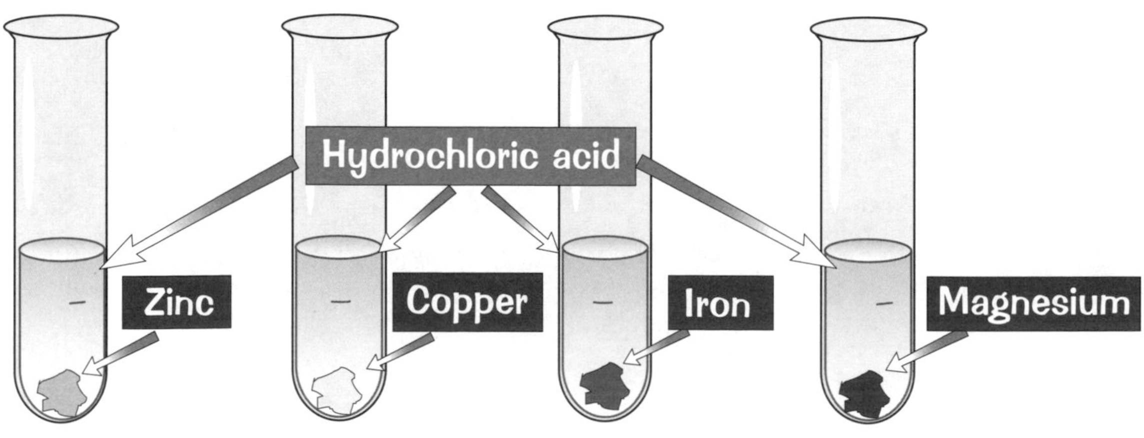

Questions on Reactions of Metals with Acids

a) Complete the table by filling in what you think he observed.

Metal	Observation of reaction after		
	2 min	4min	6min
Zinc		Moderate reaction gas given off	
Magnesium			Fast reaction now finished
Iron			
Copper	No reaction		Few bubbles slow reaction

b) Which metal do you think is the most reactive of those in the table? ....

c) If you touched the test tube containing magnesium, what would you feel?

....

Q3 Joshua put some zinc in a flask with some hydrochloric acid. He collected the gas given off as shown in the diagram.

a) Label the diagram.

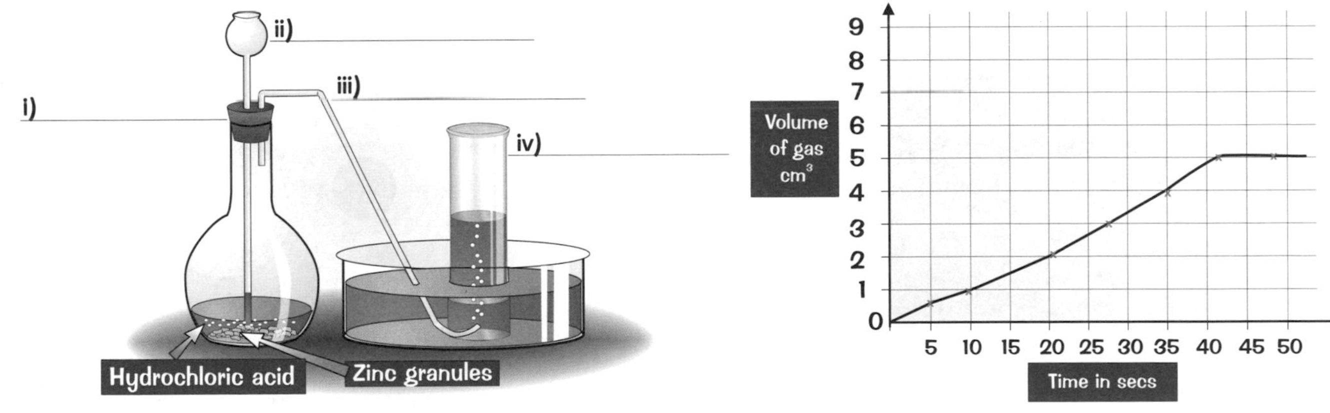

b) He collected the results of the amount of gas given off at regular intervals and plotted the results on a graph. What volume of gas had been given off after:

i) 15 seconds? ....

ii) 35 seconds? ....

c) Would gas be collected more quickly or more slowly if magnesium metal was used instead of zinc?

....

....

Questions on Reactions of Metals with Acids

Q4 Damian wanted to do an experiment using *sodium* and weak *hydrochloric acid*. He knew that they would react to make *common salt* and produce *hydrogen gas*, but he did not know how quickly they would react. His friend said that he needed to be very careful.

a) Why would Damian need to be very careful? ....

....

....

b) What would he see? ....

c) Complete this word equation to show the reaction.
(Words to use: **sodium** / **hydrogen** / **chloride**)

Sodium + hydrochloric acid → .... + ...

d) One of the products is a common salt. The salt would not exist on its own, but in *solution*. Using a diagram, explain how Damian could get a pure dry salt sample from this reaction.

Q5 In this word search you will find *seven* metals that react with an acid to give a salt and hydrogen. Find the words and then put them in order of how violently they react with acid. Start with the most reactive.

1) ....
2) ....
3) ....
4) ....
5) ....
6) ....
7) ....

F	R	Q	P	F	M	U	I	D	O	S
M	F	A	A	I	U	M	R	L	B	B
U	Q	L	A	J	D	M	O	F	T	I
I	S	U	J	O	S	N	N	D	F	T
S	V	M	A	G	N	E	S	I	U	M
S	W	I	Q	F	R	F	I	U	M	L
A	Z	N	P	T	O	S	T	P	A	N
T	Z	I	N	C	F	R	V	T	B	C
O	A	U	O	M	U	I	C	L	A	C
P	M	M	T	S	S	A	T	T	O	B

Questions on Reactions of Metals with Acids

Q6 Fill in the spaces with the clues and find the mystery word. The letters that make up this word are in the coloured boxes. (Words can go in all directions.)

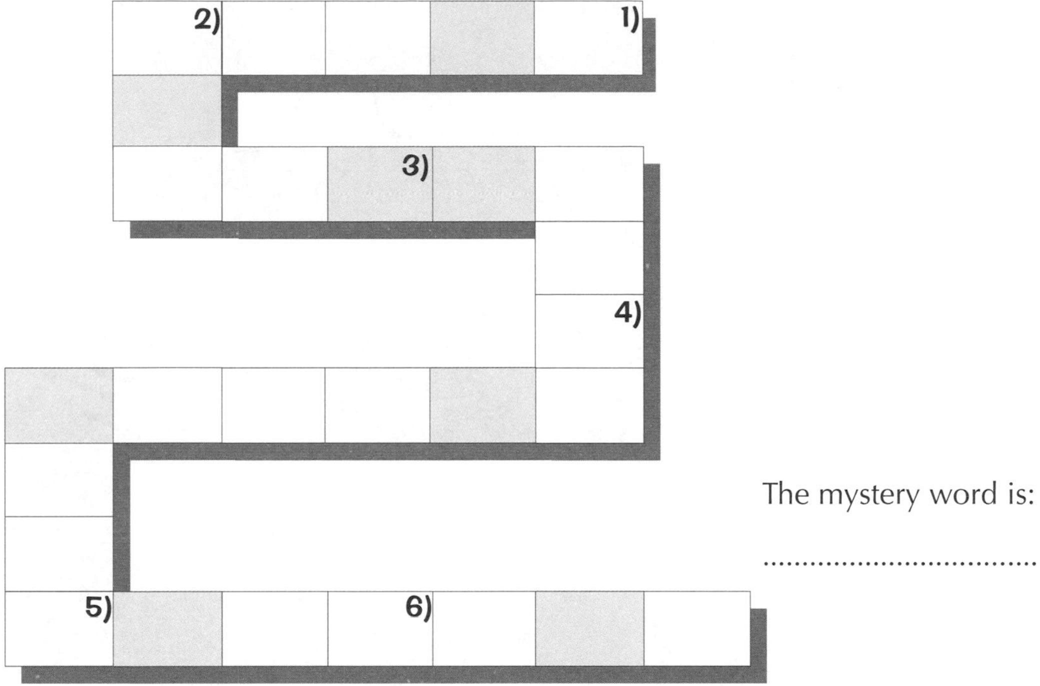

The mystery word is:

....

1. Reacts fairly well with an acid and is a common metal. *(4)*
2. A boring unreactive metal, *not* used in pencils. *(4)*
3. Hydrogen is displaced from this when you add a reactive metal. *(4)*
4. A very very very reactive metal. *(9)*
5. A lighted splint does this in hydrogen gas. *(3)*
6. The metal that reacts to give zinc sulphate with sulphuric acid. *(4)*

Q7 Below are some chemical equations. Complete the equations by linking the arrow to the correct products.

a) Potassium + Sulphuric Acid →

b) Sodium + Hydrochloric Acid →

c) Iron + Sulphuric Acid →

d) Copper + Hydrochloric Acid →

e) Magnesium + Sulphuric Acid →

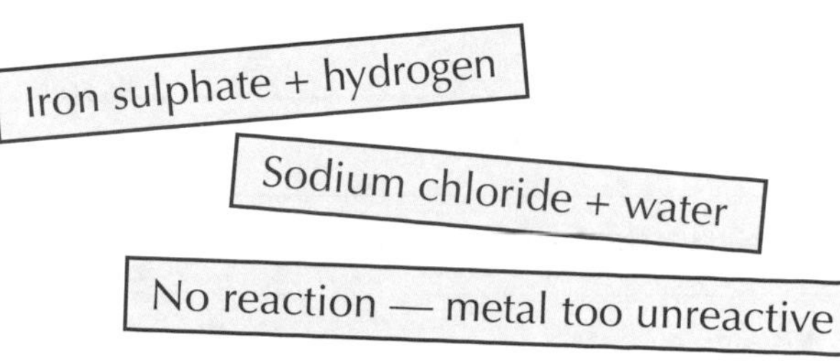

Potassium sulphate + Water

Questions on Acids and Alkalis

Q1 For each item, decide whether it's an acid, alkali, or if it's neutral.
Write your answer in the box underneath each picture.

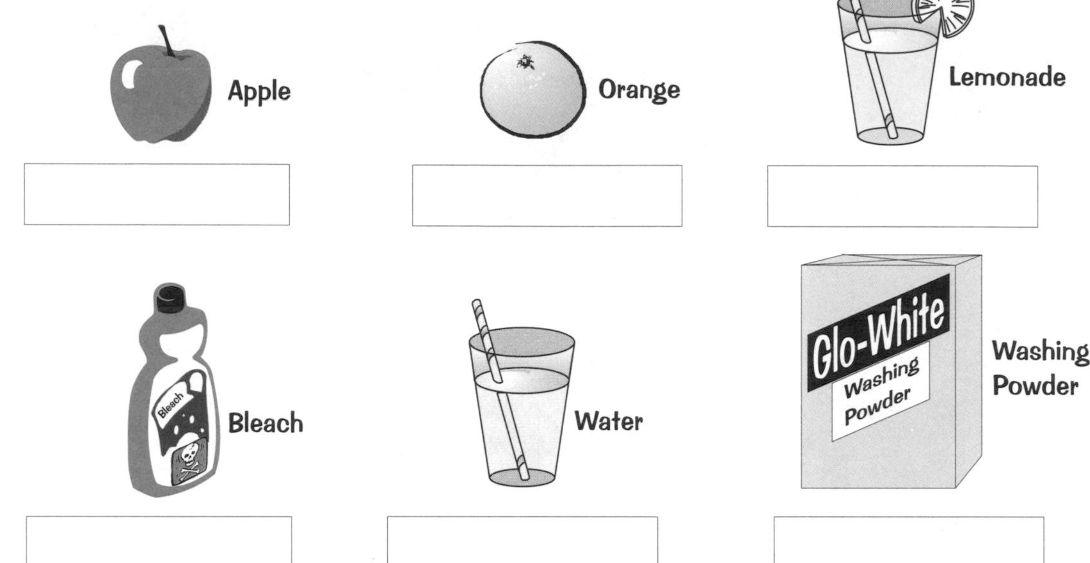

Q2 Colour the pH chart below with the Universal Indicator colours and write on it the following labels: **i)** Strong Acid, **ii)** Weak acid, **iii)** Neutral, **iv)** Strong alkali, **v)** Weak alkali.

pH Scale	1	2	3	4	5	6	7	8	9	10	11	12	13	14

Q3 Complete the table below, filling in the gaps with the words given.

pH8 dark blue red strong acid strong alkali
weak alkali pH1 pH13 pH7
pH10 strong acid purple blue green neutral

Useful Substance	pH value	Colour with Universal Indicator	Acid, Alkaline or Neutral
a) Hydrochloric acid in stomach			
b) Smelling salts (phew!) ammonia			
c) Kitchen cleaner			
d) Tap water			
e) Washing up liquid			

Questions on Acids and Alkalis

Q4 _Universal Indicator_ is one of a number of indicators that can tell us whether a substance is acid or alkaline.

a) Name one other indicator and say what colour it turns in an acid and an alkaline solution.

....

b) Why is Universal Indicator more helpful to us?

....

....

Q5 Fill in the following sentences using words from the box below.

citric acid, 1, 6, hydrogen, sour, 1 and 6, corrosive, high, bacteria, hydrogen

a) Hydrochloric acid in the stomach kills ....

b) Acids will react with metals .... in the reactivity series to give the gas ....

c) All acids contain ....

d) Some strong acids such as sulphuric and hydrochloric are very ....

e) We eat some acids such as .... which we find in fruit such as oranges.

f) The acids we eat have a .... taste.

g) The pH of an acid is between pH ....

h) pH .... is a strong acid.

i) pH .... is a weak acid.

Q6 Which are true and which must be false?

	True	False
a) All acids are dangerous.	☐	☐
b) Acids are sweet tasting.	☐	☐
c) Acids have a pH of below 7.	☐	☐
d) Acids turn Universal Indicator purple.	☐	☐
e) Acids react with alkalis in a combustion reaction.	☐	☐
f) Metal oxides are sometimes acidic.	☐	☐

Questions on Reactions of Acids and Alkalis

Q1 Anthony's teacher demonstrated an experiment to show what happened when an acid was added to calcium carbonate. The diagram shows what she did:

Tube A

Tube B

a) What is wrong with the diagram?

....

....

....

b) The liquid in tube B turned cloudy as bubbles of gas dissolved in it.

i) What was the liquid in tube B? ....

ii) What was the gas in tube B? ....

c) Complete this equation to show what has happened.

Metal carbonate + acid → Salt + W____________ + C______ d________

Q2 _Acids_ are neutralised by _bases_, to give a _salt_ and _water_.

a) What do you understand by the term "neutralised"?

....

....

b) Ethanoic acid is a weaker acid than nitric acid. Would it neutralise nitric acid? Explain your answer.

....

....

Q3 Acids react with some metals to give a salt and hydrogen.

a) Complete the diagram to the right to show how you could collect the hydrogen gas.

b) Name a safe and suitable metal that could be used in this experiment.

....

c) How could you test the gas you collected to check it was hydrogen?

....

....

Acid

Metal

Questions on Reactions of Acids and Alkalis

Q4 Alkalis are at the other end of the pH scale to acids. Fill in the missing words from the box below to complete the sentences on alkalis. Words can be used as many times as you need.

bases, burn, soap flakes, corrosive, 8, 14, bleach, neutralise

a) Alkalis are .... like acids and they can .... your skin badly.

b) The pH of alkalis is between .... and ....

c) pH .... is a weak alkali.

d) pH .... is a strong alkali

e) Alkalis are soluble .... They react with acids to .... them.

f) Alkalis are often found in cleaning materials such as .... and ....

Q5 Put the following in order of pH starting with the strongest alkali.

water, vinegar, hydrochloric acid, bleach, sodium hydroxide.

....

....

Q6 Complete the following reactions of acids.

a) zinc + nitric acid → zinc nitrate + ...

b) calcium carbonate + nitric acid → calcium nitrate + c................ d................ + ...

c) hydrochloric + sodium → .... + ...

Questions on Indigestion

Q1 Indigestion tablets are bases which neutralise acid. Sometimes if we eat or drink too much we get too much acid in our stomachs. This causes indigestion and we need tablets to neutralise the acid.

Rajit and John decided to do an experiment to find the most effective indigestion tablet. The diagrams show what they did. Their blank results sheet is also shown.

A

B

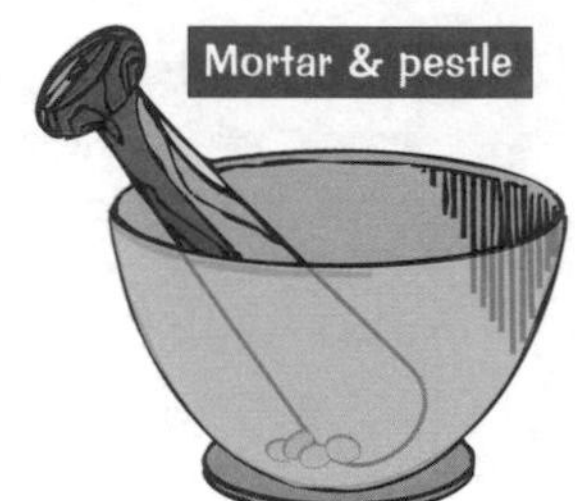

C

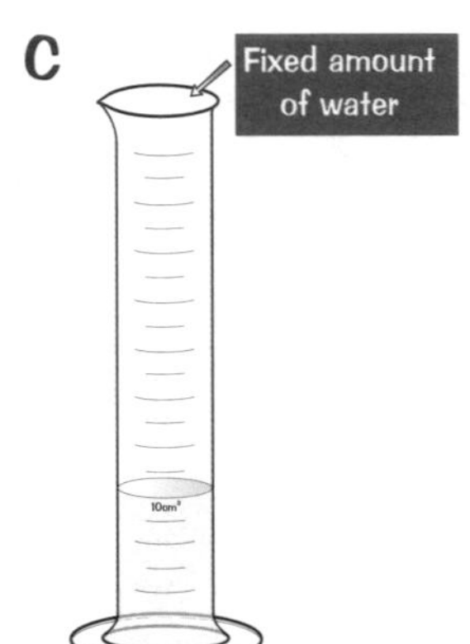

D

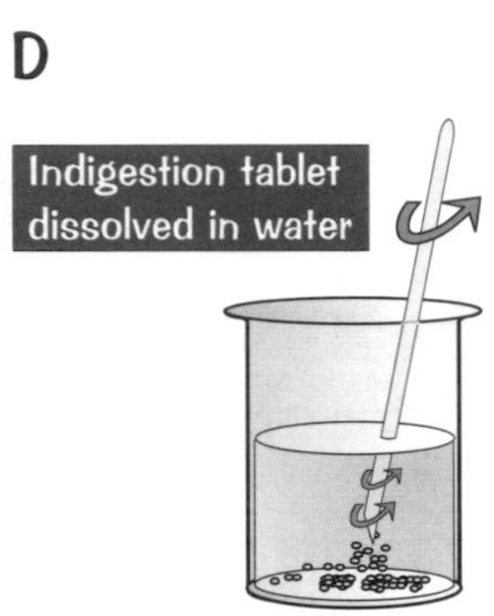

E

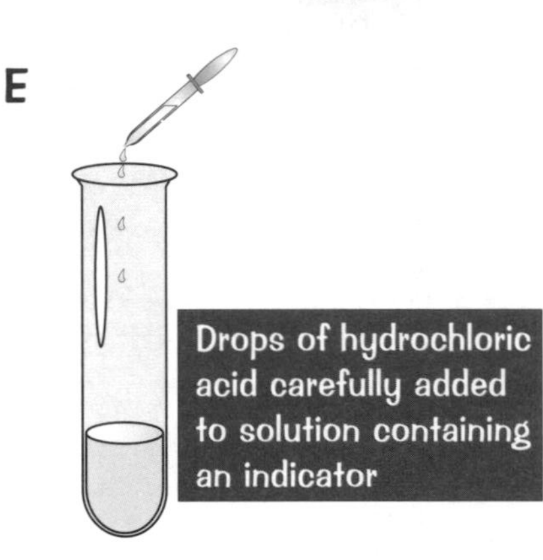

Indigestion Tablet	Amount of acid needed to neutralise (drops)		
	Expt 1	Expt 2	Average

a) They tested three indigestion tablets, with the same strength acid.

i) Why did they weigh out the tablets first?

....

ii) Why did they crush the tablets?

....

iii) Why did they have to make a solution from the tablets?

....

....

b) Name two ways in which they tried to ensure that this was a fair test.

....

....

Questions on Indigestion

c) In diagram E they used an indicator. Suggest an indicator they could have used?

....

....

d) How would they have known when they had added enough acid in E?

....

....

....

e) The table below shows the results of Rajit and John's experiment. Fill in the "average" column for each tablet.

Indigestion Tablet	Amount of acid needed to neutralise (drops)		
	Expt1	Expt2	Average
X	15	14	
Y	19	21	
Z	23	22	

f) Why did they repeat the experiment for each tablet?

....

....

g) Which is the most effective tablet? Explain the reason for your answer.

....

....

h) Enzymes in the stomach help to break down food.
Why is it not a good idea to have an indigestion tablet with a strong alkali in them?
(Hint:— what do you know about enzymes?)

....

....

....

....

Questions on Useful Acid Reactions

Q1 Answer the following questions and fill in the gaps to find the missing word in the shaded column.

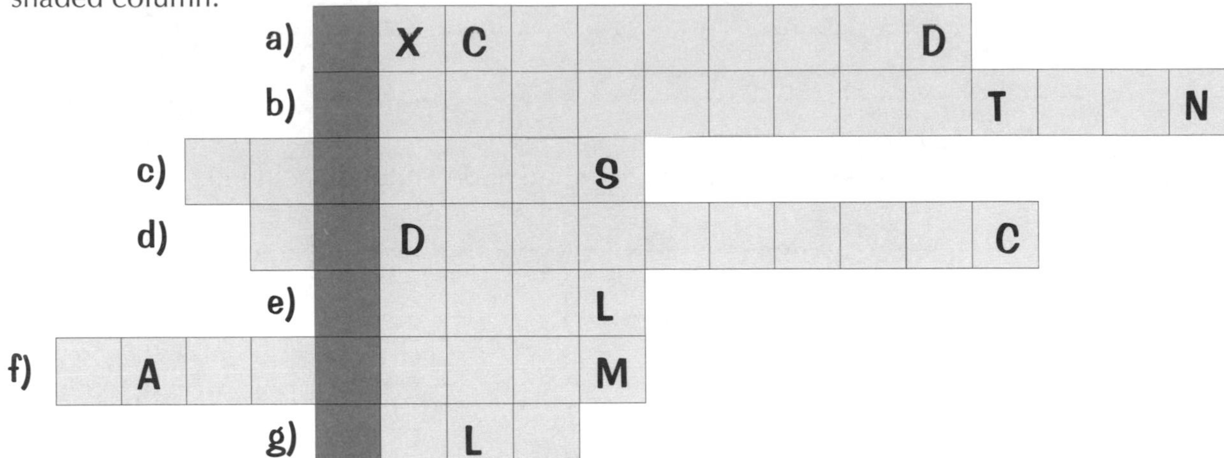

a) This causes indigestion (2 words: 6,4).

b) The reaction in your stomach when you swallow an indigestion tablet.

c) We find these in our stomachs to help with digestion.

d) The acid found in our stomachs.

e) Most salts will have a .... and a non-......................... in them (both words are the same!).

f) Some indigestion tablets have an oxide of this in them.

g) An acid and an alkali produce a .... and water.

The missing word is ....

Q2 Complete the following sentences by adding the words from the list below. You can use any word however many times you need.

liming, calcium, carbonate, minerals, acidic, neutralises, acid, alkaline, rock.

Some soils are either too .... or .... This can be because of the type of .... the soil is made from. Chalky soil contains .... which makes the soil .... rain can cause the soil to be .... Some soils are acidic because of the .... they have in them. Some plants will only grow in certain types of soil. To make the soil less acidic we use a process called .... This .... the acid.

Questions on Useful Acid Reactions

Q3 The range of pH in soils is not 1 → 14 but 4.5 → 7.5. The diagram below shows the scale we use.

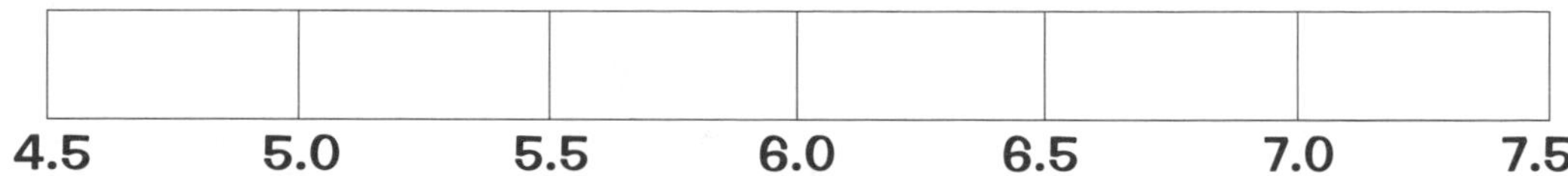

4.5 5.0 5.5 6.0 6.5 7.0 7.5

a) Mark in the words acid, neutral and alkaline on this scale.

b) Here is a list of some plants and what soil they like:

Carrot pH6

Potato pH5

Onion pH7

If a soil where a farmer wanted to grow onions was pH5, what would have to be done to the soil to make it suitable for growing onions?

....

....

....

....

c) Colour in the pH chart for soil, using the colours shown by standard universal indicator.

Q4 Lime (calcium hydroxide) is put on acidic soil by farmers.

a) Would you expect its pH to be greater or lesser than seven?

....

....

b) Quicklime will neutralise acid rain. Why is acid rain a problem to the environment?

....

....

....

....

Questions on Acid Rain

Q1 Use the words from the box to complete the sentences on acid rain.

trees, marble, gases, nitrogen, car fumes, weathering, sulphur dioxide, industry, plants, fish.

Acid rain attacks rocks such as chalk, ... and limestone. This is called .... Acid rain is formed by .... such as .... and oxides of .... joining with water in the atmosphere. The gases that form acid rain come from .... and .... Acid rain damages .... and .... It also pollutes water, killing ....

Q2 Acid rain can weather rocks and damage buildings. Paul and Jane set up the experiment below to look at how bench acids might affect three rock samples.

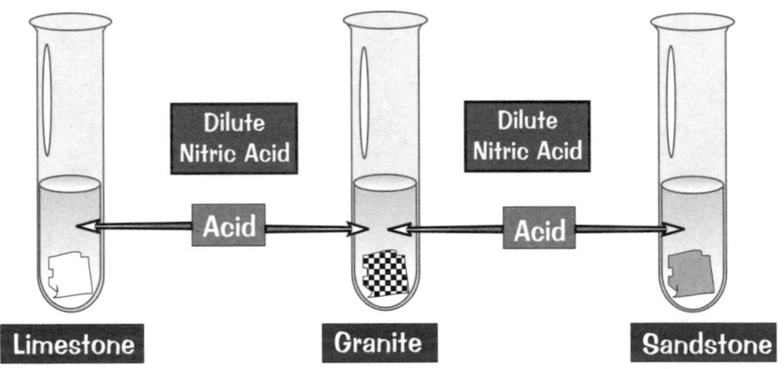

Test Tube contains:	Observation after 30 mins
Limestone	Bubbles and froth
Granite	No reaction
Sandstone	No reaction

a) Which rock type reacted with the acid?

....

....

b) What gas do you think was be given off in the reaction in **a)**?

....

....

Questions on Acid Rain

c) Draw and label a diagram to show how you could test for this gas.
Name any chemicals you may use.

Q3 Emily and Miriam did a study of some graves in a graveyard to look at the effects of weathering. The table below shows some of their results. All the graves were the same age.

Grave Stone Made from	Amount of Weathering
a) Iron	A lot
b) Granite	Very little
c) Marble (caloium carbonate based)	Some

a) Why is it important that all the graves were the same age?

....

....

b) They thought that acid rain could have caused the corrosion.
Why did it effect two of the graves but not the third?

....

....

c) If you wanted to make a statue that would last, which metal would you choose from these three:— iron, copper or zinc? Explain why you chose the metal you did.

....

....

....

More Questions on Acid Rain

Q4 Acid rain can alter the pH of soil by making it more acidic. From the chart below, pick:

pH	
4.5	Potatoes
5.0	
5.5	
6.0	Parsley
6.5	Carrot
7.0	Cauliflower Broad bean / cabbage
7.5	
8.0	

a) Two plants that could survive more acidic conditions.

....

b) Two plants that would need the soil neutralised if they were to grow successfully.

....

c) How can soil be neutralised?

....

....

d) Some fish can live in more acidic waters than others.

Name from the table two fish that could live in fairly acidic water and two that could not.

....

pH	Fish
6 - 7	Salmon, roach, char.
5.5 - 6.0	Perch.
4.5 - 5.0	Eel, trout.

Q5 Read the passage below and answer the questions.

> The more the levels of carbon dioxide increase in the atmosphere, the more the levels of carbonic acid increase. This leads to the formation of the acid rain. Trees and plants use carbon dioxide to produce food for themselves. In this way they keep the balance of carbon dioxide in the atmosphere correct. Carbon dioxide is also a product of the burning of fossil fuels.

a) Name one way in which levels of carbon dioxide can increase in the atmosphere.

....

....

b) If we destroy forests of trees worldwide, what effect will this have on the levels of carbon dioxide?

....

Questions on Less Useful Acid Reactions

Q1 The questions below are all about less useful acid reactions.

a) Why is it not sensible to put food like pickled onions in a can made of steel?

....

b) Cans are coated with another type of metal.

i) Explain why this is.

....

....

ii) Which metal could they be coated with?

....

....

Q2 Sodium metabisulphide is a chemical which when mixed with water produces an acidic gas, sulphur dioxide. Some cress seeds were set up as shown in the diagram below. Both were watered and put in plastic bags but only one had a container of sodium metabisulphide.

a) Why did it need to be a clear plastic bag?

....

b) Why was it important that *both* sets of cress seeds were in cotton wool?

....

c) What did you expect to see in each plastic bag after a few days?

....

d) What would this tell you about the effect of acid on the growth of the cress seeds?

....

e) What do you think the sulphur dioxide combines with in the bag to make an acid?

....

....

Questions on Making Salts

Q1 Acid and alkali combined will give a salt and water, if they are mixed in the right amounts.

a) What is the name given to this reaction?

....

b) What is the pH of the resulting solution of salt and water?

....

c) Put the correct acid into each equation. Some acids may be used more than once.

Nitric acid produces *nitrate* salts.

Sulphuric acid produces *sulphate* salts.

Hydrochloric acid produces *chloride* salts.

i) Sodium hydroxide + ... → Sodium sulphate + water

ii) Sodium hydroxide + ... → Sodium nitrate + water

iii) Calcium hydroxide + ... → Calcium chloride + water

iv) Calcium hydroxide + ... → Calcium sulphate + water

Q2 To make pretty blue copper sulphate crystals we use copper oxide and sulphuric acid.

a) Why would you gently heat the sulphuric acid and copper oxide?

....

....

b) Why would you filter the mixture?

....

c) How could you get crystals of copper sulphate from the solution of copper sulphate?

....

....

....

....

Questions on Making Salts

Q3 Fill the blanks using the words below.

alkali, neutralisation, acid, green, water, nitrate, universal indicator, indicator, sulphuric acid, chloride
Salts are prepared by the .... of an .... and an .... This also gives .... To make sure acid and .... are added in the right amounts an .... is needed. .... is a good indicator to use. It goes .... in a neutral solution. The type of acid used will give a particular salt. For example .... will give a sulphate, hydrochloric acid will give a .... and nitric acid will give a .... All these are types of salts.

Q4 We can make sodium chloride by neutralising sodium hydroxide with hydrochloric acid, as shown.

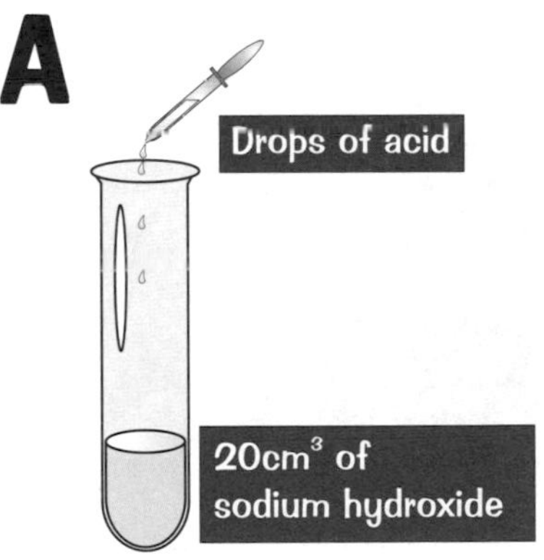

B — After adding a few drops of acid, remove a small sample and check the pH is neutral.

C — When you have a neutral sample, evaporate a little of the water over a Bunsen burner (see diagram).

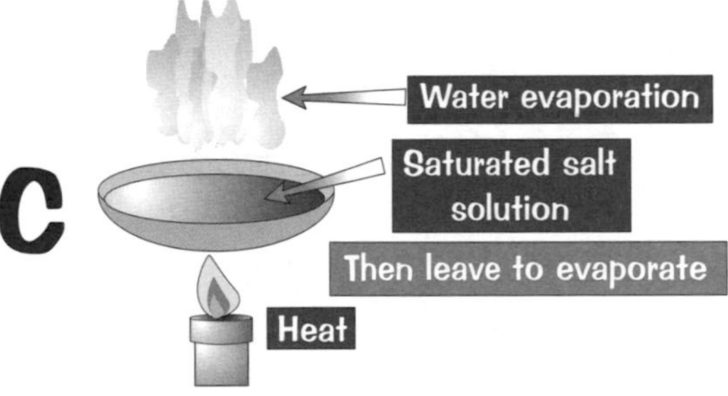

a) Why do you keep checking the pH?

....

b) What indicator would be suitable to use?

....

c) Why do you not add the indicator to the test tube at the beginning, instead of taking samples of the mixture out?

....

d) Complete this sentence.

The faster the cooling of the solution, the .... the crystals.

The slower the cooling of the solution, the .... the crystals.

Questions on Weathering Rocks

Q1 Here is a picture of a *test-tube* with some *water* in it.

Water Level

a) If the test-tube is put into a freezer so that all the water turns to *ice*, will the level of the ice be *higher* or *lower* than the level for water?

....

b) If a glass screw-top bottle is *completely filled* with water and put in a freezer, it can break. *Why* is this?

....

....

....

Q2 The picture below shows a rock on the Earth's surface during day and night-time.

a) What happens to *solids* when they *heat up*? ....

....

b) What happens to them when they *cool down*? ....

....

c) During the day, what causes rocks to *warm up*? ....

....

d) When are the rocks likely to *cool down*? ....

....

e) Which part of the rock is likely to be *most* affected by this heating and cooling?

....

Questions on Weathering Rocks

f) What name is given to this type of *weathering*? ....

....

g) In which parts of the *world* is this weathering effect seen the most? ....

....

Q3 Dave and Tracey are carrying out a study of a dry stone wall near their school. The wall has been there for some time, and shows evidence of weathering. Look at what they found, and say whether the evidence points to *physical*, *chemical* or *biological* weathering by putting a tick in the correct column.

	Physical	Chemical	Biological
a) Some of the stones used to build the wall show streaks. When they test the rock with dilute acid the rock fizzes.		✓	
b) Rabbits have dug burrows under one bit of the wall. One burrow has collapsed, and the wall has started to fall into the hole.			
c) There are cracks between the stones, and also in some of the stones. It's been a cold night, and they see that some of yesterday's rain has frozen in the cracks.			
d) They look closely at some of the stones, and find that they can peel away the outside layer.			
e) A tree has been planted by the wall. The roots have grown both through the wall and under it. Some stones have been pushed out of the way.			
f) Due to the rain, a stream has formed in the field. It flows by the side of the wall. Where the banks have moved, some stones have fallen away from the wall.			

Q4 Explain the following in terms of problems associated with *weathering*.

a) *Marble* statues wear away more *quickly* in towns and cities.

....

b) There has to be a *minimum* distance between a large *tree* and a new *house*.

....

....

c) Large *scree* slopes (areas of small rocks) are found under cliffs in *mountainous* areas.

....

Questions on The Rock Cycle

Q1 Solve the anagrams to identify the words that are all part of the rock cycle.

Anagram	Description	Word
a) STNARTNOIPROAT	Moving rocks from one place to another	
b) OXRUSEPE	Result of uplift on rocks	
c) PEDSIOGTNI	Putting down sediment	
d) GAWTNIREHE	Breaking down rocks	
e) LARIBU/SNERPMOCSIO	Covering and squashing layers to form rock	
f) TEMGLIN	Change to liquid caused by intense heat	
g) SOENIOR	Wearing down of rocks	
h) GOLOCNI	Causes the solidification of molten rock	
i) THAE/RUSPEERS	Cause further changes to rock inside the Earth	

Q2 Tick the box to indicate whether the statements about the rock cycle are true or false.

	True	False
a) Igneous rocks change into sedimentary rocks.	☐	☐
b) Sedimentary rocks are formed by the weathering of other rocks.	☐	☐
c) Molten rock in the Earth is known as lava.	☐	☐
d) Crystallisation of magma forms metamorphic rocks.	☐	☐
e) Burial of sediment makes igneous rocks.	☐	☐
f) Erosion is weathering and transportation of sediment.	☐	☐
g) Extrusive igneous rocks form on the Earth's surface.	☐	☐
h) Intrusive igneous rocks form on the Earth's surface.	☐	☐
i) Exposure happens inside the Earth.	☐	☐

Q3 Give a definition of the following:

a) An igneous rock. ....

....

b) A sedimentary rock. ....

....

c) A metamorphic rock. ....

....

Questions on The Rock Cycle

Q4 The diagram below is a simplified picture of the Rock Cycle. On the picture, the numbers represent *rock types* and *changes* that are happening to the rocks or other material.

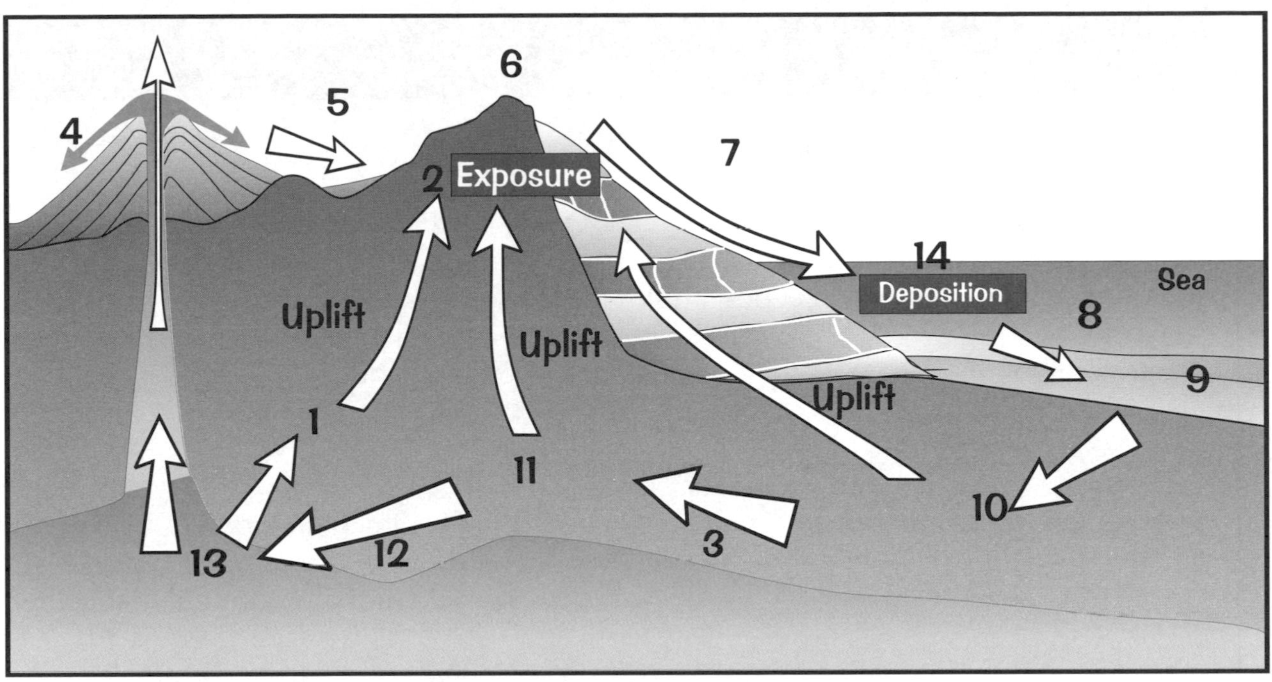

Which *numbers* match the following *labels*? (Lower case words are processes.)

Type of rock or change	Number
IGNEOUS	
SEDIMENTARY	
METAMORPHIC	
SEDIMENTS	
MAGMA	
Weathering	
Transportation	
Deposition	14
Exposure	2
Heat + pressure	
Cooling	
Melting	
Burial + compression +cementation	
Lava	

Stick a number In here

Questions on Rock Types

Q1 Here are some sentences about different types of rocks.
Put the following words in the gaps so that the sentences make sense.

layers changes seas crystals randomly fossils millions age cooled crystals pressure three molten long layers minerals heat volcano older minerals

There are ____________ different types of rock.

Igneous rocks are made from ____________ magma which has ____________ and solidified. Where the rock reaches the surface we sometimes get a ____________.

The rocks contain ____________ which are made from various ____________.

The crystals are arranged ________________.

Sedimentary rocks are formed from ____________ of sediment laid down in lakes or __________ over ____________ of years. The particles are then cemented together by other ____________. Sometimes the remains of long dead plants and animals are found in the rock. These are called ______________. Scientists study the fossil type to work out the ____ of the rock. In general, the deeper the rock, the ____________ it is.

Metamorphic rocks are formed by ____________ to other types of rock. They can be caused by ____________ or ______________ effects, or both together. The changes take a __________ time. Metamorphic rocks can contain tiny ________________ and may also have __________________.

Q2 Although *sedimentary* and *metamorphic* rocks are formed deep underground, they can be found on the Earth's surface. What *two* things make this possible?

....

....

....

Q3 Explain briefly why *igneous* rock is more *resistant* to weathering than *sedimentary* rock. (Consider how each rock is formed.)

....

....

....

Questions on Rock Types

Q4 Look at the descriptions of various rocks below. Try to identify each type of rock as *Igneous*, *Sedimentary* or *Metamorphic* by ticking the correct column in the box below.

Basalt
Chalk
Slate
Grit
Granite
Marble
Breccia
Obsidian
Pumice
Sandstone
Marl
Quartzite

A dark rock with small crystals, formed on the surface of the Earth.

A white rock formed from the shells of sea animals which collected at the bottom of shallow seas.

A dark rock showing crystals and layers. It was formed by shale being changed by heat and pressure.

Rock formed from small particles stuck together.

A speckled rock. The speckles are different crystals that have formed from melted rock which cooled slowly inside the earth.

A white sugary rock. It is made from crystals, but also shows layers. It is formed from chalk or limestone by heat and pressure.

A rock made from different sized angular particles which have collected together and been cemented.

A glassy rock formed by volcanoes. The melted rock has cooled very quickly, so the crystals are tiny.

A rock that contains air bubbles. It is formed by volcanic rock cooling and trapping air inside.

A rock formed from small grains of sand which have been squeezed tightly together.

A rock made from small, dark grey fragments which have been squeezed together.

A crystalline rock which has been formed by changes due to heat and pressure within the earth.

Rock	Igneous	Sedimentary	Metamorphic
Basalt			
Chalk			
Slate			
Grit			
Granite			
Marble			
Breccia			
Obsidian			
Pumice			
Sandstone			
Marl			
Quartzite			

Questions on Recognising Rock Types

Q1 Harry and Kevin go on a science trip to a quarry. There they see a rock face made up of different rocks. Here is a sketch of what they saw. Their teacher tells them that the rocks 1, 2, 3, 4 and 5 are all *sedimentary* rocks.

Look at the sketch and answer the following questions.

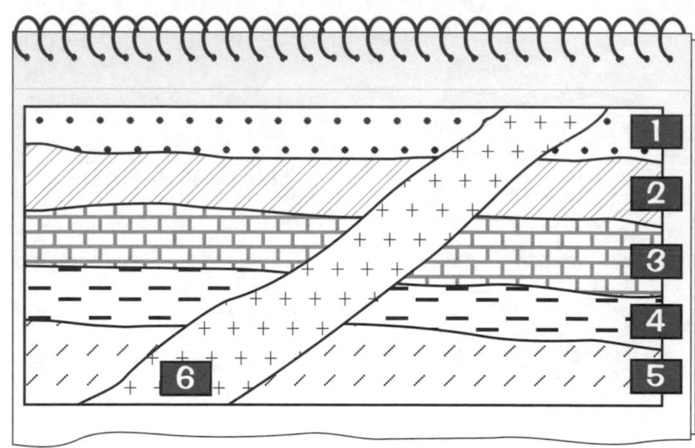

a) How is a sedimentary rock *formed*?

....

....

....

b) Which of the six rock types was formed *last*? Give a reason for your answer.

....

....

....

c) If *all* the sedimentary rocks contained fossils, in which rock would you expect to find the *oldest* fossils? Explain your answer.

....

....

....

The teacher tells them that *Rock 6* is an *igneous* rock called *rhyolite*.

d) How is *igneous* rock formed?

....

....

....

....

Questions on Recognising Rock Types

Harry and Kevin are given a sample of the rock to take back to their science laboratory. When they get back, they compare the *rhyolite* with two other *igneous* rocks they are given.

Name of Rock	Average Size of Crystals
Rhyolite	1.5mm across
Syenite	2mm across
Basalt	1mm across

e) Which type of rock has cooled the *fastest?*

....

....

....

f) Put the three rocks in order of *increasing* distance from the surface at the time of their formation.

....

....

....

g) What do we call igneous rocks that form:

i) at the *surface*.

....

....

iii) *within* the Earth.

....

....

Questions on Recognising Rock Types

h) Harry and Kevin have also brought back samples of rock 3. Some of it was taken from *near* the *igneous* rock, some was taken from much *further* away. They are told that the original rock 3 is *limestone*.

What would you expect to happen if dilute acid was added to the limestone?

....

....

....

i) Would there be a *reaction* if you added *acid* to the rock that had come from near the igneous rock?

....

....

....

....

j) What do we call a rock that has been changed by heat?

....

....

k) What is the *name* given to the rock formed from limestone in this way?

....

....

l) Limestone is made from calcium carbonate.
Give the *equation* for limestone reacting with dilute hydrochloric acid.

Use the following words to construct your equation:
(**calcium**, **carbon**, **hydrochloric**, **dioxide**, **acid**, **chloride**, **water**, **carbonate**).

....		....		....				....
	+		→		+	....	+	
....		....		....				....

Questions on Common Physics Apparatus

Below are shown various apparatus often used in physics experiments.

a)

b)

c)

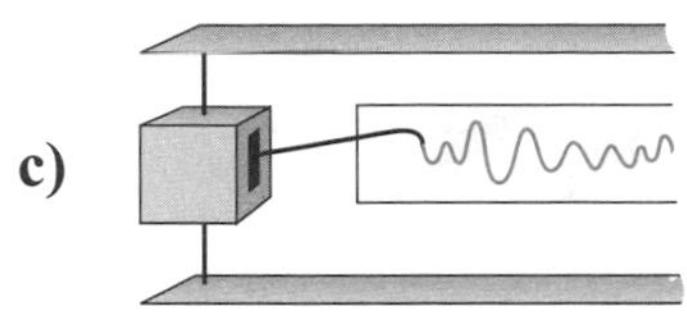

d)

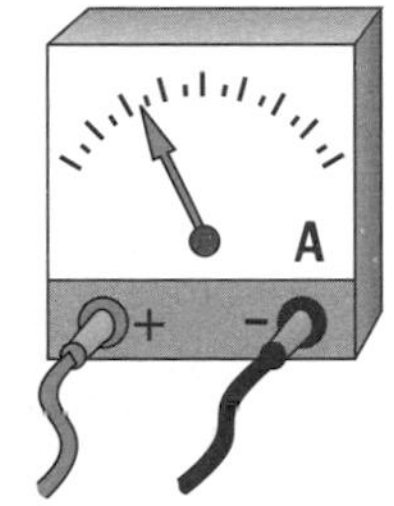

e)

f)

g)

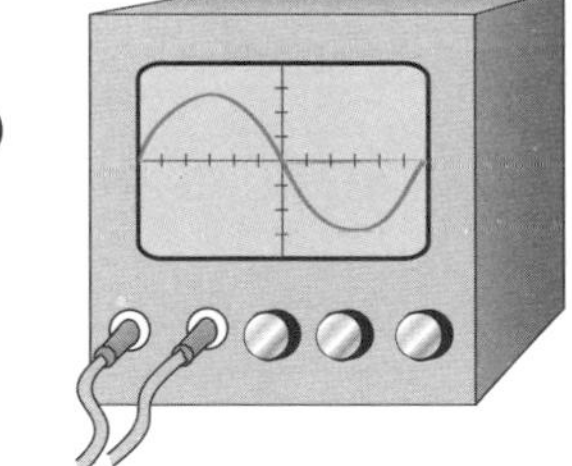

h)

i)

j)

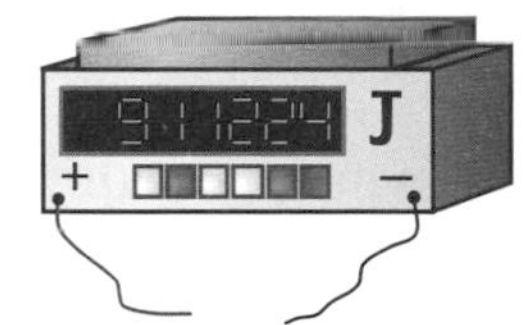

k)

Which of the above would you use to...

Q1 measure force? ....

Q2 measure electrical energy? ....

Q3 measure electrical current? ....

Q4 measure voltage? ....

Q5 detect electric charges? ....

Q6 measure seismic wave strength? ....

Q7 measure time? ....

Q8 collect light from distant objects? ....

Q9 measure pressure? ....

Q10 measure temperature? ....

Q11 measure newtons? ....

Q12 display electrical signals? ....

Questions on Reading Scales

Q1 A student carries out an experiment with a resistor. An ammeter and voltmeter are used to measure the current and the voltage across it.

The meter reading taken in the experiment is shown opposite.

a) What *current* does the meter read? ....

b) What *voltage* does the meter read? ....

Q2 Angela carried out an experiment to find the electrical energy used by a light bulb. She ran the experiment for 2 minutes. The reading on the joulemeter she used is shown below.

a) What is the meter reading rounded to the nearest joule?

....

b) What is the meter reading rounded to the nearest kilojoule?

....

Q3 The dial display opposite shows the pressure reading of a vacuum pump. The units are measured in pascals.

a) What is the symbol for pressure when measured in pascals?

....

b) What is the pressure reading on the meter?

....

Q4 A group of students is carrying out an experiment on pressure. They use a Bourdon gauge to measure the pressures.

a) What is the reading on the Bourdon gauge (shown opposite)? Give your answer in *kilopascals*.

....

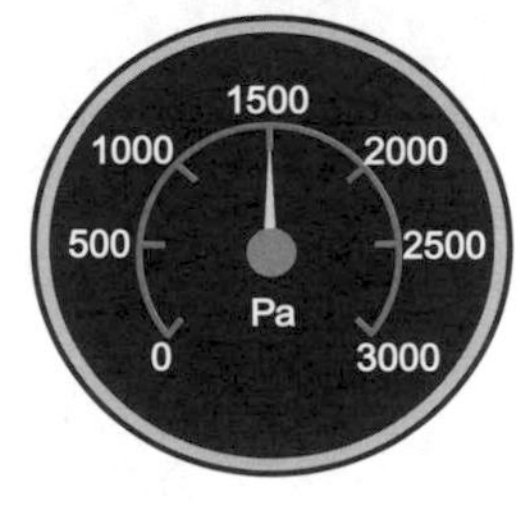

b) The pointer on the gauge does not return to zero when they disconnect the gauge from the apparatus. Why is this?

....

....

Questions on Reading Scales

Q5 An old forcemeter is being used to measure weights.

Before any weights on

Abbie looks at the scale of the forcemeter (shown opposite) before any weights have been hung on.

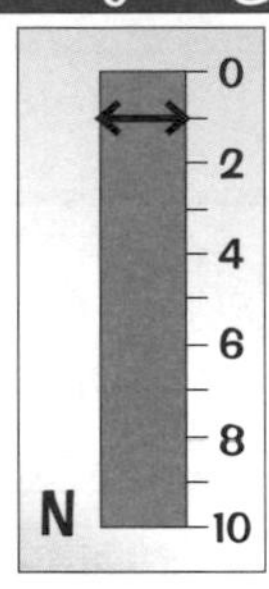

With first weight on

Then the first weight is attached...

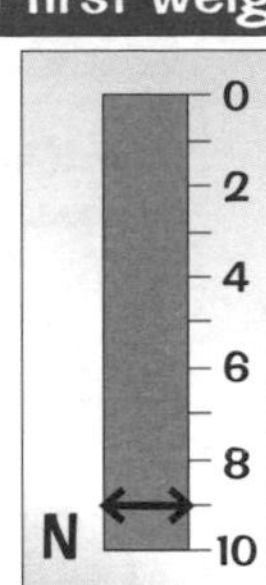

a) What is the force pulling the weight downwards? ....

b) What is the <u>cause</u> of this downward force? ....

Q6 An astronomer is taking a long exposure photograph of a distant galaxy. The time at the top shows when he started the exposure, and the time at the bottom is the current time. He wants the exposure to be 20 minutes long.

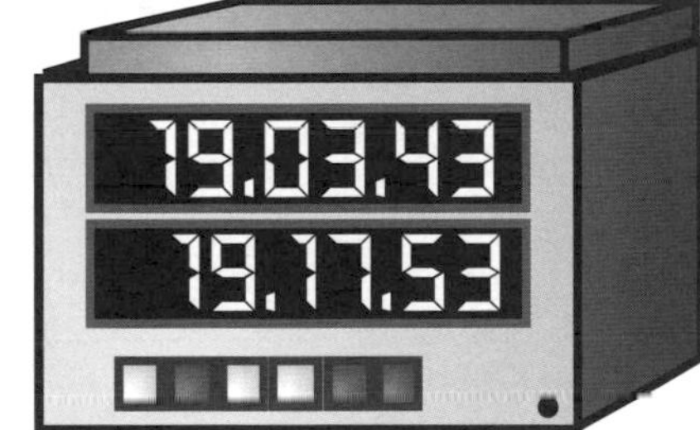

a) How long has he been exposing the photograph for?

....

b) How long is there to go before the finish of the exposure?

....

Q7 Round the following numbers up or down.

a) 3,645N to the nearest kN. ....

b) 195 seconds to the nearest minute. ....

c) 13.27 cm to the nearest mm. ....

d) 2,493 kW to the nearest MW. ....

e) 12.56 Nm to the nearest joule. ....

f) 9,854,399 amps to the nearest kiloamp. ....

Questions on Units and Equations

Q1 In the table below, write down the standard unit for each of the quantities.

Quantity	Voltage	Force	Speed	Frequency	Current
Standard Unit					

Q2 In the table below, write down the quantity for each of the standard units.

Standard Unit	ohms	joules	kilograms	pascals	seconds
Quantity					

Q3 Write down the name and symbol of the unit for:

a) one thousand metres. ....

b) one thousandth of a watt. ....

c) one million joules. ....

d) one thousandth of a second. ....

e) one thousandth of a kilonewton. ....

f) one million millivolts. ....

Q4 Consider the equation A = B ÷ C, which can be represented by the general formula triangle opposite.

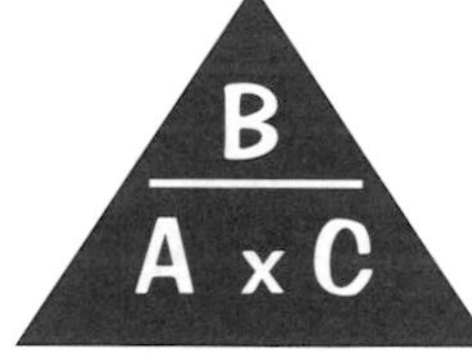

Draw your own formulae triangles for the following equations.

Density = Mass ÷ Volume

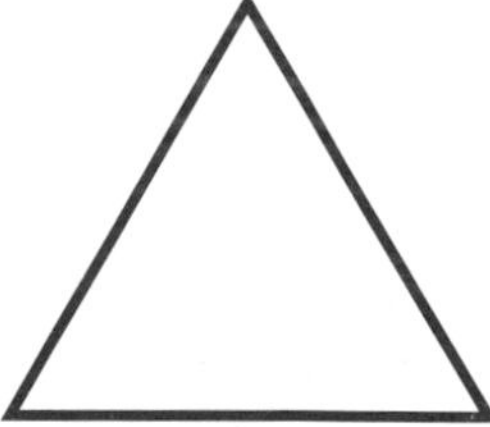

Speed = Distance ÷ Time

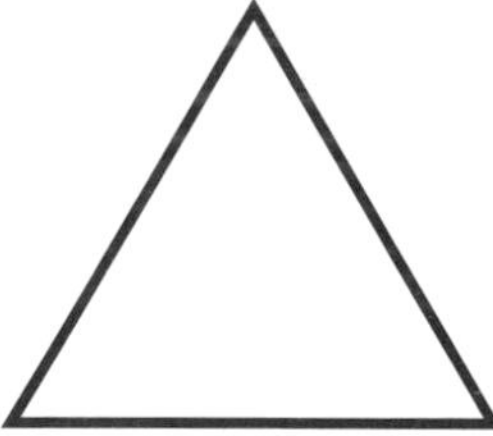

Pressure = Force ÷ Area

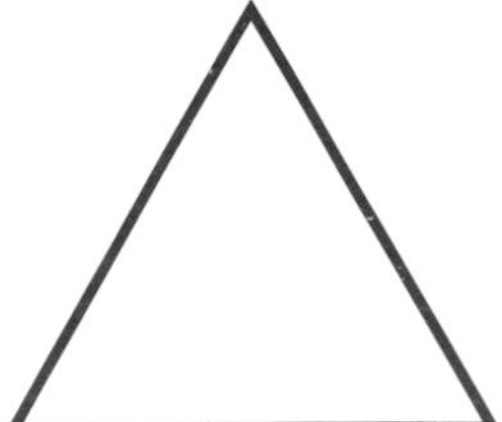

Moment = Force x Perpendicular Distance

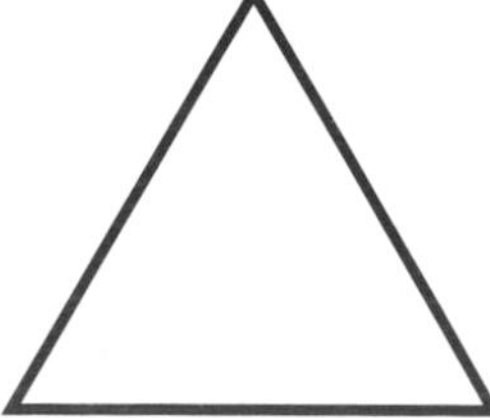

Questions on Electricity and Conductors

Q1 List five things which use *electrical* energy at home. ....

....

Q2 For each of the five things you listed in Question 1, say what form the electrical energy is converted to. (E.g. A speaker changes electrical energy to kinetic and sound energy.)

....

....

Q3 From these lights, circle the *odd* one out. Explain briefly your choice.

TORCH HEADLAMP CANDLE TABLE LAMP

....

....

....

Q4 Name a device which produces electrical energy. ....

Q5 Complete the following sentences by circling the correct word.

a) Electricity will only flow if you have a *series* / *parallel* / *complete* circuit.

b) A complete circuit has *no* / *one* / *two* gaps in it.

c) Electricity can only flow through *an insulator* / *a conductor.*

Q6 Complete this sentence:

'All ________________ are conductors, but not all ____________________ are metals.'

Q7 Circle the statements below which you think are *true*.

a) A working circuit must contain a power supply, or battery.

b) A complete circuit does not have an open switch in it.

c) If there is a gap in a circuit, current can only flow on one side of the gap.

d) A gap in the circuit can be filled with an insulator to make it work.

Q8 Why do we use the words *electric current* when describing electricity? (HINT: Think about where else the word "*current*" is used.)

....

....

Questions on Static Charge

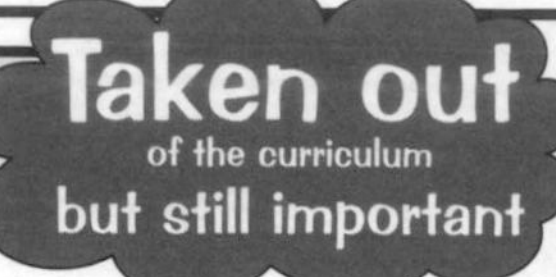

Q1 Complete the sentences by circling the correct word:

a) Materials that you can charge up by rubbing are types of *conductor* / *insulator*.

b) Rubbing causes *friction* /*smoothness* between a duster and a polythene rod.

c) There are *two* /*three* types of charge.

d) The names of the different types of charge are *positive* /*neutral* and *negative* /*neutral*.

e) Positively charged objects will attract *negatively* /*positively* charged objects.

Q2 Describe an experiment you could do to show whether a plastic rod was charged or not.

....

....

....

....

....

Q3 *Tick* the boxes of the following sentences which you think are *true*, and put a *cross* in the boxes of those which you think are *false*.

a) Rubbing a polythene rod with a duster gives the rod extra *negative* charge. ☐

b) Rubbing a polythene rod with a duster takes away *positive* charge from the duster. ☐

c) The duster will have the *same* charge as the polythene rod it has rubbed. ☐

d) The duster will have the opposite charge to the polythene rod it has rubbed. ☐

e) The duster will be *attracted* to the polythene rod. ☐

f) The duster will be *repelled* by the polythene rod. ☐

g) When an acetate rod is rubbed with a duster it *gains* charge. ☐

h) When an acetate rod is rubbed with a duster it *loses* charge to the duster. ☐

Q4 Before a thunderstorm a huge voltage difference is created *between* the *ground* and the *clouds*. Before the lightning begins to strike, is the ground *positively* or *negatively* charged?

....

Questions on Static Charge

Taken out of the curriculum but still important

Q5 Complete the table. One row has been done for you.

	Charge 1	Charge 2	Force between
1	Positive	Positive	
2	Positive	Negative	Attract
3	Positive	Uncharged	
4	Negative	Positive	
5	Negative	Negative	
6	Negative	Uncharged	

a) Why is the fourth row down in the table not really necessary?

....

....

b) Complete the following sentence by circling the correct words.

'Like charges <u>attract</u> / <u>repel</u>, unlike charges <u>attract</u> / <u>repel</u> '.

Q6 Use the ideas on this page and the previous one to explain the facts below.

a) A plastic rod will pick up small pieces of paper when it has been rubbed with a cloth.

....

....

b) A balloon rubbed on a jumper will stick to a wall.

....

....

c) The gold leaf on an electroscope will lift when a charged object is brought near.

....

....

....

Questions on Electric Current in Circuits

Q1 Draw arrows to match these symbols with the correct name.

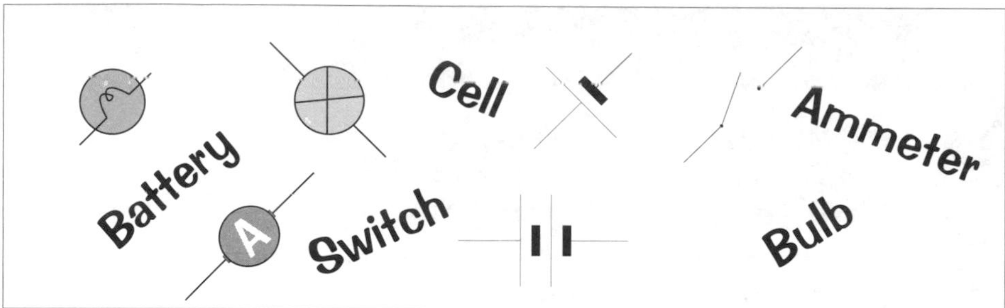

Q2 Draw a circuit diagram to show a *series* circuit in the box below having two bulbs, a single cell and a switch.

Q3 Draw a circuit diagram to show a *parallel* circuit with a single cell and *three* bulbs in the box below.

Q4 Mark with a cross on your diagram for Question 3 the position where a switch could be placed that would turn off *all three bulbs*.

Q5 What is the *unit* of current? ....

Q6 What is the *symbol* for the unit of current? ....

Q7 What *device* can measure the flow of current? ....

Q8 Draw the *circuit symbol* for the current-measuring device.

Questions on Electric Current in Circuits

Q9 Choose parts from the box below to make a circuit that measures the current through the bulb.

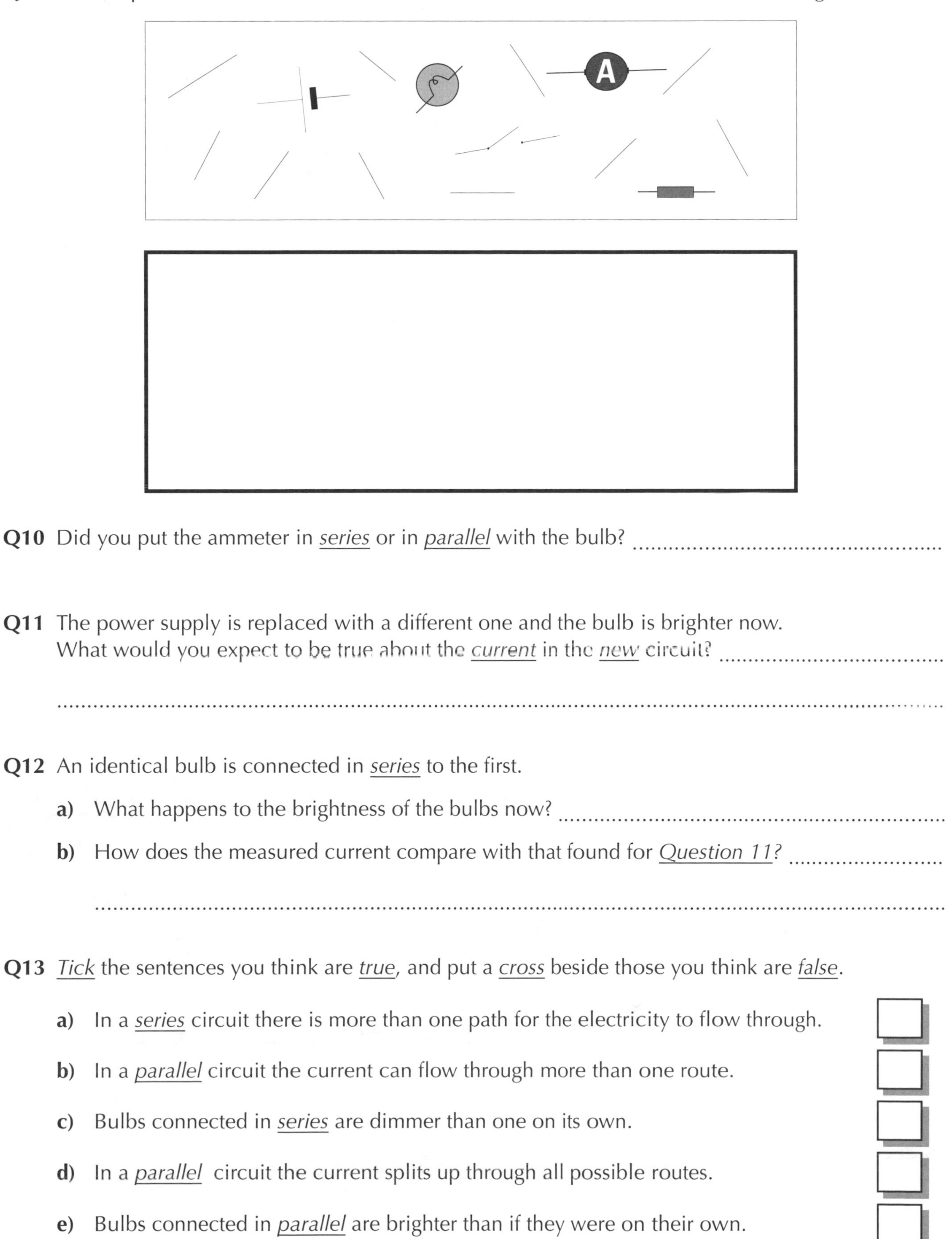

Q10 Did you put the ammeter in *series* or in *parallel* with the bulb? ....

Q11 The power supply is replaced with a different one and the bulb is brighter now.
What would you expect to be true about the *current* in the *new* circuit? ....

....

Q12 An identical bulb is connected in *series* to the first.

a) What happens to the brightness of the bulbs now? ....

b) How does the measured current compare with that found for *Question 11?* ....

....

Q13 *Tick* the sentences you think are *true*, and put a *cross* beside those you think are *false*.

a) In a *series* circuit there is more than one path for the electricity to flow through. ☐

b) In a *parallel* circuit the current can flow through more than one route. ☐

c) Bulbs connected in *series* are dimmer than one on its own. ☐

d) In a *parallel* circuit the current splits up through all possible routes. ☐

e) Bulbs connected in *parallel* are brighter than if they were on their own. ☐

Questions on Electric Current in Circuits

Q14 Both the arrows in the diagram are pointing in the 'correct' direction. How can this be true? (*HINT*: your explanation should include the words *'conventional current'*.)

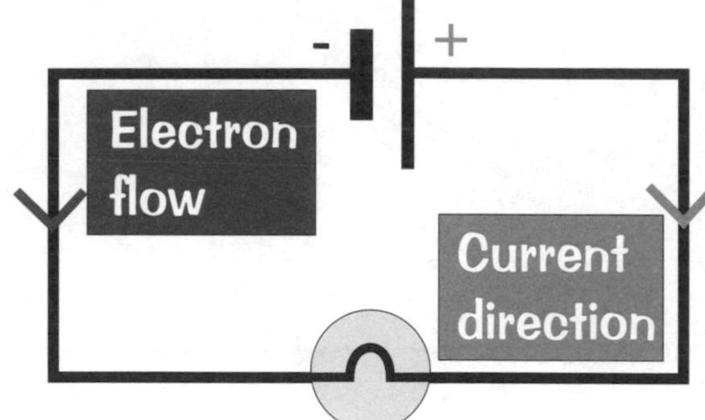

a) Would you connect a *voltmeter* in *series* or *parallel* with the bulb in order to measure the *voltage* across it? ....

b) Would you connect an *ammeter* in *series* or *parallel* with the bulb in order to measure the *current* passing through it? ....

Q15 The flow of current around a circuit may be likened to the flow of water around a central heating system. The diagram below shows a "*water circuit*" and an "*electrical circuit*".

Draw lines in the table to link up the water circuit components to their equivalent electrical circuit components. (The first link has been done for you.)

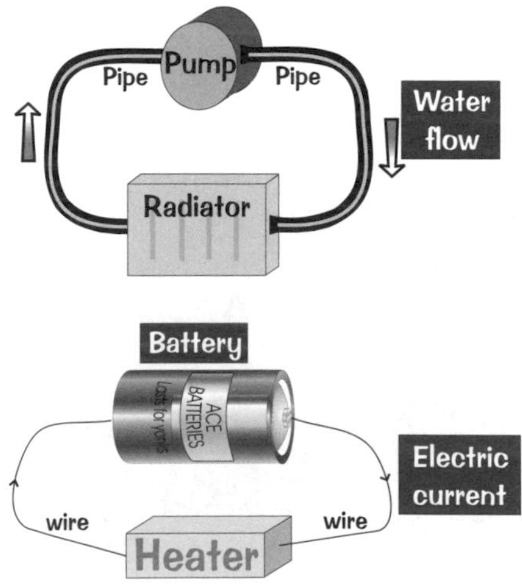

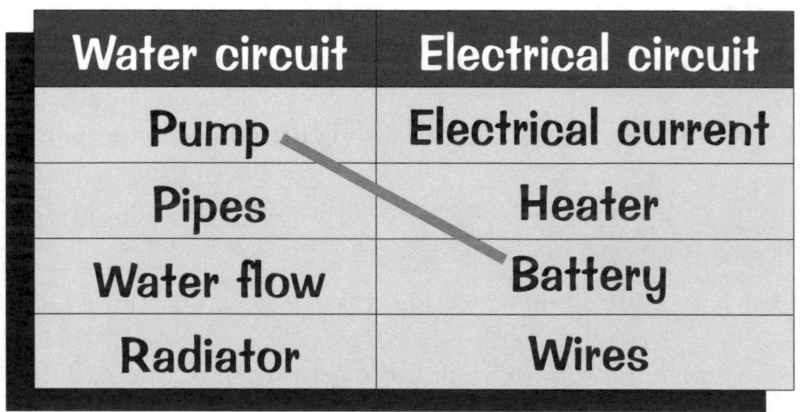

Water circuit	Electrical circuit
Pump	Electrical current
Pipes	Heater
Water flow	Battery
Radiator	Wires

Q16 As you should know, current is not used up (charge is *conserved*) — so what are we actually paying for when we pay our electricity bills? ....

....

Questions on Series Circuits

Q1 This circuit has components in it. Name the components?

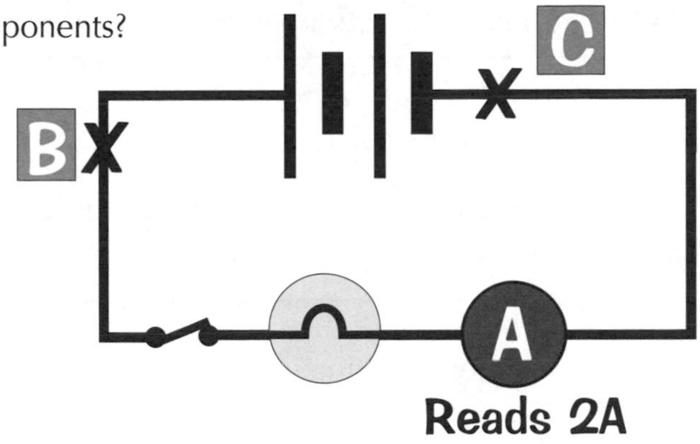

a) ....

b) ....

c) ....

d) ....

e) ....

Q2 What is the *'job'* of each component?

a) ....

b) ....

c) ....

d) ....

e) ....

Q3 If you added an ammeter at *point B*, what *current* would it read when the switch is closed?

....

Q4 What would an ammeter placed at *point C* read when the switch is closed.

....

Q5 Write a sentence which sums up what you know about the current in a series circuit.

....

....

Q6 If you added another bulb *in series* with the first bulb in the circuit above, how bright would each bulb appear compared to the first bulb *on its own?*

....

....

Q7 If you then connected another cell in *series* to the two cells, how bright would the bulbs appear compared to those in Question 6?

....

....

Questions on Series Circuits

Q8 Complete the following text by circling the correct answers.

More *voltage* /*resistance* in a *series circuit* means there is more push for the charge and so *more* /*less* current flows, making the bulbs *brighter* /*dimmer*.

More bulbs in a series circuit means there is more *push*/*resistance* to the flow of current, so *more* /*less* current flows, making the bulbs *dimmer* /*brighter*.

Q9 Draw the following *series* circuits. Below each one say whether the bulbs are *brighter*, *dimmer*, or *the same* as one bulb connected to one cell.

three bulbs and one cell ....

three bulbs and three cells ....

three bulbs and four cells ....

Q10 In the circuit shown opposite the ammeter reading is 2A.
What will be the current reading in each of the circuits below?
(Assume all the circuits in this question have identical bulbs and cells).

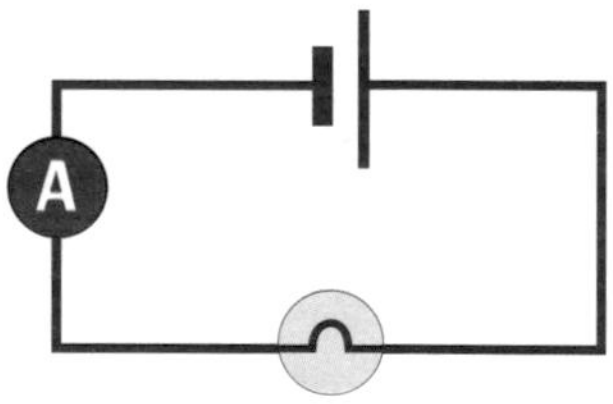

1. ....

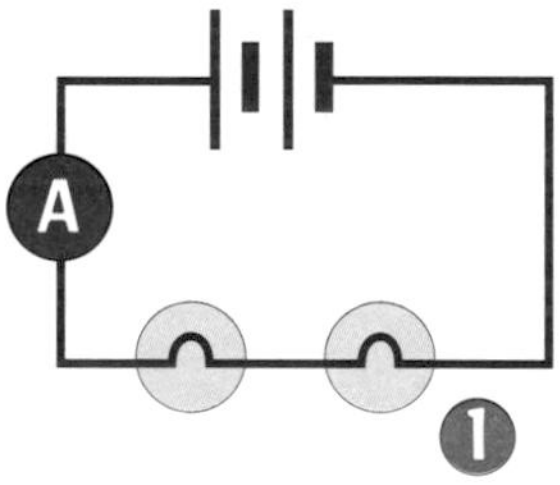

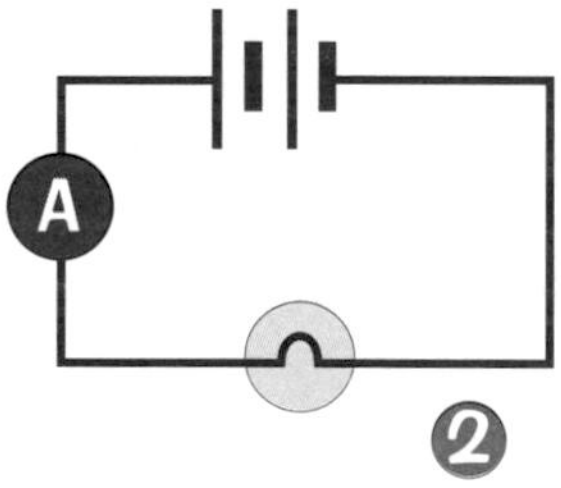

2. ....

3. ....

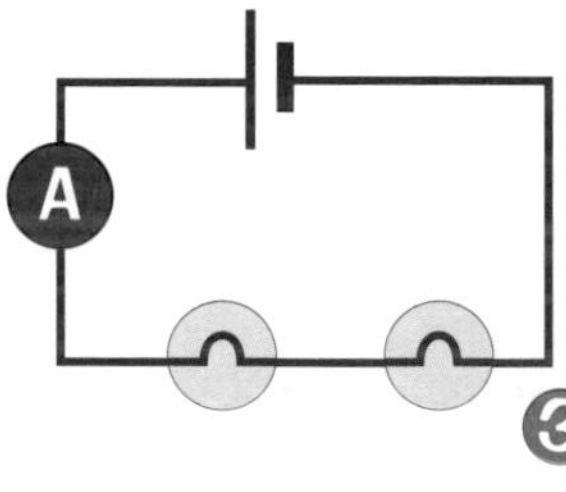

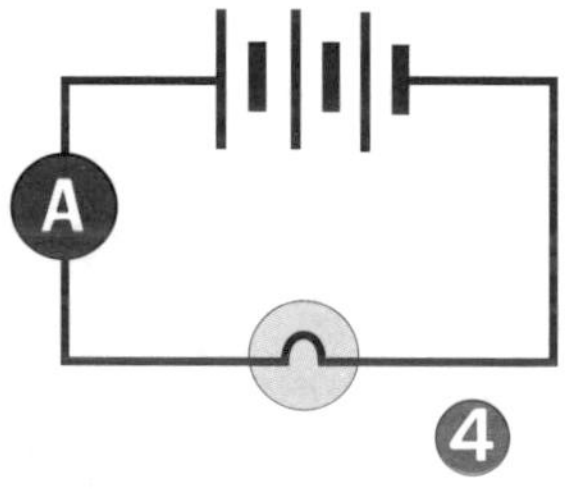

4. ....

Q11 What *type* of material will you find all the way around the outside of an electric circuit to *protect* it?

....

Q12 What is the 'job' of an ammeter in a circuit? ....

....

Q13 How does a change in the *size* of the *current* through a bulb affect its *light output?*

....

Questions on Parallel Circuits

Q1 Look at this circuit below which has a switch in parallel with a bulb.

Bulb1 Bulb2

a) Are the bulbs in *parallel* with each other?

....

b) Would *Bulb 2* be alight when the switch is open?

....

c) Would *Bulb 2* be alight when the switch is closed?

....

d) Would *Bulb 1* be alight when the switch is open? ....

e) Would *Bulb 1* be alight when the switch is closed? ....

f) What do we call the sort of connection you make by closing that switch?

....

g) If *Bulb 2* is removed and the switch is closed, would *Bulb 1* appear brighter, dimmer, or the same as it would for the situation in Question **e**)? ....

Q2 This circuit diagram shows two lamps (A and B) connected in parallel.

Write down A and B in the correct boxes in the table below to indicate what will happen to each bulb when the various changes are made to the circuit.

(Assume the original circuit is in place before each change is made).

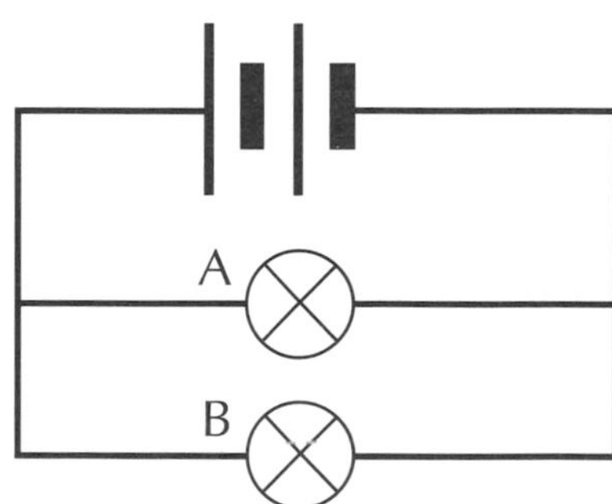

What is done to the circuit	The lamp(s) is(are):			
	Off	Dim	Normal	Bright
a) lamp A is unscrewed				
b) another cell is added in series				
c) another bulb is added in parallel to the first two				

Questions on Parallel Circuits

Q3 Look at this circuit diagram showing a circuit containing R1 and R2 and a bulb. Say which of the following statements are true (T) or false (F) by circling the appropriate letter.

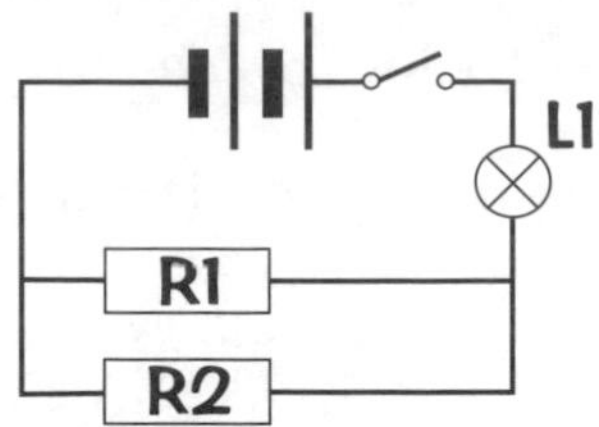

a) The lamp L1 and the switch are connected in parallel. (T / F)

b) The electric current is the same everywhere in the circuit. (T / F)

c) The potential difference across each resistor is the same. (T / F)

d) If resistor R1 has a higher resistance than R2, its current will be lower. (T / F)

e) If the switch is open, current will still flow through resistor R1. (T / F)

Q4 Look at this diagram of a parallel circuit.

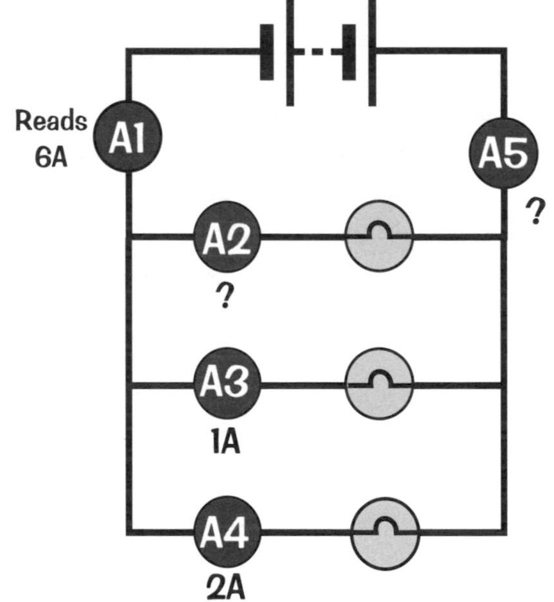

a) What would ammeter *A5* read?

....

b) What would ammeter *A2* read?

....

c) The *currents* in the bulbs are all *different*. What difference in the bulbs causes this difference in the currents?

....

....

d) If the power supply is a 4V battery, what is the *voltage* across each bulb?

....

e) Tick the following sentence(s) which you think are *true*. Cross them if they are false.

i) In any circuit the current *leaving* the power supply is *greater* than the current *returning* to it. ☐

ii) In a *parallel circuit* the current in the branches adds up to the same amount as the current from the supply. ☐

iii) In a *series circuit* the current through the different bulbs adds up to the same amount as that coming from the supply. ☐

Questions on Magnets

Q1 Answer the following questions concerning magnets.

a) Name _one_ object which would be attracted to a magnet. What _material_ is it made of?

....

b) Name _one_ object which would _not_ be attracted to a magnet. What is it made of?

....

c) Circle the set below that contains _three_ objects that would each be attracted to a magnet.

Set A

Gold ring, Iron nail, Nickel coin

Set C

Iron nail, Nickel coin, Steel spring

Set B

Copper bracelet, Gold ring, Iron nail

Set D

Copper bracelet, Steel spring, Nickel coin

Q2 Name four magnetic substances. ....

....

Q3 Steel is magnetically _'hard'_. What is meant by this? ....

....

Q4 Some 1p and 2p pieces contain nickel and some don't — it depends on the year in which they were made. How could you find out which years the coins containing nickel were made in?

....

....

....

Q5 Complete the following:

"Materials which are attracted to a magnet are called m________________ materials.

They all contain one of three elements: ____________ , ________________ or

______________________ .

If a magnetic material is magnetised it becomes a ____________________ ."

Questions on Magnets

Q6 A *magnetic field* is the region around a magnet where a *magnetic force* may be detected. What sort of material do you need to use to detect the force?

....

Q7 What is the *name* given to the type of magnet shown in the diagram opposite?

....

On the diagram opposite mark the poles for this magnet (N and S).

Q8 It is possible to map the direction of a magnetic field.

a) What *materials* could you use to 'see' the field lines around a magnet?

....

b) What could you use to find the *polarity* of the magnet?

....

c) What does it mean when the field lines are *close* together?

....

Q9 A careless student (there are some, you know) breaks a *bar magnet* in half.

Label the broken ends of the magnet N & S (North and South).

Copy and complete these sentences.

— Magnetic *poles* always come in

p_________________ .

— The broken ends of the magnet will

a_________________ each other.

— The broken end of one piece will

r__________ the unbroken end of the other.

Questions on Magnets

Q10 Circle any of the sentences below which you think are *true:*

a) A N-pole will *repel* a S-pole.

b) A N-pole will *attract* a S-pole.

c) A N-pole will *attract* a piece of unmagnetised steel.

d) A S-pole will *attract* a S-pole.

e) A S-pole will *attract* a N-pole.

f) A S-pole will *repel* a piece of unmagnetised steel.

Q11 John is a small boy with a wooden train set. The coaches each have magnets at either end, with the north pole facing outwards at one end and the south pole facing outwards at the other. The engine has one non-magnetised disc and one disc that is magnetised. John has made a line of three coaches which stick together. His big sister, Sally, finds that the engine can be put at either end to pull or push the coaches. How would Sally find out which disc on the engine is magnetised and which pole was facing outwards?

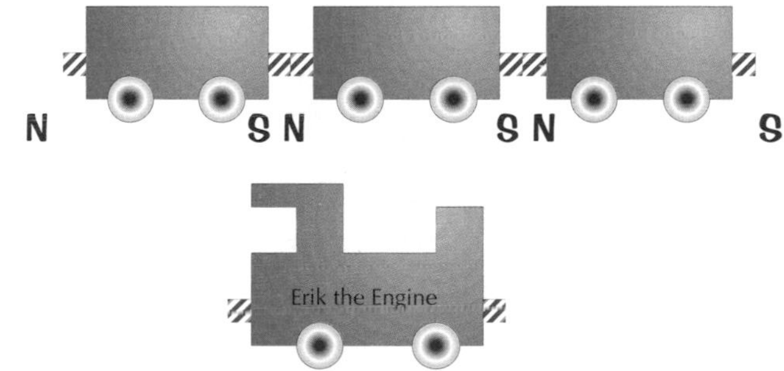

....

....

....

....

Q12 Complete these sentences about magnets using the words provided.

stronger two repel poles attract field

Any magnet has ______________ "ends" called ______________.

Opposite poles ______________ but like poles ______________.

The area around a magnet is known as the magnetic ______________.

The stronger the magnet, the ______________ the field.

Questions on Magnets

Q13 A compass needle is a small magnet. It lines up with the Earth's magnetic field lines. What must be true about the polarity of the compass needle which points *Northwards* (geographically)? (Remember that magnetic North is located pretty much at the geographical North pole.)

....

....

Q14 Complete:-

> "You only need a magnet and a piece of magnetic material for the two to be ______________ together. For two magnets to ________________ or ________________ each other, they must be suitably orientated."

Q15 Magnets can be many different shapes. Beside each of the magnets shown below, *write* which letters mark which poles (North or South).

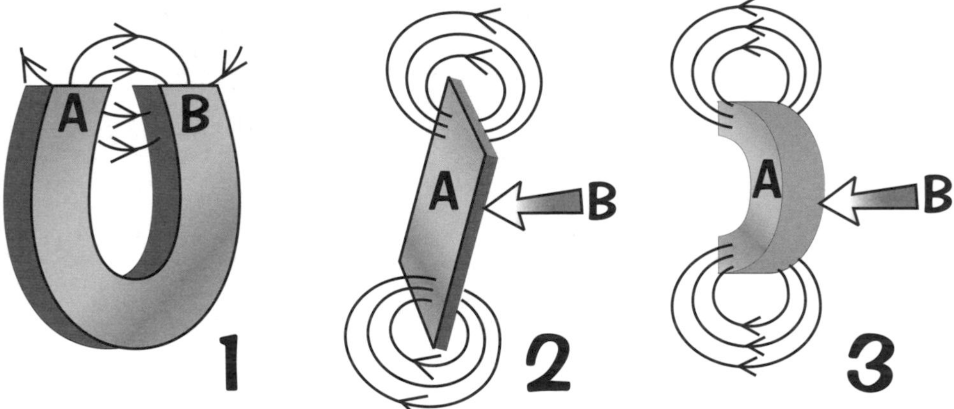

Q16 Look at the pictures below showing various magnetic field lines. Match each diagram to the appropriate statement.

1. Two south poles repelling each other ....
2. A single bar magnet ....
3. A north pole attracting a south pole ....

Stick a) b) or c) in here

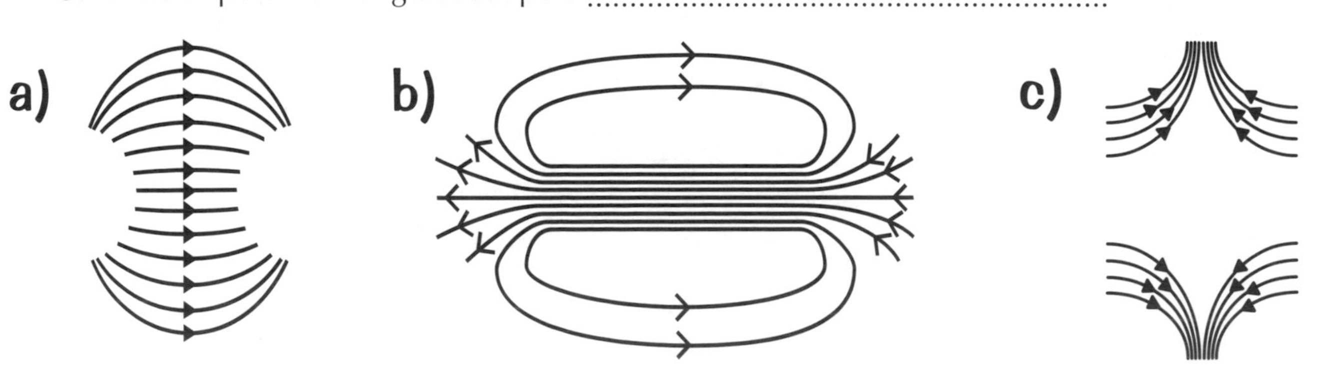

Questions on Electromagnets

Q1 The diagram below shows the magnetic fields around different arrangements of wire.

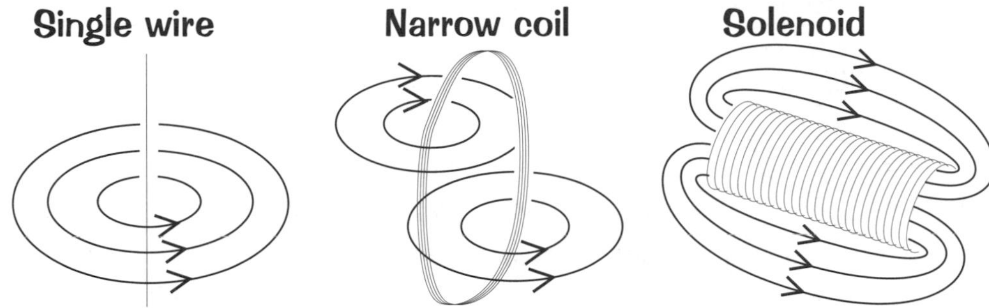

a) The field around the long coil (solenoid) is the same as that for something you have seen before. What was it?

....

b) What would happen to the *direction* of the *field* if the direction of the current was *changed?*

....

c) What would happen to the *strength* of the *field* if the *current* was *increased?*

....

d) How would a change in the *strength* of the *field* change the pattern you see?

....

....

Q2 An electromagnet is basically a coil of wire with a current flowing through it, like in the diagram above. The flow of current creates a magnetic field around the coil.

Circle any of the following statements that you think are true.

a) Inserting an *iron metal core* will *increase* the strength of the magnetic field.

b) Making the coil *wider* will *increase* the strength of the magnetic field.

c) Changing the *direction* of the current will *swap the poles* of the magnetic field.

d) Increasing the *number of coils* of wire will *increase* the strength of the magnetic field.

e) Increasing the *resistance* of the wire will make the magnetic field *stronger*.

f) Increasing the *current* flow will make the magnetic field *stronger*.

Questions on Electromagnets

Q3 One use of electromagnets is to move pieces of metal about in scrap yards. What is the main *difference* between *electromagnets* and *permanent magnets* which makes electromagnets better for this job?

....

....

Q4 Electrical appliances either utilise the *heating* effect of an electric current, or the *magnetic* effect of an electric current. Complete the table below by choosing which of these two effects is being used.

Electrical Appliance	Magnetic or Heating effect?
Toaster	
Drill	
Iron	
Light Bulb	
Blender	

Electrical appliances containing moving parts rely on the electromagnetic effect to make the device work. The next question details a device which also uses electromagnets.

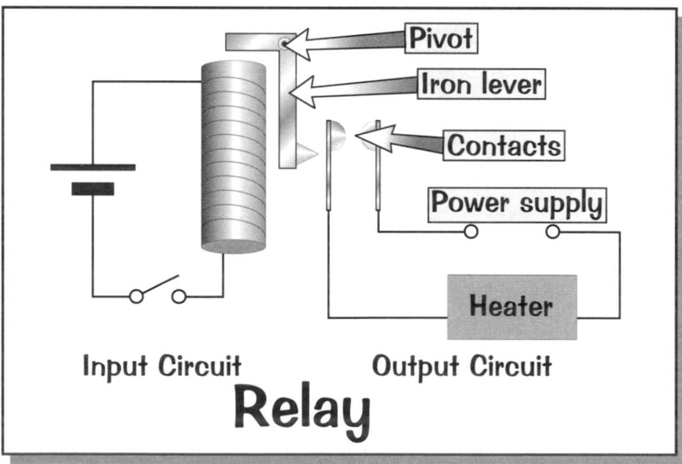

Q5 This above diagram shows a *relay*. Fill in the gaps in the steps below.

a) The switch in the input circuit is closed.

b) This causes a c________________ to flow in the i________________ circuit.

c) This makes the coil become an e______________________.

d) The coil then a____________________ the iron lever.

e) The lever tips and the contacts t___________________ each other.

f) This causes a c___________________ to flow in the o___________________ circuit.

g) This current makes the __________________________ work.

Questions on Electromagnets

Q6 Complete the following:

'A relay uses a s____________ current in one circuit to switch on a much l____________ current in another circuit.'

Q7 Opposite is a diagram of an electric bell. Try to write your own 'steps' for how this one works. The first one is done for you and there is a key letter given for the others.

a) The switch is closed.

b) There is a c________________ in the coil.

c) The coil becomes an e________________________.

d) The electromagnet a______________ the spring armature.

e) The clanger moves away from the b________.

f) The contacts separate and the circuit is b_________________.

g) The armature s _________ back and the clanger hits the bell

h) The contacts c_____________ the circuit.

i) Current then f____________ in the circuit.

j) An then the process r________________ itself.

Electric Bell

Contacts

Bell

Clanger

Q8 A Revision Puzzle — Fill in the squares. The letters in the bright squares make up a word when read downwards. What is it?

....

Clue	Squares
Magnetic metal in coins	N
Like poles ______	R
More current more field _____	S
Adding an iron _____ increases strength	C
Repelled by a S-pole	S
Magnetic element in steel	I
Attracted by a S-pole	N
Relies on magnetism for movement	M
Input circuit controls the __	R
Small pieces of iron	F
The magnet in a compass	N
The area of force round a magnet	F
Magnetic element	C

Questions on Forces

Q1 Fill in the blanks.

repel	newtons	attract	buoyancy	weight
magnetic	electrostatic	attract	friction	surface tension

a) Forces are measured in ____________________.

b) ________________ is the name given to the force of gravity acting on you.

c) A plastic rod rubbed with a duster will ____________________ bits of paper because of an ____________________ force.

d) The force which makes things float is called ___________________.

e) The force between two magnets is a _________________ force and can make them _________________ or _________________.

f) Water droplets are held together by _____________ _______________.

g) _____________________ between a moving object and the surface it moves on is a force which slows the object down.

Q2 Describe what will happen to the toy trucks in each of these diagrams when the force shown by the arrow(s) is applied. Use words like "accelerates", "slows down", "steady speed" and "stationary".

a) ....

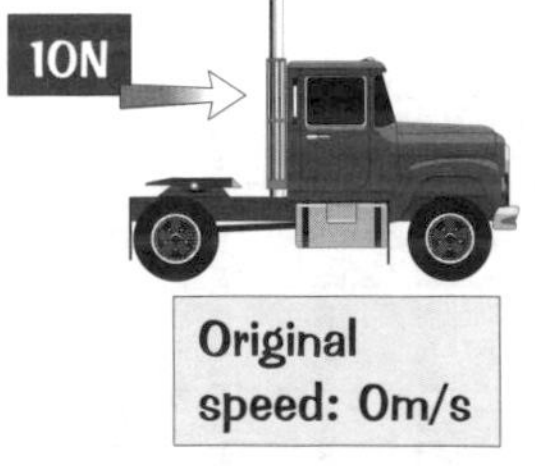

b) ....

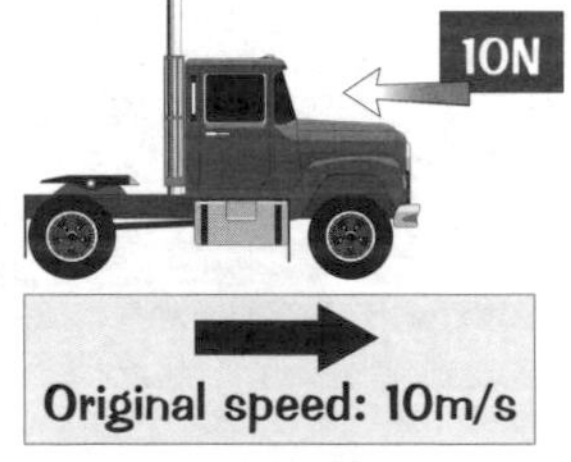

c) ....

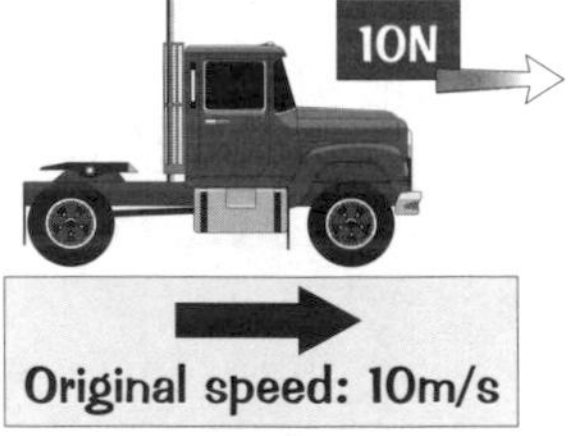

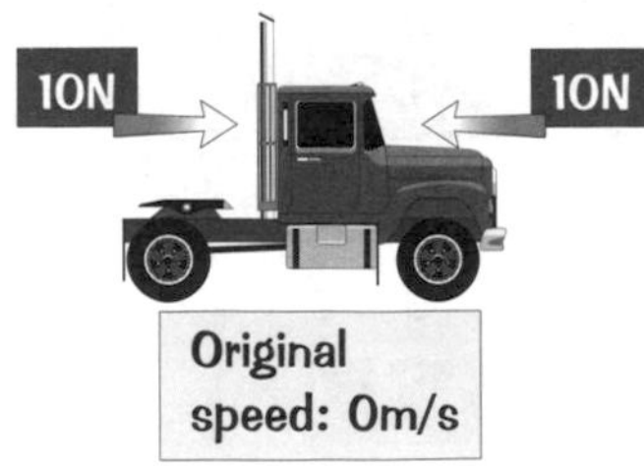

d) ....

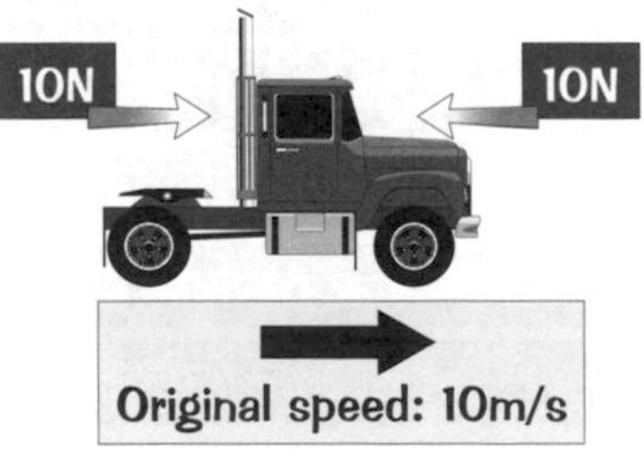

e) ....

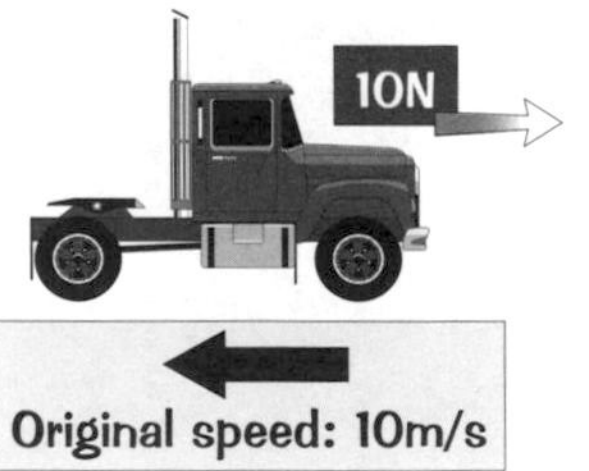

f) ....

Questions on Forces

Q3 *Complete* the sentences using the following words:

balanced	direction	speed	stationary
constant	slow		direction

If an object has an *unbalanced force* acting on it, it will ________________ up, ____________________ down, or change ____________________.

If an object has ___________________ forces acting on it, it will either move at a ____________________ speed in the same ___________________ , or, if it was stationary to start with, it will remain _________________.

Q4 When constructing force diagrams, it is important to draw pairs of forces acting along the *same line* (as in Question 2 on the previous page). What would be the effect upon an object if the two forces acting *were not* lined up?

....

....

....

....

Q5 *Complete* the following sentences by circling the correct words.

a) Mass is measured in *N* / *kg* / *Pa*.

b) Weight is a *pressure* / *force* and is measured in *N* / *kg* / *Pa*.

c) One kilogram weighs approximately *0.1* / *10* / *100* newtons on the Earth.

Q6 A car is moving in a straight line with a steady speed.

a) Draw and label the two *vertical forces* on the diagram.

b) Draw and label the two *horizontal forces* on the diagram.

Questions on Forces

Q7 a) Complete the table, noting that the strength of the Earth's gravity is 10N/kg at its surface, while that of the Moon is 1.6N/kg at its surface. (i.e. 1kg is pulled down with a force of 10N on Earth and a force of 1.6N on the Moon.)

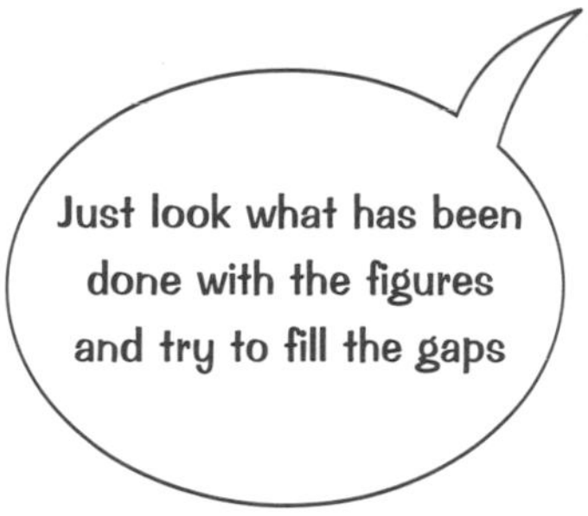

Just look what has been done with the figures and try to fill the gaps

Mass on Earth	Weight on Earth (N)	Mass on the Moon	Weight on the Moon (N)
2kg	2×10=20N	2kg	2×1.6=3.2N
0.1kg			
500g			
1000kg			
10g			

b) Why is the *weight* of an object on the Moon different from that on the Earth?

....

....

c) On Jupiter one kilogram weighs about 25N. What would be the *weight* of the 500g object in the table if it were on Jupiter?

....

....

d) The diagram opposite shows a satellite in orbit around the Earth. Which arrow shows the *direction* of the gravitational *force* acting on the satellite?

....

....

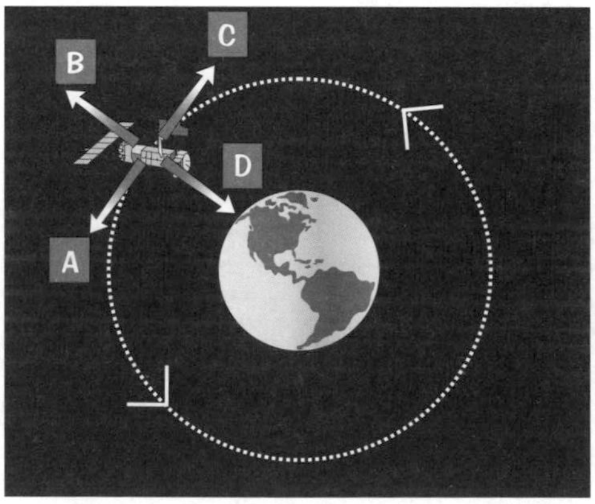

e) If the force was suddenly removed, which arrow shows the *direction* the satellite would move in?

....

f) The force acting on the satellite is *not* balanced by a force in the *opposite* direction. How do we know this?

....

....

Questions on Forces

Q8 As well as changing the direction or speed of movement, forces can cause changes of shape. *State* the names of *three* forces under which the shape of an object can be changed.

....

Complete the following:

When an object is being *stretched* it is said to be in ____________________.

When an object is being *squashed* it is said to be in ____________________.

Q9 The table below shows the results for a stretching experiment where a *spring* has been *loaded* by applying a weight to it.

Force (N)	0	1	2	3	4	5	6	7	8	9	10
Extension (cm)	0	2.1	3.9	6.2	7.9	10	12.1	13.9	16	17.9	20.1

Plot a graph of these results and explain what the shape of the curve tells you about the relationship between extension and load applied.

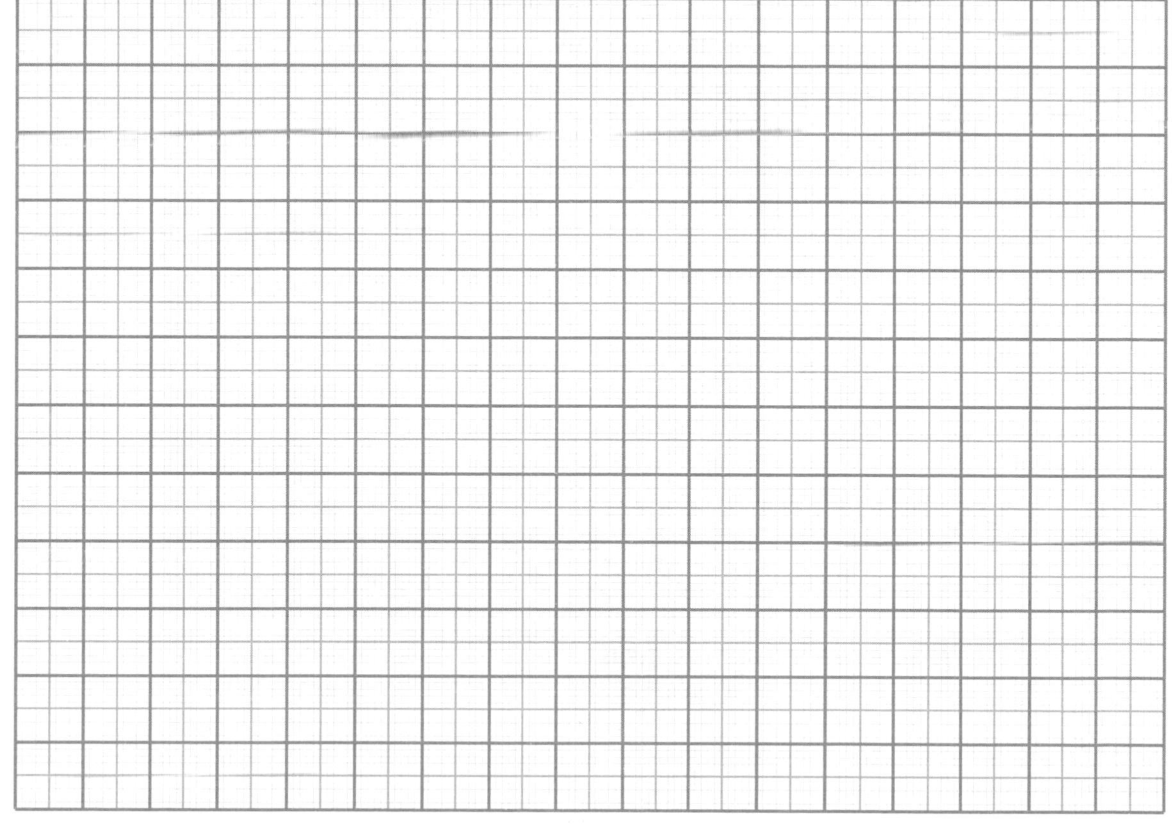

The larger the load, the ....

....

Questions on Speed

Q1 Fill in the blanks.

a) Speed is usually measured in ________________.

b) Average speed is worked out from dividing ______________ by ______________.

c) An increase in speed is called __________________.

d) A decrease in speed is called _________________.

e) To change speed you need to have an __________________ force acting.

Q2 Michael and his mother have just finished a long car journey. 'We did 160 miles in four hours, so we did 40 miles per hour.' she said. 'That can't be right' said Michael, 'I never saw the speedo say 40, it was usually much more than that!'

Explain the cause of their confusion.

....

....

....

....

Q3 Draw a line to link the correct word equations on the left with the *correct* symbol equations on the right.

SPEED = DISTANCE ÷ TIME	$t = d \div s$
TIME = DISTANCE ÷ SPEED	$d = s \times t$
DISTANCE = SPEED × TIME	$s = d \div t$

Q4 Speed is often confused with velocity — the two *aren't* quite the same. Explain briefly the *difference* between *speed* and *velocity*.

....

....

Questions on Speed

Q5 Use the equations from Question 3 (previous page) to complete the following table.

DISTANCE (m)	TIME (s)	SPEED (m/s)
10	5	
0.5	2	
1,000	10	
20	0.1	
500		10
	4	12
1		100
10		0.2
	15	15
200		0.02

Q6 This question is a bit harder than question 5 because the units are all mixed up. Use the equations from Question 3 again to fill in the blanks. Don't forget to sort the units out!

(Do the rough work on some scrap paper).

DISTANCE	TIME	SPEED
50km	s	10km/h
2m		2cm per year
150,000,000km	500s	
1km		3m/s
	1 year	300,000,000m/s
1km		50m/s
600m	1 minute	m/s
72km	2h	m/s
360km	s	100m/s
360km	minutes	100m/s

Questions on Speed

Q7 The movement of an object can be described using a distance/time graph. One such graph is shown below for the motion of a cat.

Distance — Time Graph

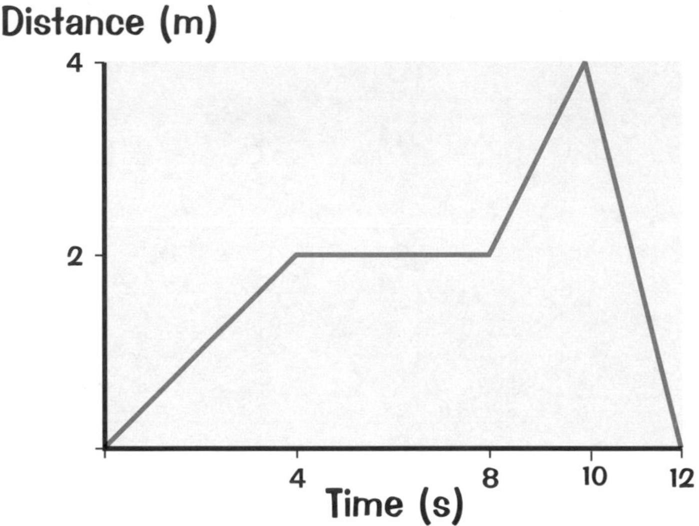

a) What does a *horizontal line* mean in a *distance-time* graph?

....

....

b) What does a *line sloping upwards* mean in a *distance-time* graph?

....

....

c) What does the above *distance-time* graph tell you about the *motion* of the cat it describes.

(HINT: do it in four separate parts: 0-4s, 4-8s, 8-10s and 10-12s and remember, *speed = distance ÷ time)*

0-4s: ....

4-8s: ....

8-10s: ....

10-12s: ....

Questions on Air Resistance and Friction

Q1 *Circle* the correct words that make the following sentences *true:*

a) Friction is a type of *pressure* / *force* / *momentum*.

b) The force of friction is measured in *kg* / *cm*^{2} / *newtons*.

c) Friction always acts to make moving objects travel more *quickly* / *slowly* / *smoothly*.

d) Friction occurs when two *rough* / *smooth* surfaces rub together.

e) Air and water both exert *accelerating* / *decelerating* forces upon moving objects.

f) When an object moves through air the force of friction is called *gravity* / *drag* / *weight*.

g) Friction forces in a fluid increases as an object travels more *quickly* / *slowly* through it.

h) As an object accelerates through air, the force of friction will *decrease* / *increase*.

Q2 *Circle* the correct ending to this sentence:

'When the force of friction equals the accelerating force the object will ....

- ....speed up'
- ....continue at the same speed'
- ....slow down'
- ....stop'

Q3 During winter in very cold areas of the world people put chains around their car wheels when they go driving in the snow. Explain why they may need to do this.

....

....

....

....

Q4 Complete the table below using the words "LOW" or "HIGH" to show what the ideal amount of friction should be.

Example of Friction	Friction should be...
A car tyre in contact with a road surface	
A skater moving over the ice	
Brake blocks pressing against a wheel rim	
Rock climbing boots in contact with the rock	

Questions on Air Resistance and Friction

Q5 The diagram below shows a car at *three* stages near the start of its journey. The *thickness* of the arrows represents the *size* of the force acting on the car, so a *thicker arrow* means a *bigger force*. Answer the following question about the car's motion.

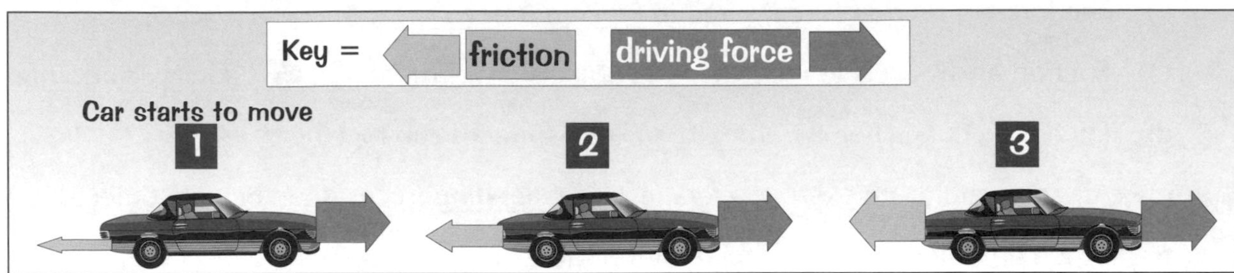

a) Which of the two forces is *biggest* when the car is *starting off?* ....

b) What will happen to the car's *speed* at this time? ....

c) What has happened to the *frictional force* by picture 2?

....

d) Which is the *biggest* force acting on the car in picture 2? ....

e) Are the forces on the car *balanced* or *unbalanced* in picture 3? ....

f) What happens to the car's *speed* now? ....

g) What must happen to the forces if the car's motion is to *change?*

....

h) The forces drawn are the ones which actually affect the way the car moves along the ground. What *other* forces are there which act on the car that have not been drawn?

....

Q6 Say the car discussed in Question 1 was to slow down from the time of picture 3.

a) How can the driving force be *changed* for this to happen?

....

b) Will the *air resistance* increase or decrease as the car slows down?

....

c) What overall change in the *shape* of a car would *reduce* the effect of air resistance?

....

....

Questions on Air Resistance and Friction

Q7 This diagram shows a sky-boarder in free-fall (that is before she opens her parachute). The arrows show the forces acting on her. Thick arrows mean big forces.

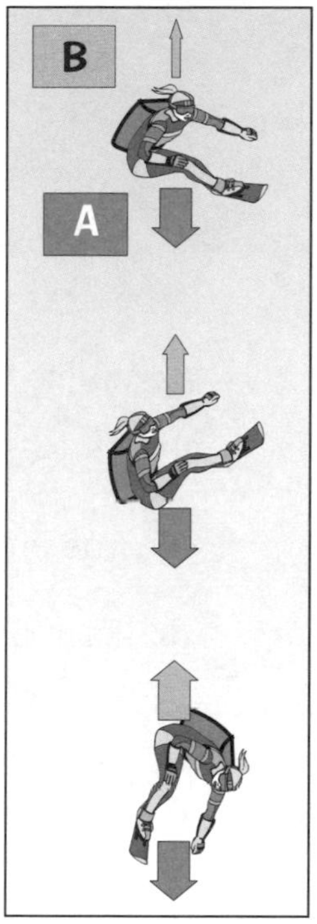

B

A

a) What is the name given to force A? ....

b) What is the name given to force B? ....

c) Does force A change as the sky-boarder falls towards the ground?

....

d) Explain why force B *does* change. ....

....

e) Which force will *change* when she *opens* her parachute?

....

f) What will happen to her speed after the parachute opens?

....

g) What will be true about her *speed* in the last picture?

....

Q8 Sohail is investigating friction through liquids. He lowers different shaped plasticine lumps into a measuring cylinder of wallpaper paste and times how long they take to reach the bottom. He lowers them on a piece of cotton to the top of the paste and then lets them go.

a) What must be *true* about the lumps of plasticine if it is going to be a *fair* test?

....

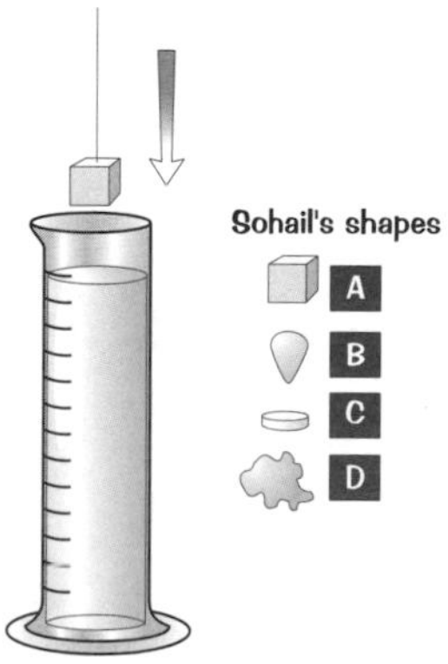

b) Why is *wallpaper paste* used instead of water or air?

....

....

Sohail's shapes

A

B

C

D

c) Which shape would you expect to take the *shortest* time?

....

Why? ....

....

Questions on Moments (Force and Rotation)

Q1 Answer these questions on moments.

a) The sails of the windmill in the picture are rotating. Give *three* other examples of objects you might often see *rotating*.

....

....

Complete these sentences by filling in the blanks.

b) The sails are rotating which means that they are moving in a c________________.

c) The end of the sail travels f___________ than the centre of it.

d) Each part of the sails takes the s_______________ time to complete one rotation.

e) The sails are rotating about a f______________________.

f) Another name for this point is a p__________________.

g) Overall the forces on the sails must be un______________________. How do you know?

....

....

Q2 The objects shown below are all stationary to start with.
What will happen to the objects shown in the picture below when the forces are applied?
Draw lines connecting each phrase with the appropriate picture(s).

- It will accelerate to the left.
- It will accelerate downwards.
- It will rotate anticlockwise.

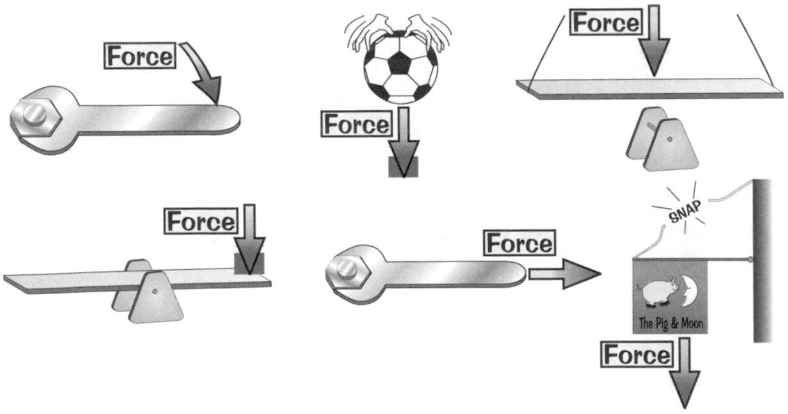

Force

Force

Force

Force

Force

SNAP

The Pig & Moon

Force

- It will rotate clockwise.
- It will accelerate to the right.
- It will accelerate upwards.

Questions on Moments (Force and Rotation)

Q3 Complete these sentences by filling in the blanks.

force turning greater Nm distance increased pivot

a) Moments are a measure of the ______________________ effect of a force.

b) The moment is increased if the size of the force is ______________________.

c) The moment is also increased if the force acts at a ________________ distance from the ______________________.

d) Moments are calculated using:

Moment = F________________ x D________________.

e) Moments are measured in ________________.

Q4 What would you do to calculate a moment if you knew the size of the force and the distance from the pivot?

....

....

Q5 In the previous section we looked at the speeding up and slowing down of a car. When the brakes are applied to slow a car down, brake pads press against rotating discs that are attached to the wheels.

a) What is the name given to the *force* that is produced when the pads rub against the discs.

....

....

b) Would it be easier or harder to slow the car down if the pads rubbed at the top of a larger disc? (Explain your answer.)

....

....

Questions on Moments (Force and Rotation)

Q6 The diagram shows a seesaw with two children on it, each positioned 2m from the centre.

m
F x d

4m

ANNA
mass = 30kg
weight = 300N

AARON
mass = 40kg
weight = 400N

a) What is Anna's *mass?* ....

b) What is her *weight?* ....

c) Calculate the *moment* caused by Anna's weight.

....

....

....

d) What is Aaron's *weight?*

....

e) Calculate the *moment* caused by Aaron's weight.

....

....

f) Which way will the seesaw move? (clockwise or anticlockwise.) ....

g) Who should move and which way, (away from the pivot or towards the pivot), to balance it?

....

h) Complete the following by completing the words.

'A seesaw will balance if the cl____________________ and anti— cl____________________ moments are equal.'

Q7 A DJ is mixing tracks using two turn-tables and needs to spin one record *backwards* to get its beat in the right place. Would it be easier for the DJ to spin the record with his fingers placed near the middle of the record, or with them placed towards its edge?

Explain your answer using the idea of moments.

....

....

....

....

Questions on Moments (Force and Rotation)

Q8 Look at the diagram on the right.

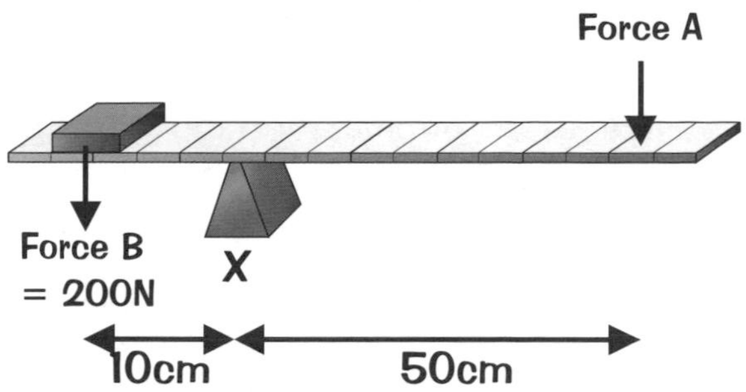

Force A

Force B = 200N

X

10cm

50cm

a) What is the *name* given to force A?

....

b) What is the *name* given to force B?

....

c) What is the *name* given to point X?

....

d) What is the *size* of the *load?*

....

e) What is the *distance* between the load and the pivot?

....

f) What is the *moment* of the load? (i.e. force × distance from pivot)

....

g) If the moments from forces A and B are to balance, what must be the *moment* of the *effort?*

....

....

h) What *size* must the effort be to *lift* the load?

....

....

Q9 Mark on each diagram where the *loads*, *efforts* and *pivots* are.
The first has been done for you as an example.

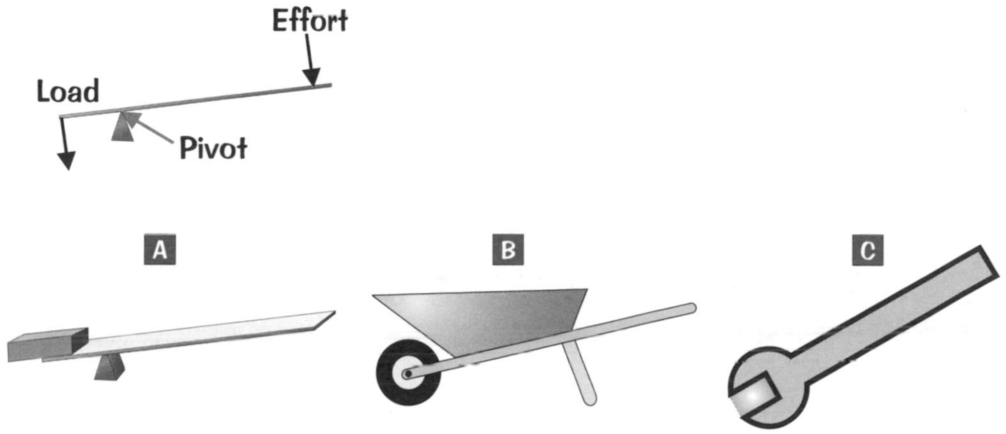

Effort

Load

Pivot

A

B

C

Questions on Pressure

Q1 Complete the questions by circling the correct words.

a) Pressure measures the *mass* / *force* per unit *volume* / *area*.

b) The more force there is, the *greater* / *smaller* the pressure.

c) The greater the area over which the force acts, the *greater* / *smaller* the pressure.

d) Pressure is worked out from dividing *force* / *area* by *force* / *area*.

e) Force is measured in *pascals* / *newtons*.

f) Area is measured in cm^3 / m^2.

g) Pressure is measured in *pascals* / *newtons*.

Q2 Alice wants to find the pressure she exerts upon the floor. She measures the length and width of her shoe and multiplies them together to get a rough area. She then doubles the answer. She divides her weight in newtons by the total area she has worked out.

a) Why won't her area measurement be very accurate?

....

....

....

b) Will it be *too big* or *too small*?

....

c) Why did she *double* the measurement she made?

....

....

d) What *result* does she get for the pressure? Remember the *units*.

....

....

e) Suggest one *improvement* to this experiment to make it more accurate.

....

....

Questions on Pressure

Q3 Circle the equations that you think are *correct* for calculating *pressure*.

PRESSURE = FORCE ÷ AREA

$p = F \times A$

$F = p \div A$

AREA = PRESSURE ÷ FORCE

$A = F \div p$

FORCE = PRESSURE × AREA

Q4 Use the *correct* equation for pressure to help you to answer the questions below.

a) What *force* is Box A exerting upon the ground?

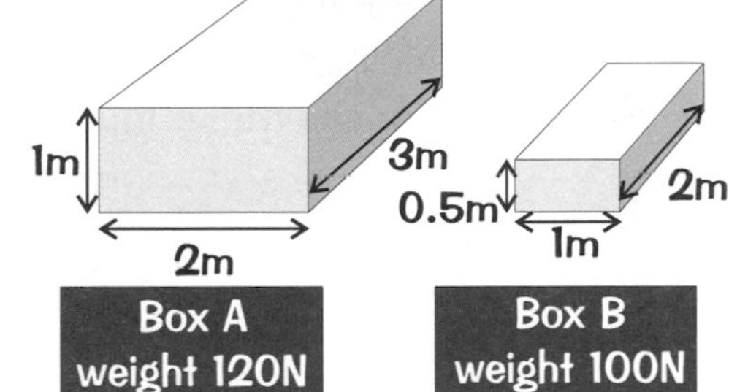

b) What *area* is this force spread over?

c) What *pressure* is Box A putting on the ground?

d) What *pressure* is Box B putting on the ground?

e) If you stood Box A on its smallest area, what would the value of the new *pressure* be?

f) What is the *greatest* pressure Box B could exert upon the ground?

g) If Box A is put on top of Box B, so that their largest areas are in contact, what would be the *pressure* upon the ground?

Questions on Pressure

Q5 The following questions concern the pros and cons of pressure in various situations. Include the word "pressure" in each of your answers.

a) Why are *blunt* scissors *poor* at cutting things out?

....

....

Happy finger Unhappy finger

b) Why can you push one end of a drawing pin in, but not the other? (*Remember* that the pressures acting at each end are different!)

....

....

c) Why are caterpillar tracks better than wheels when driving over snow or muddy ground?

....

....

....

....

Q6 For each of these, write whether the area should be LARGE or SMALL and the pressure HIGH or LOW.

Object	Area should be: (small / large)	Pressure will be: (small / large)
A knife to cut meat		
Shoe heels that don't damage floors		
A sewing needle		
Tractor tyres for use on soft ground		
Snow skis		

Q7 A man has a weight of 900N and his shoes have a total area of $0.1m^2$.

What pressure does he exert on the ground?

....

....

....

Questions on Pressure

Q8 Fill in the gaps in the questions, by finding the words in the word search. They can be in any direction.

a) The forces on a stationary object are b______________________.

b) A name for the highest speed when falling is t______________________ velocity.

c) Force is measured in n______________________.

d) The force of gravity on an object is its w ______________________.

e) A stretched spring is in t ______________________.

f) A moment is the t______________________ effect of a force.

g) A force which slows things down is f______________________.

h) Gases and liquids are both f______________________.

i) Pressure = force / a______________________.

j) The force keeping boats afloat is b______________________.

D	E	Y	C	N	A	Y	U	O	B	A	P
S	T	E	N	S	I	O	N	E	F	V	S
A	D	L	O	H	I	L	D	D	R	E	N
F	E	P	L	O	R	V	E	C	I	R	O
E	C	R	T	A	R	C	S	S	C	A	T
E	N	W	A	Q	N	P	D	U	T	G	W
R	A	T	Y	A	U	I	O	P	I	E	E
S	L	F	L	G	U	H	M	K	O	L	N
S	A	A	D	L	A	Z	X	R	N	C	V
Q	B	M	F	N	T	H	G	I	E	W	B
W	N	E	T	P	I	H	M	U	S	T	R
I	U	G	N	I	N	R	U	T	U	Y	T

Questions on Light

Q1 Complete these sentences by filling in the missing words.

a) Light travels in S__________ lines.

b) Light travels as a type of electromagnetic R__________.

c) Light travels at a speed that is much F____________ than that of sound.

d) The speed of light in a vacuum is ______________________________ m/s.

e) Some things can be seen through. These are said to be T________________.

f) Some things just don't let light through at all. These are called O__________ materials.

g) Some things give out their own light. These are said to be L_____________.

h) All other things we see because they R____________ light.

i) For us to see something, light from it must enter our E__________.

j) Areas where light can't reach because something is in the way are called S___________.

Q2 Choose suitable words to describe each of the things listed **a)** to **i)**. You may find that more than one word will fit.

OPAQUE, TRANSPARENT, SHINY, LUMINOUS, DULL, TRANSLUCENT

a) A window ....

b) A mirror ....

c) The Sun ....

d) The Moon ....

e) Air ....

f) Greaseproof paper ....

g) Water ....

h) Carpet ....

i) Aluminium foil ....

Questions on Light

Q3 Complete the following sentences by circling the correct words in the brackets.

a) Most things are able to be seen because they (bend / reflect) light into our eyes.

b) Objects with rough surfaces give a (clear / diffuse) reflection.

c) Objects with smooth surfaces give a (regular / irregular) reflection.

d) Usually we think of reflection using a flat mirror.
This sort of mirror is called a (concave / convex / plane) mirror.

e) When we are thinking about reflections in a mirror, we are interested in two angles, called the angle of (incidence / transmission) and the angle of (reflection / absorption).

f) These angles are not measured from the mirror but from the (parallel / normal) line.

g) This line is at (45° / 90°) degrees to the mirror's surface.

Taken out of the curriculum **but still important**

Q4 Look at the diagram opposite that shows how shadows are made.

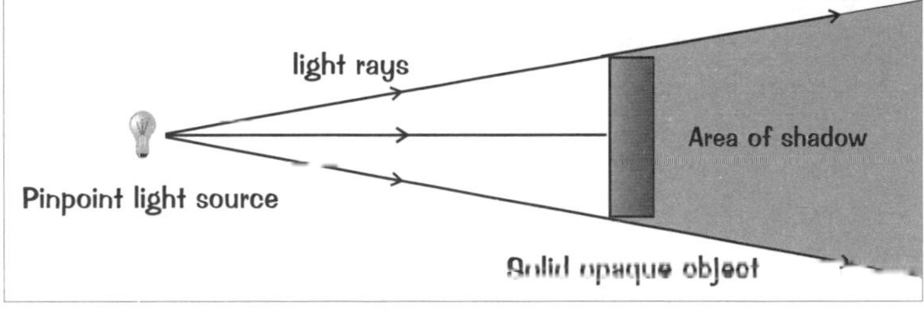

a) What must be true about the *object* if it is going to cause a shadow?

....

....

b) What fact about the way light *travels* explains why *shadows* are made? ....

....

Q5 When the light source is not a point source, but a larger object, the shadows produced are different.

By continuing the light rays, complete this diagram.

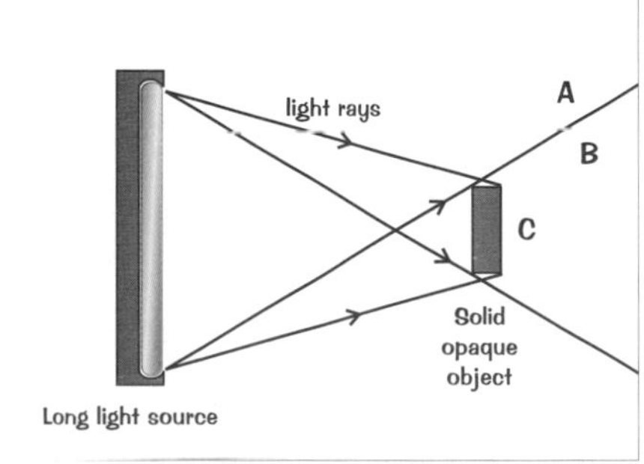

a) In terms of *brightness*, describe how regions A, B and C will be *different* from each other.

....

b) What are the *names* given to the regions B and C? ....

Questions on Light

Q6 Shadows produced by astronomical eclipses can be described in the same way as other shadows. Look at the diagram on the right. Here S is the Sun, M is the Moon and E is the Earth (not to scale!).

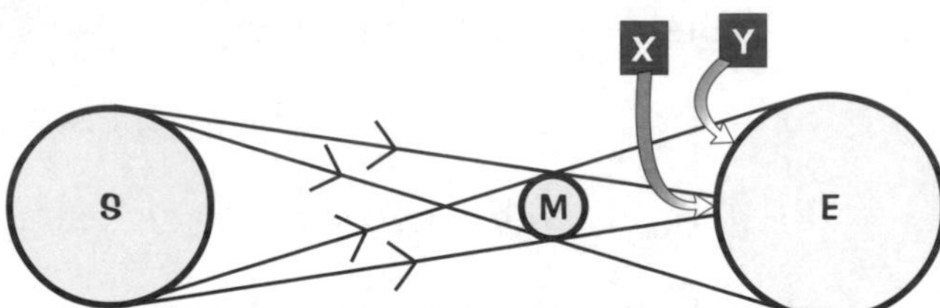

a) What would you see if you were at X? ....

....

....

b) What would you see if you were at Y? ....

....

....

Q7 The diagram below right shows a *lunar eclipse*, but *two* of the light rays have been missed out. *Complete* the diagram. (The above diagram might help you.)

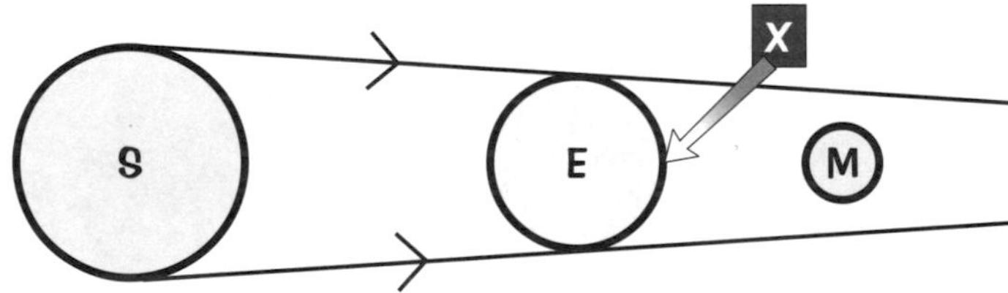

a) What would you see if you were at X?

....

b) Onto what will the Earth cast its shadow?

....

Q8 During a lunar eclipse, the Moon changes from its usual *bright white* colour to a *slightly pale white* colour. This lasts for some time before the Moon finally turns *very dark*. What is it about the Earth's *shadow* that causes this *sequence* of changes?

....

....

....

Questions on Reflection

Q1 Look at the diagram to the right.

a) When a ray of light hits a surface, *two* things will happen to the light. What are they?

....

....

b) Use this to explain the *difference* between *transparent*, *opaque* and *shiny* objects.

....

....

....

Q2 Not all the light that reaches our planet from the Sun makes it to the ground.

a) *Name* an important *visible feature* of the Earth's atmosphere that is a significant *reflector* of sunlight.

....

....

Some of the light that does reach the surface is reflected upwards and the rest is absorbed, causing the ground to warm up.
The warm ground emits its own special 'light', which we can't see.

b) *What* is the *name* of this type of special 'light'?

....

c) On Earth on a clear night the temperature drops more quickly than on a cloudy night. Explain why this is the case.

....

....

....

(*HINT:* Heat radiation is reflected in the same way as light.)

Questions on Reflection

Q3 Follow these instructions:-

- Draw a straight line on the page
- Label this line *MIRROR*

} These two are done for you

- Draw a line from the *middle* of the mirror at *right angles* to it.

  Label this line with its correct *name*.

- Draw a *ray of light* hitting the mirror where the two lines join.

  The angle between the ray and the mirror should be 40° *(40 degrees)*.

- Label the angle of *incidence* and write what its value is.
- Draw in the *reflected* ray.
- Label the angle of *reflection* and say what its value is.

Questions on Refraction

Q1 Complete these sentences by circling the correct word in the brackets:-

When light is travelling through a medium it travels in a (*straight* / *curved*) line.

When light moves from one medium into another, its speed (*isn't* / *is*) changed.

In the new medium it continues to travel in a (*curved* /*straight*) line, but with a new direction. This change happens because the speed of light is (*the same* / *different*) in different materials. The name given to this effect is (*reflection* / *deflection* / *refraction*).

Q2 Which two of the diagrams below are correct?

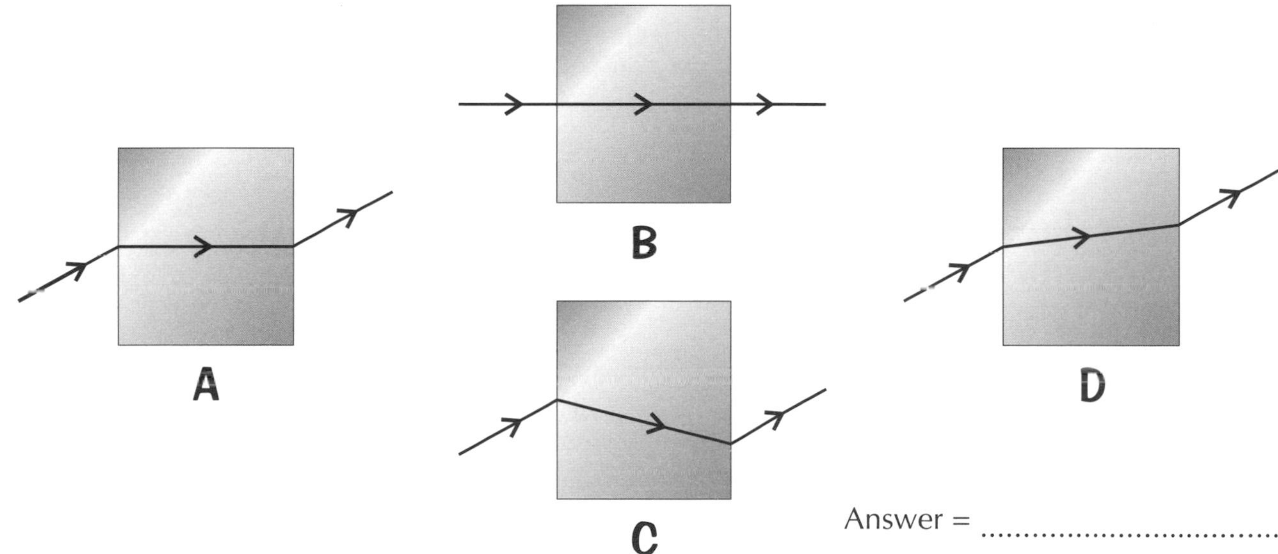

Answer = ...

Q3 Complete the following sentences by circling the correct word(s) in the brackets:-

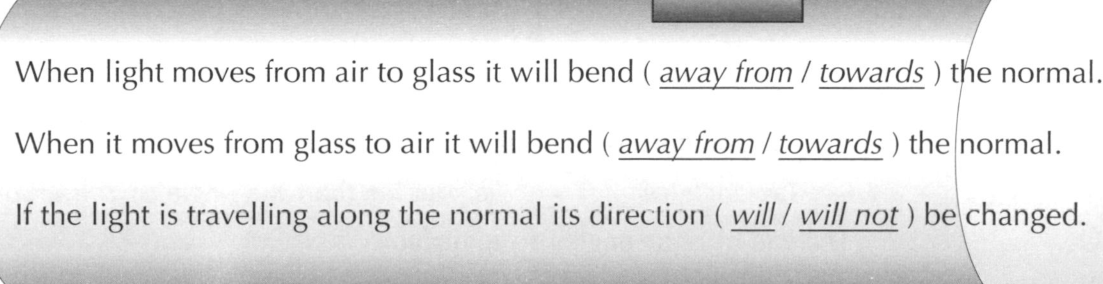

When light moves from air to glass it will bend (*away from* / *towards*) the normal.

When it moves from glass to air it will bend (*away from* / *towards*) the normal.

If the light is travelling along the normal its direction (*will* / *will not*) be changed.

Questions on Refraction

Q4 You have probably seen diagrams like this one on the right, showing what a converging lens (like in a camera or in your eye) does to light. You know enough about *refraction* to be able to explain why it works like that. It's easier if you split the lens up into bits, like in the lower diagram.

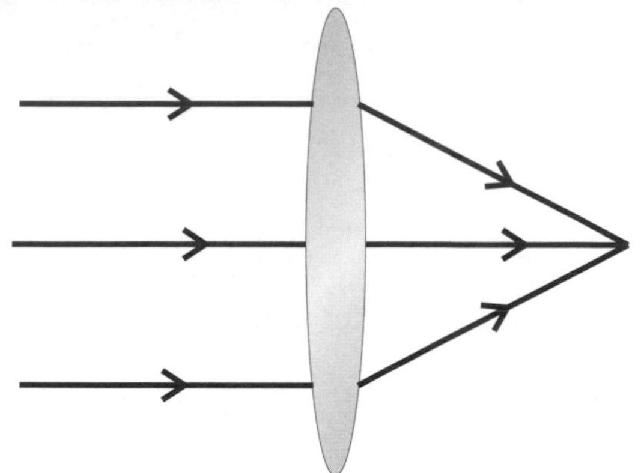

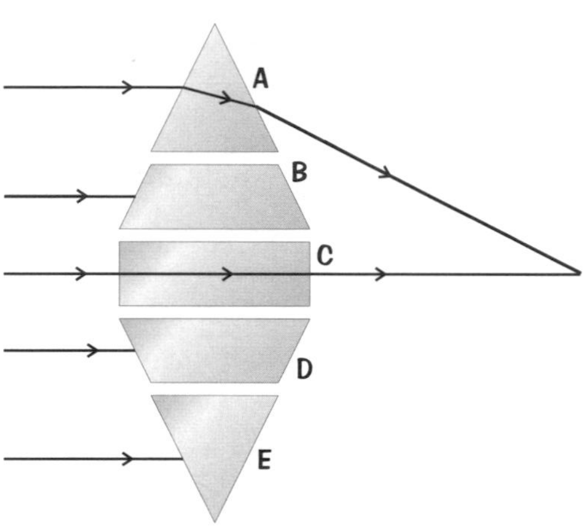

a) Complete the ray entering section B (you will need to draw this section fairly carefully, the others you can sketch quickly).

b) Draw in the rays for sections D and E (you shouldn't need to think about them very much)

c) List five things which work by refraction (*HINT*: anything with lenses or prisms)

....

....

Q5 Find the missing words.

Letter	Clue
R	Used to bend light in binoculars
E	Used to focus light in a camera
F	When it moves from one material to another light will _______
R	A thin beam of light
A	_____ of incidence = _____ of reflection.
C	Where light travels fastest
T	Going from air to glass light bends ______ the normal
I	The angle of _______ is greater than the angle of refraction
O	The line at right-angles to a surface
N	Light travels slower in a material with greater _______

Questions on Refraction

Q6 Follow the instructions to complete the diagram of *monochromatic* light passing through a prism. *(Monochromatic light = one colour.)*

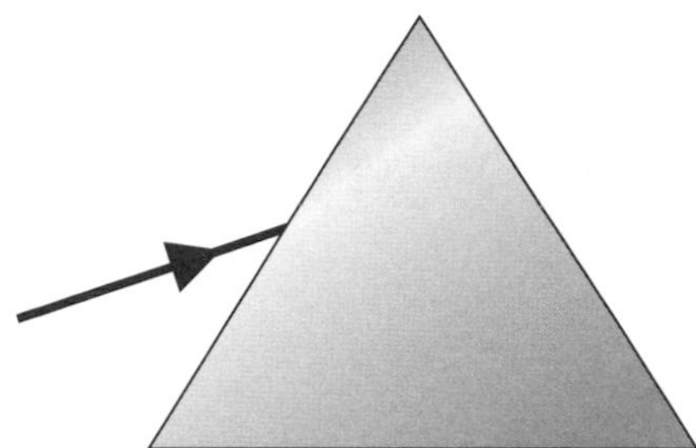

a) Draw in the "*normal*" to the prism's side where the light ray enters.

b) Continue the normal *inside* the prism.

c) Draw the ray of light crossing the prism. *(HINT: there are two things to get right about this ray.)*

d) The ray hits the other side of the prism. Draw in the *normal* to the surface at that side.

e) Draw the ray *leaving* the prism.

f) When you look through a prism you don't see what is directly in front of you. Why?

....

....

Q7 Fred the fisherman has been told that, because of refraction, a fish in water will appear to be nearer the water's surface than it really is.

He draws a diagram to try to work this out.

'I think it will look lower, not higher.' he says.

Where has he gone *wrong?*

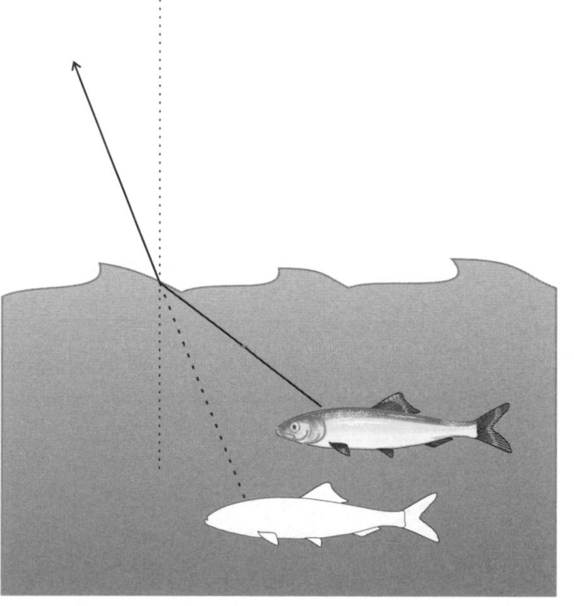

....

....

....

....

Questions on Colour

Q1 Complete these sentences by circling the correct answer in the brackets or writing the correct word in the spaces provided:

a) Light from the Sun and light bulbs is often called (*coloured* / *white*) light.

b) This light is made up from (*five* / *nine* / *many*) different colours.

c) Different colours are caused by light waves having different (*speeds* / *frequencies*) and (*speeds* / *wavelengths*).

d) The main colours making up sunlight are ____________, ____________, ____________, ____________, ____________, ____________ and ____________.

e) Light can be split into its colours using a (*mirror* / *prism*).

f) This splitting is called (*deflection* / *reflection* / *dispersion*).

g) The pattern of colours made like this is called a ____________.

h) Our eyes can be fooled into seeing any of the different colours by mixing together different amounts of just three of them. These three colours are _______, ________, and _________.

i) These three colours are called the ____________ colours.

j) Mixing these three colours in equal amounts gives __________ light.

Q2 Complete the following sentences using the box of words below.

REFLECTS	ABSORBS	RED	BLUE	GREEN

A post box is red because the paint on it ________________ red light and ________________ all the other colours. A dandelion appears yellow because it absorbs __________ light but reflects ___________ and _______________ light.

Questions on Colour

Q3 Label the missing colours on the diagram below, then answer the following questions.

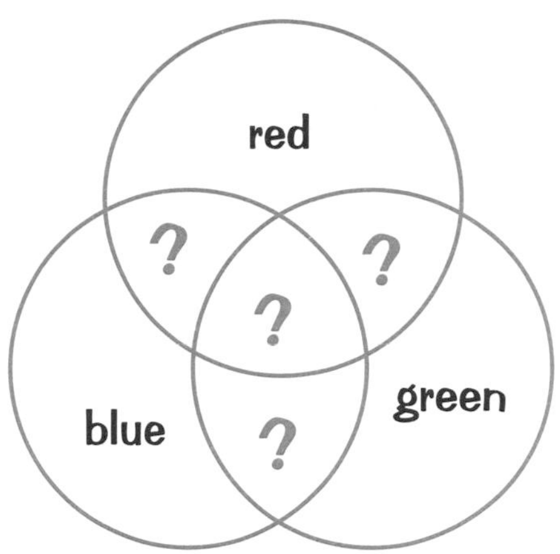

a) What do we call colours which are made by mixing *two* of the *primary* colours? ....

....

b) Use the diagram to find which colour gives *white light* when it is mixed with green? ....

....

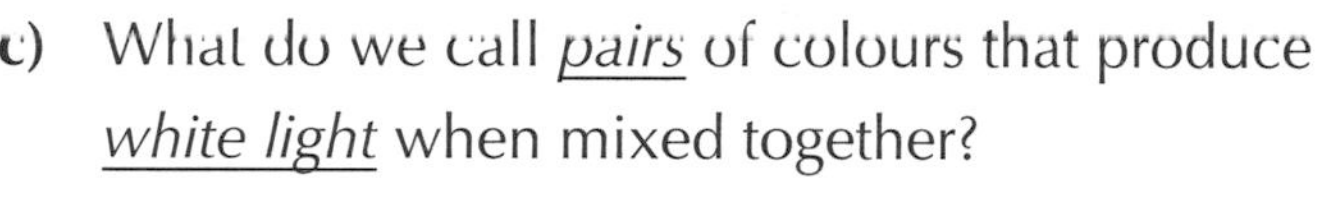

c) What do we call *pairs* of colours that produce *white light* when mixed together?

....

Q4 Pieces of *coloured* plastic or glass can be used as colour *filters*.

a) Why are they called '*filters*'? ....

....

b) Explain why a *red* filter tints colour the way it does. (*HINT*: you should need to use the words '*reflects*', '*absorbs*' and '*transmits*') ....

....

c) Complete the labelling on the two diagrams below. (Assume a white light source.)

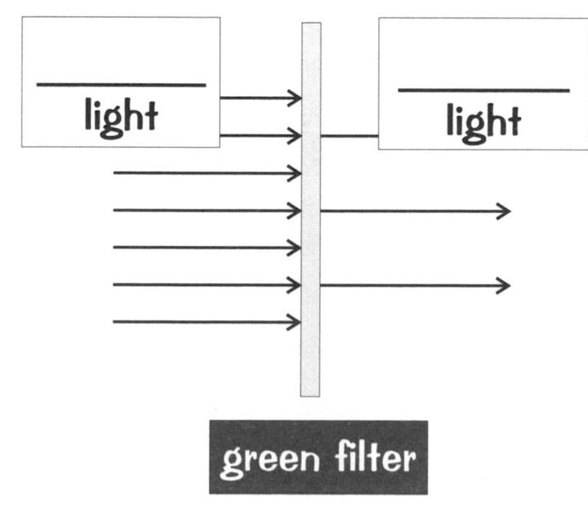

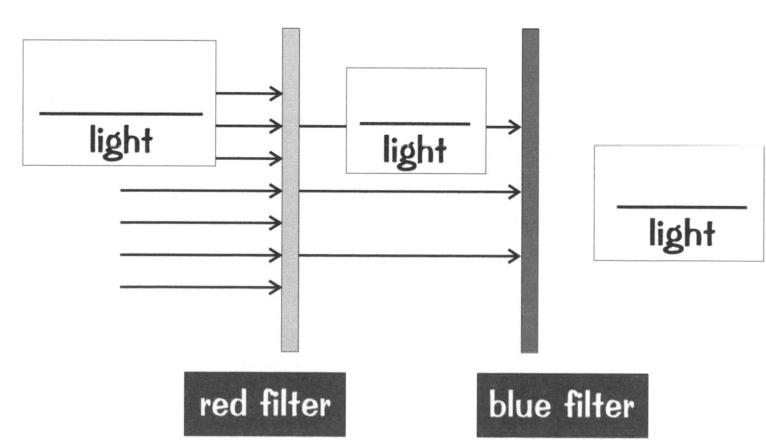

Questions on Colour

Q5 Mick is looking at different plastic cubes in different *coloured light*. The table is only partially complete.

a) Fill in the missing words to complete Mick's table.

Colour of cube	Colour of light	Colour cube seems to be
....	Red	Red
	Blue	Blue
	Green	Green
Red	Red	....
	....	Black
	Green	....
Blue	....	Black
	....	Blue
	Green	....
....	Red	Red
	Blue	Black
	Green	Green
Green	Red	....
	Blue	....
	Green	....

b) If you were to look at the cubes through *coloured filters* while *white light* was shining on them instead of coloured light, would you get the same results? (e.g. white light + red cube + red filter = ?)

Give reasons for your answer.

....

....

....

c) Sodium street lights emit mainly orange light and little else. Why does this make them poor for seeing the colours of cars at night?

....

....

....

....

Questions on Colour

Q6 Answer the questions below, then find the answers in the word search.

- The *bending* of light at the edge of a material. ....
- The *angle* a ray arrives at. ....
- The *spreading* of light into its different colours. ....
- *Red*, *green* and *blue* are ___________ colours. ....
- An object which gives out its own light. ....
- The *property* of light that we need to see most things. ....
- Something you can see through. ....
- A *flat* type of mirror. ....
- The colour you get if you mix *blue* and *green* light. ....
- Something light *can't* get through. ....
- An area where light does not *reach*. ....
- A *cyan* bead seen through a *magenta* filter. ....

I	N	O	I	T	C	E	L	F	E	R	S
T	N	E	R	A	P	S	N	A	R	T	U
G	D	C	H	N	M	C	Y	C	A	B	O
S	B	D	I	S	P	E	R	S	I	O	N
A	R	Y	G	D	S	H	A	D	O	W	I
T	E	R	H	U	E	D	O	W	A	R	M
E	N	A	L	P	O	N	U	F	C	E	U
B	A	M	T	L	I	O	C	Y	A	N	L
N	O	I	T	C	A	D	F	E	R	T	U
T	U	R	E	P	S	K	I	B	L	U	E
S	O	P	A	Q	U	E	G	B	A	W	T
A	N	O	I	T	C	A	R	F	F	I	D

Questions on Sound

Q1 Fill in the blanks using these words:

EARDRUMS	SOLIDS	LIQUIDS	HIGH	
WAVE	AMPLITUDE	LOUD	ULTRASOUND	
330	FREQUENCY	VACUUM	LESS	HIGH

a) The propagation of sound can be described in terms of motion of a ______________.

b) Sound cannot travel through a ____________________.

c) Sound can travel through gases, __________________ and __________________.

d) A high ____________________ of vibration makes a ____________ pitched sound.

e) A large ___________________ of vibration makes a _________________ sound.

f) Sound travels ________________ quickly than light.

g) The speed of sound in air is about _____________________m/s.

h) We hear sound when a sound wave causes our __________________ to vibrate.

i) Some sounds have too _____________________ a frequency to hear.

These are called ___________________.

Q2 What would be vibrating to cause a sound in the following instruments?

Drum. ....

Guitar. ....

Flute. ....

Keyboard. ....

Questions on Sound

Use these facts to answer the following questions:

Q3 These points are true about violins:

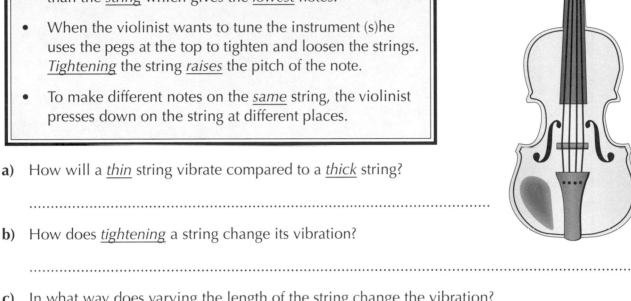

- The *string* which gives the *highest* notes is much thinner than the *string* which gives the *lowest* notes.
- When the violinist wants to tune the instrument (s)he uses the pegs at the top to tighten and loosen the strings. *Tightening* the string *raises* the pitch of the note.
- To make different notes on the *same* string, the violinist presses down on the string at different places.

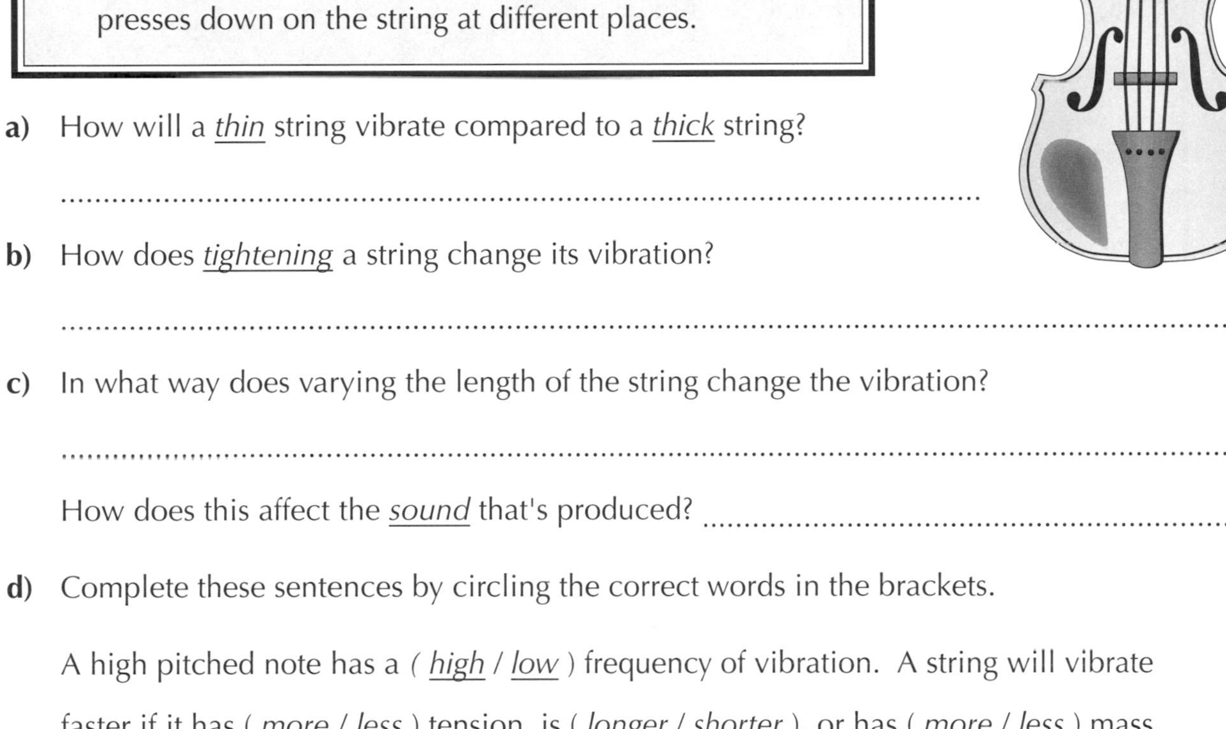

a) How will a *thin* string vibrate compared to a *thick* string?

....

b) How does *tightening* a string change its vibration?

....

c) In what way does varying the length of the string change the vibration?

....

How does this affect the *sound* that's produced? ....

d) Complete these sentences by circling the correct words in the brackets.

A high pitched note has a (*high* / *low*) frequency of vibration. A string will vibrate faster if it has (*more* / *less*) tension, is (*longer* / *shorter*), or has (*more* / *less*) mass.

Q4 This experiment is one you are very likely to have seen (probably more than once)!

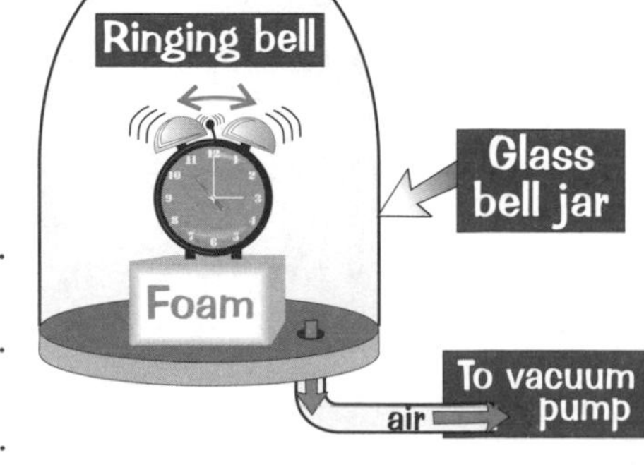

a) What are the 'jobs' of each of:

the *vacuum pump* and the *foam block?*

....

....

b) What is the *result* of this experiment? ....

....

c) What is the *conclusion* of this experiment? ....

....

Questions on Sound

Q5 Felicity is doing an experiment with two tuning forks — one large one and one small one. She has these instructions.

> **(i)** Hold the tuning fork handle and strike the prongs firmly on the heel of your shoe.
>
> **(ii)** Touch the edge of a sheet of paper with the prongs.
>
> **(iii)** Strike the fork again and this time dip it into a plastic beaker of water.
>
> **(iv)** Do the same again but with the other fork.
>
> **(v)** Strike the forks again and listen carefully to the sound they make.
>
> SAFETY: Do not touch the prongs of the fork on any part of your body, particularly your teeth!

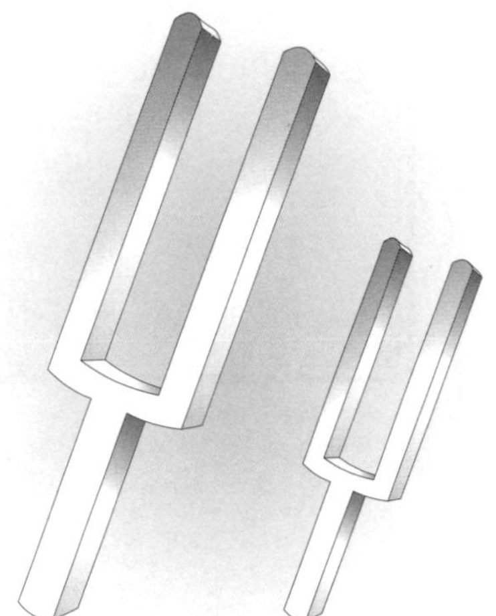

Answer these questions about the experiment.

a) Why *shouldn't* you hit the tuning fork on a bench? ....

b) What happens when the tuning fork *touches* the paper? ....

c) What happens when the tuning fork is *dipped* into the water? ....

d) Why must it be a *plastic* beaker? ....

e) Why *mustn't* you touch your teeth with a *vibrating* tuning fork? ....

f) How would the sound of the two forks in the diagram *compare?* ....

g) Why would there be this difference? ....

h) Why can't you *see* the vibration of the forks? ....

i) Tuning fork sounds can be made louder by standing them on an empty wooden box.

Why? ....

....

Questions on Sound

j) The teacher uses an *oscilloscope* to examine the sounds produced by the tuning forks. She gets the four pictures below on the oscilloscope.

Felicity gets the titles mixed up when she writes up her report.

Which *title* should go with each of the oscilloscope traces, A, B, C and D?

....

....

Titles:- SHORT FORK NO BOX   SHORT FORK WITH BOX
LONG FORK NO BOX   LONG FORK WITH BOX

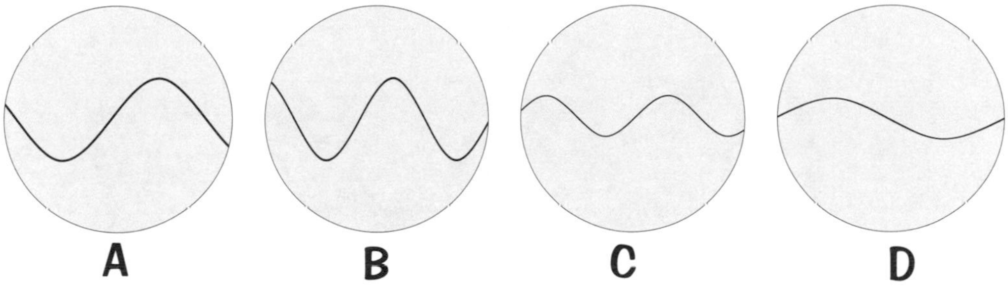

A   B   C   D

Q6 The class is doing experiments on sound and Peter is measuring the highest frequency people can hear.

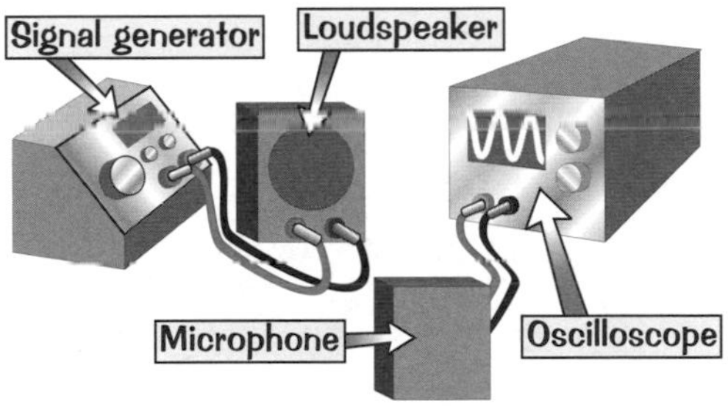

Signal generator
Loudspeaker
Microphone
Oscilloscope

He has a *signal generator*, *loudspeaker* and an *oscilloscope*. He tries different frequencies, uses the oscilloscope to check the amplitudes and asks each person if they can hear the sound. Sometimes he increases the frequency, sometimes he decreases it, and sometimes he turns the sound off altogether.

Answer the following questions about the experiment.

a) What *sort* of signal does the *signal generator* make? ....

b) What is the 'job' of the *loudspeaker?* ....

c) What should he be looking for when he checks the *amplitudes?* ....

d) Why does he sometimes turn the experiment *off* while people are being tested?

....

e) How could he *prove* to someone that there was a signal when they couldn't hear it?

....

f) What *result* would you expect to get for most of the students in the class?

....

Questions on Hearing

Q1 Name the parts of the ear labelled in the diagram below.

A — ....

B — ....

C — ....

D — ....

E — ....

F — ....

G — ....

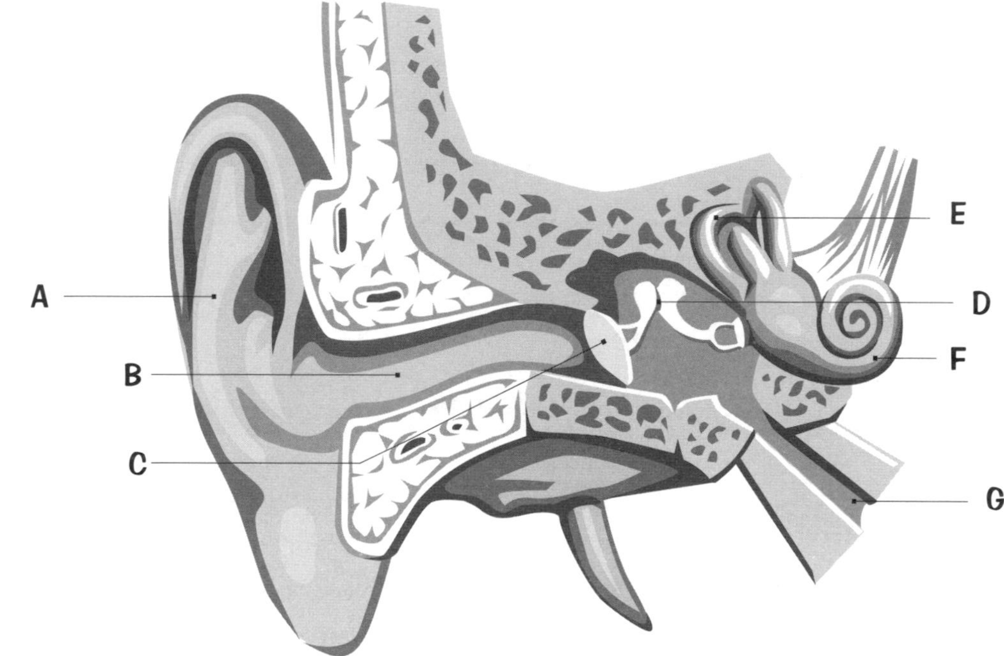

Q2 Answer these questions about the ear.

a) What is the 'job' of the outer part of the ear (the *pinna*)? ....

b) What is the 'job' of the *ear canal?* ....

c) The ear canal can often get blocked with wax. What *effect* does this have on hearing?

....

d) What is the eardrum *made of?* ....

e) Which part of the *inner ear* does not play a part in hearing? ....

What is its 'job'? ....

f) Where does the *eustachian tube* lead to? ....

....

Questions on Hearing

Q3 Jenny and Louis have an electronic noise meter and are doing a survey of noise levels around their school. They make a table of the following values.

Lesson	Noise Level (dB)
Science	65
French	40
Art	50
Technology	115
P.E.	90
History	45

a) What is/are 'dB'? ....

b) Why are *science*, *technology* and *P.E.* classes likely to be *noisier* than the others?

....

c) Which lesson(s) are near levels where *damage* could be caused to the ears?

....

....

d) Why is this really more of a concern for the *teachers* rather than the *students?*

....

e) Jenny says, "I suppose too much noise is why Mr. Jones, our science teacher, can't hear as high a frequency as I can." There is a more likely reason. *What* is it?

....

....

f) Mr. Jones says the high value measured during *P.E.* is a consequence of the wooden surfaces of the hall in which the lesson takes place. *Explain* briefly what he means by this.

....

....

....

Questions on Day, Night and the Four Seasons

Q1 This diagram shows the motion of the Sun across the sky on a Spring day. Answer the questions that follow.

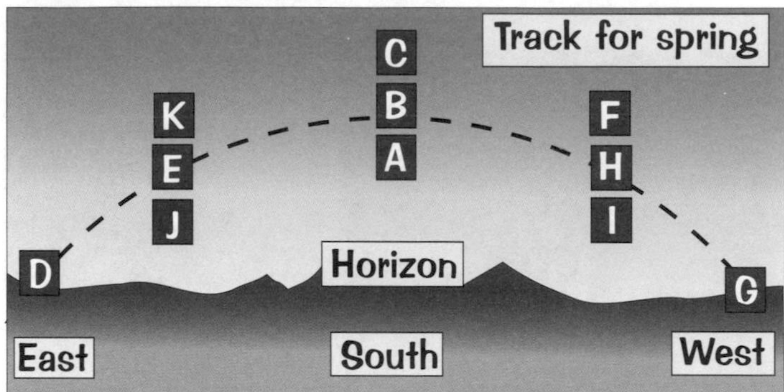

a) *Choose* the letter that shows where the Sun *rises*. ....

b) *Choose* the letter showing where the Sun is on a *summer's* morning. ....

c) *Choose* the letter showing where the Sun is on a *winter's* morning. ....

d) *Choose* the letter that shows where the Sun *sets*. ....

e) What is the *cause* of the Sun's motion across the sky? ....

f) If you were positioned a bit *further south*, would the *curve* traced out by the Sun be *higher* or *lower* in the sky? ....

Q2 Here are some dates. Match up the dates with the sentences that follow. The dates can be used once, more than once or not at all.

June 21st	March 21st	September 21st
December 21st	March 30th	September 30th

a) At noon in Britain, the Sun is at its *highest* point for the year. ....

b) This is the *nearest* date to the *shortest* day of the year in Britain. ....

c) Here, the length of *day* and *night* is 12 hours long exactly. ....

d) This is *midwinter's* day for someone in the *southern* hemisphere. ....

e) In Britain, this day is slightly *longer* than that of March 21st. ....

f) In Britain, this date will have the *shortest* night. ....

g) Somewhere on the *equator*, the Sun will be directly *overhead* at midday on these *two* dates. ....

Questions on Day, Night and the Four Seasons

Q3 Harold and Sadie have a tree outside in their garden in Kent. They noticed that every day at *noon*, they could see the shadow cast by the tree, provided the Sun was shining. They decided to measure the *length* of the shadow, and recorded it day by day. The table of their results is shown below. During this time the tree's height remained approximately constant.

Date	Length of Shadow
March 21st	4.9 metres
April 21st	4.5 metres
May 21st	4.2 metres
June 21st	4.0 metres
July 21st	4.2 metres

a) What causes the *length* of the tree's shadow to *change* over the months?

....

b) If they measured the length of the tree's shadow on *September 21st*, how long would it be?

....

c) If they measured the length of the shadow on *December 21st*, would it be *longer* or *shorter* than all the measurements in the table?

....

d) In which direction would the tree's shadow point at *noon* each day?

....

Q4 The picture below shows the Earth in its orbit during early January. Study it and then answer the following questions by writing the appropriate letters down.

a) Where is it dark? ....

b) Where is summer being experienced?

....

c) Which of the five marked places will experience the most intense heat during its daytime?

....

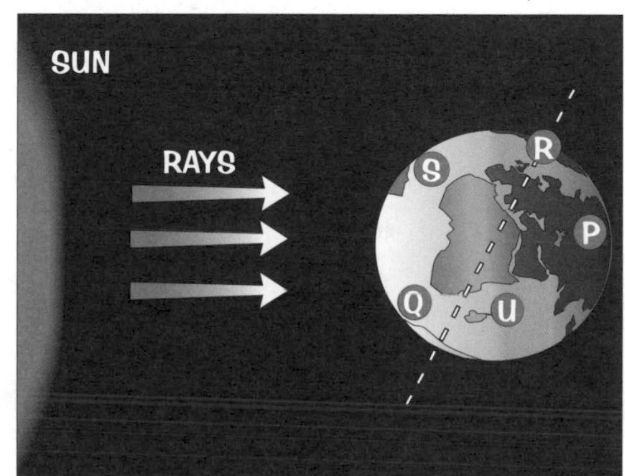

Questions on Day, Night and the Four Seasons

Q5 Some of these statements are _true_, some are _false_. Say which is which.

a) In June, the _northern_ hemisphere of the Earth points _away_ from the Sun. ....

b) For Britain, the Sun appears to rise in the _east_. ....

c) The Sun is always highest in the sky at midday. ....

d) The Sun's rays are concentrated over a smaller surface area in _winter_. ....

e) In _winter_, a country spends more time in the sunlight than in the dark. ....

f) The stars appear to _move_ across the sky at night time. ....

g) Places on the equator get _seasons_ just like we do in Britain. ....

h) The Earth takes just over _365_ days to orbit the Sun. ....

i) Spring is the only season in which days are always getting _longer_, and nights _shorter_.

....

Q6 Use the following words to complete the sentences below.

Day Four Axis Orbit Beach
Nights Seasons Year Days

a) The Earth spins on its __________ in 24 hours.

b) We call this time one __________ .

c) It takes a __________ for the Earth to complete one revolution of the Sun.

d) We call the track followed by the Earth an __________ .

e) The tilt of the Earth's axis causes the __________ .

f) In summer, __________ last longer than __________ .

g) There are __________ seasons every year.

h) In parts of Australia, some people eat their Christmas dinner on the __________ because it's so warm there at that time.

Questions on the Moon

Q1 This diagram shows the Moon orbiting around the Earth. The Moon takes 28 days to complete one orbit and appears to change shape as it does so.

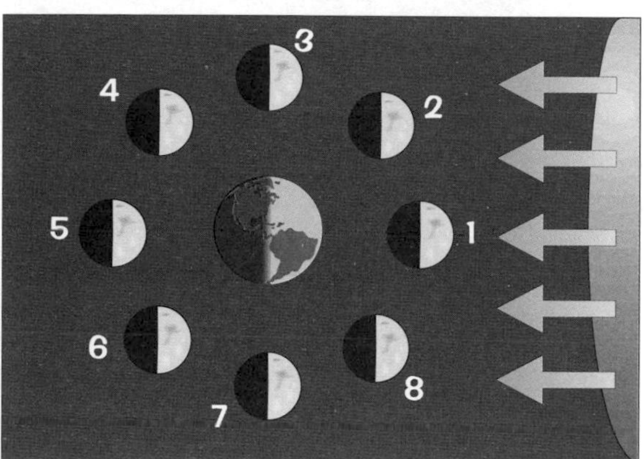

a) Why does the Moon appear *luminous*? ....

b) When the Moon is at position 8 in its orbit, it looks like a *crescent* when seen from *Earth*. This is shown in the diagram. Draw a similar picture showing what the Moon looks like 14 days later, when it is at position 4.

c) What position is the Moon in when it is *"full"*? ....

d) What position is the Moon in when it is at last quarter? ....

e) The Earth rotates in an *anti-clockwise* direction in the diagram above, so night begins when your view into space points towards position 3. If at this time the Moon is at position 2, it again appears as a thin *crescent* when seen from Earth. But will the Moon be seen in the *morning* or *evening* sky?

....

Questions on Satellites and Gravity

Q1 This diagram shows the Earth and some Global Positioning System (GPS) satellites in orbit around it. The satellites transmit information that can be received on Earth that tells you exactly where you are. Information from at least <u>three</u> satellites is needed to get an accurate position.

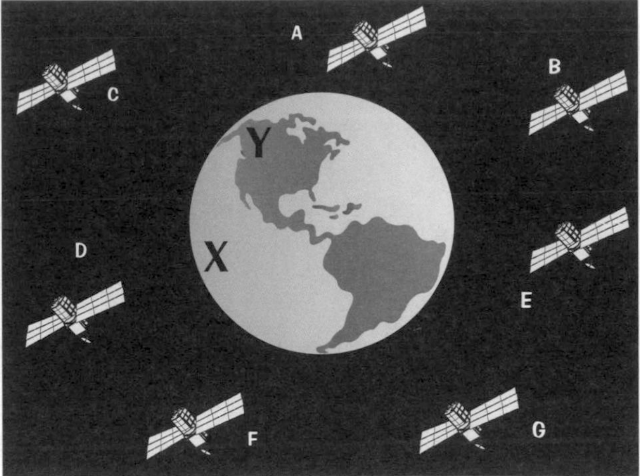

a) A sailor is in the Pacific Ocean at point X. Which satellites must he receive data from to get an accurate position?

....

b) To find out your altitude using the GPS system, information from four of the satellites is needed. Could a climber at position Y find out his altitude?

....

c) Name *four* uses for the Global Positioning System. ....

....

Q2 This diagram shows a moon orbiting around a planet which is much more massive than the Moon. There are some *arrows* on the diagram. Study the diagram and answer the questions that follow.

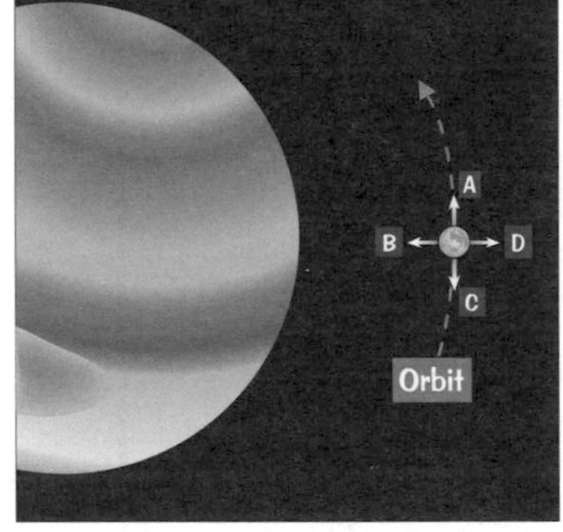

a) In which direction does the *gravitational force* acting on the moon point? (Write down a letter from the diagram)

....

b) There is also a *gravitational force* acting on the *planet* due to the moon. How does this force *compare* to that acting on the moon due to the planet?

....

Q3 This picture shows the Earth with two identical artificial satellites in circular orbits around it.

Satellite 2 is further away from Earth than Satellite 1.

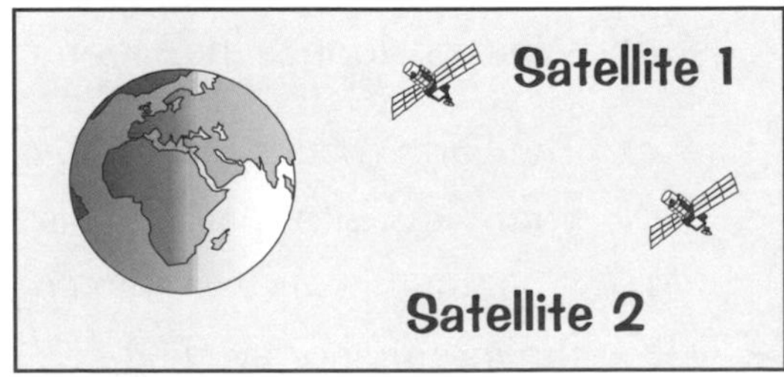

a) Which satellite is being pulled towards Earth with the greater gravitational force?

....

b) Which satellite will take longer to orbit the Earth?

....

Questions on the Solar System

Q1 For the first part of this question, the names of six of the planets in the Solar System have been mixed up. Work out the names of each of the planets.

a) NARSUU ....

b) RATHE ....

c) RUNTAS ....

d) SARM ....

e) REYRMUC ....

f) PUNTEEN ....

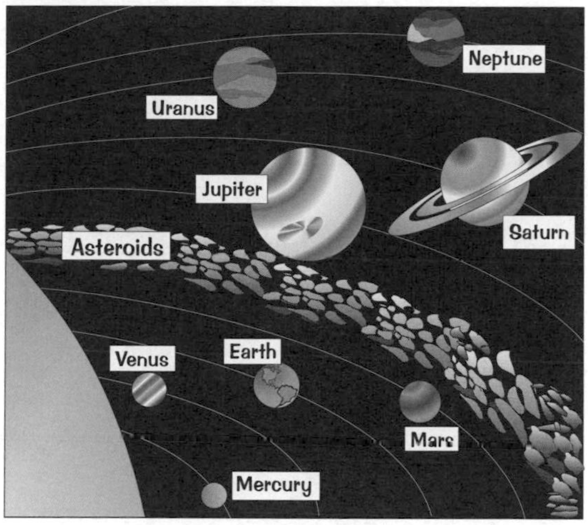

g) *List* the six planets (a to f) in order of *increasing* distance from the Sun.

....

....

h) Which *two* planets are missing from the list? ....

i) Which of the eight planets is the most massive? ....

Q2 Name the *planets* that fit the following descriptions. (No planet appears more than once.)

a) The second largest planet in the Solar System. It was the first planet that was known to have *rings*. ....

b) A rocky planet that is just smaller than the Earth. It has a thick atmosphere, and is very hot due to the *greenhouse effect*. ....

c) This planet is, on average, the *furthest* away from the Sun. It is seventeen times bigger than earth, and it's very cold. ....

d) This planet is rocky, and has an atmosphere made up of mainly nitrogen and oxygen. It has *one* natural moon. ....

e) This is a large, *gaseous* planet. It is a long way from the Sun, and it was the first planet to be discovered using a telescope. ....

Questions on the Solar System

Q3 Match up the statements (A to D) with the time periods.

A) How long Mercury takes to orbit the Sun	i) 365 days
B) How long the Moon takes to orbit the Earth	ii) 88 days
C) How long Jupiter takes to orbit the Sun	iii) 28 days
D) How long the Earth takes to orbit the Sun	iv) 12 years

A) ....

B) ....

C) ....

D) ....

Q4 Pick a planet, any planet...

a) Name the *two* largest planets in the Solar System. ....

....

b) Which planets in the Solar System are *smaller* than the Earth? ....

c) How many planets do not have *natural* satellites? ....

d) Which planets were observed by the two *Voyager* spacecraft? ....

....

e) Which planet takes about *165 Earth years* to orbit the Sun? ....

Q5 Complete the following text by filling in the spaces using the words from the box.

heat **reflects** **gas** **nuclear**

The Sun shines because ________________ reactions inside it produce huge amounts of _____________ and light. This energy radiates out from the Sun and some of the light ________________ off the planets, allowing us to see them. Sunlight also causes comets to warm up when they approach the inner Solar System, making them produce huge tails of ________________ and dust.

Q6 Answer these general questions about stars and planets.

a) What do we call the *path* that a planet follows around a star?

....

b) What do we call the *shape* of the *path* of a planet around a star?

....

c) What is the main *difference* between stars and planets? ....

....

Questions on the Solar System and Beyond

Q1 Complete the following sentences using the words provided.

increases rock gas Jupiter Mercury decreases

There are eight planets in the Solar System. The most massive planet is ________________ and the least massive is ____________.
The time taken for a planet to orbit the Sun ________________ the further out you go, while the gravitational pull of the Sun ___________________ the further out you go. The inner planets Mercury, Venus, Earth and Mars are made mainly from ____________, while the rest are made up mostly from __________ .

Q2 The Solar System lies in the Milky Way.

a) What is the *Milky Way*? (Circle the correct answer).

i) A universe **ii)** A solar system **iii)** A galaxy

iv) A type of comet **v)** A planet

b) Do all the stars visible in the night sky belong to the Milky Way? ....

c) How many stars are there in the Milky Way? Choose the closest answer:

☐ **HUNDREDS** ☐ **THOUSANDS** ☐ **MILLIONS** ☐ **BILLIONS**

Q3 Look at the following objects. Tick those that could be seen on a clear night with the naked eye and tick those that are inside the Solar System.

VISIBLE?		INSIDE SOLAR SYSTEM?
☐	**a)** Distant galaxies	☐
☐	**b)** The Moon	☐
☐	**c)** Artificial satellites	☐
☐	**d)** Planets	☐
☐	**e)** Stars	☐
☐	**f)** Nebulae	☐

Questions on Different Types of Energy

Q1 The following words are all mixed-up names of different energy types. Unscramble the letters to find the types of energy **a) - h)**

a) glith **b)** tacslie **c)** duons **d)** tenpliato **e)** hamlert **f)** cleerlicat **g)** nicekti **h)** clahicem

....

....

....

Q2 Choose a type of energy which fits the descriptions **a)** to **h)** below.

a) The type of energy that *moving objects* have. ....

b) A very useful type of energy that *flows* along wires. ....

c) A type of energy stored due to *gravity* and height above ground. ....

d) *Luminous* objects give off this energy. ....

e) The potential energy stored in a *stretched* rubber band. ....

f) Energy that can be released by a type of *reaction*. ....

g) Energy that *noisy* objects transmit. ....

h) Energy that everything above a temperature of *absolute zero* possesses.

....

Q3 This question is to find out whether you appreciate the difference between heat and temperature. Put a tick in the correct column for each row in the table below.

Statement	Applies to heat	Applies to temperature
measures how hot something is		
is a form of energy		
measured in °C		
measured in joules		
a difference in this causes heat to flow		
a flow of this causes a change in temperature		

Questions on Generating Electricity

Q1 All of the non-renewable energy sources have associated environmental problems. Complete this table by putting *ticks* for each environmental problem the source(s) cause.

Problem	Coal	Oil	Gas	Nuclear
Release of CO_2 adding to the Greenhouse Effect				
Acid rain production				
Devastation of landscape caused by mining				
Production of dangerous, long lasting waste				
Danger of major catastrophe due to human error				

Q2 In America and Canada, electricity is generated using several different energy sources. Some of these are listed below.

coal tidal wind oil solar hydroelectric natural gas waves

a) *Circle* all the sources that are going to be more difficult and expensive to obtain in the next few hundred years.

b) Name *one* other *non-renewable* energy resource. ....

c) Name *one* other *renewable* energy resource. ....

Q3 Clive has read that some power stations burn a liquid. He reckons that the liquid must be *petrol* as it is so easy to burn.

a) Is he likely to be right? ....

b) If so, why is petrol used, if not, why is it not used? ....

....

Q4 a) Name an energy source used in power stations that produces *carbon dioxide* and *water* when burned. ....

b) Which of the non-renewable sources of energy used in Britain today *doesn't* produce pollution directly? ....

c) Which fossil fuel creates the *widest* range of pollution? ....

Questions on Transfer of Energy

Q1 We only make use of energy when it changes from one type to another. Try to work out what the *'starting'* energy is, and what the *'finishing'* energy is for each of the following. The first one is done for you.

a) A cyclist *freewheeling* up a hill.

Starting Energy = KINETIC

Finishing Energy = GRAVITATIONAL POTENTIAL

b) A *burning* match. ....

c) An *electric* light bulb. ....

d) A pop group's *microphone*. ....

e) *Wood* on a log fire. ....

f) A solar *cell* on a student's calculator. ....

g) A motorcyclist *braking* to a halt. ....

h) A sledge and its passengers sliding *down* a slope, starting from rest.

....

i) The *loudspeaker* on a radio. ....

j) A *windmill* connected to a *generator*. ....

k) A *battery* connected to a car *headlamp*. ....

Q2 Which of the following statements are *true*, and which must be *false?*

		T	F
a)	Heat is only transferred if there is *no* temperature difference.	☐	☐
b)	The particles in a hot solid vibrate *more* than those in an identical but cold solid.	☐	☐
c)	Conduction is when vibrating particles *pass on* energy to neighbouring particles.	☐	☐
d)	Substances like wood and plastic are *better* heat conductors than metals.	☐	☐
e)	Convection is where energy is transferred *without* any movement of particles.	☐	☐
f)	Heat radiation can travel through a *vacuum*.	☐	☐
g)	Air above a hot fire will *rise*.	☐	☐

Questions on Transfer of Energy

Q3 Electricity is an energy source that is very useful. This is because it can be changed into many other types of energy.

Tick in the table below the types of energy that are produced by each of the devices listed. Include all types of energy produced, not just the ones which are utilised.

Example	Kinetic	Light	Heat	Sound
a) Fan heater				
b) Electric motor				
c) LED				
d) Torch bulb				
e) Loudspeaker				
f) Computer monitor				
g) Computer disk drive				

Q4 In the question above, what type of energy is produced *most often*?

....

Why is this type of energy *less useful* than other types of energy?

....

Q5 Think about things that people use to stop heat being lost from their houses. Choose three methods, and say what type(s) of heat transfer — *conduction*, *convection* or *radiation* — they are designed to cut down on.

Method 1

....

....

....

Method 2

....

....

....

Method 3

....

....

....

Questions on Energy Resources

Q1 Fill in the gaps in the following paragraph. Use the words that are given.

FOSSIL, BURIED, LIGHT, CHEMICAL, SEDIMENT, COAL
PLANTS, NATURAL GAS, PHOTOSYNTHESIS, CREATURES, MILLIONS, OIL

The Sun produces a great deal of _________ energy and heat energy. Some of this reaches the Earth. __________ can trap this energy and change it by a process called _________________. Some of the energy becomes locked in them, in the form of ____________ energy. Over many years, loads and loads of plants grew. Some were ____________ underground. Their energy became trapped as they were turned into _______________. Tiny _____________ can feed on plants and absorb some of the energy. This happened ______________ of years ago. They then fell to the bottom of the seas. They were buried under ______________ and chemical changes occurred to make _____________ and_____________ _____________. We call fuels formed from living things in this way _____________ fuels.

Q2 **a)** Circle the *renewable* energy resources from this list.

FOOD	COAL	BIOMASS	WIND
OIL	WAVES	NATURAL GAS	

b) Each of the energy resources listed above can have its energy traced back to *one* source. What is the mysterious '*one source*' ? ....

c) Name an energy resource that relies on *burning* to produce light and heat.

....

d) List *two* energy resources that do *not* rely on photosynthesis.

....

....

....

Questions on Energy Resources

Q3 Traditional electricity generating power stations all work in pretty much the same way.

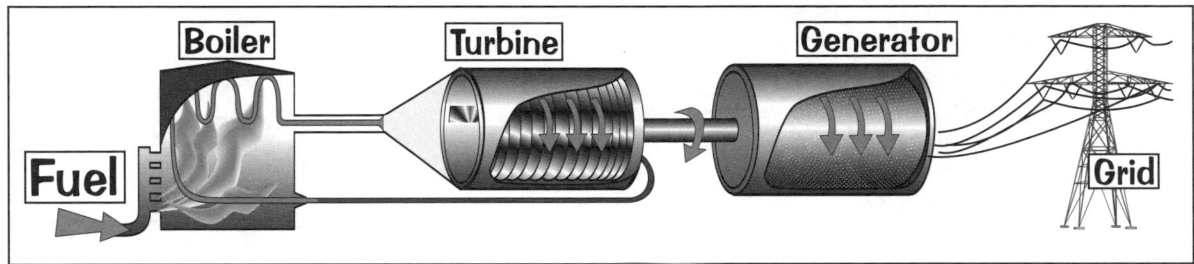

a) What *type* of energy is contained in the power station's fuel supply? ....

b) This energy is *changed* into another form of energy in the boiler.
What *type* of energy is this? ....

c) What *machine* does this new energy drive? ....

d) What *type* of energy is brought about by *this* machine? ....

e) What other *machine* is this energy used to drive? ....

f) This last machine sends electricity along the national ....

Q4 Power stations have great big *cooling* towers. What are these for?

....

Q5 Name *two* ways in which we can reduce the use of fossil fuel energy. ....

....

Q6 Fossil fuel is still being created on the Earth, so why should we be *worried* about reducing our use of it?

....

....

....

Q7 Wind energy, biomass energy and wave energy are examples of renewable energy resources, and are all consequences of energy emitted by the Sun. What aspect of the Sun's energy allows us to consider the above resources as *renewable?*

....

....

....

Questions on Fuels

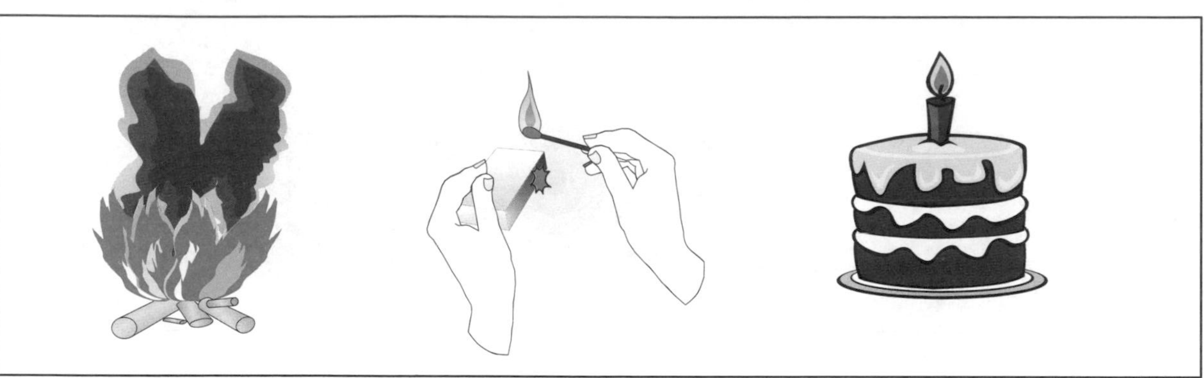

Q1 A fuel is a substance that can be burned to release energy.

a) What *substance* in the *atmosphere* is needed for a substance to burn? ....

b) Coal is made mainly from *carbon*. What *substance* is made when coal is burned with *oxygen?* (Assume plenty of oxygen is present.)

....

c) Complete the equation showing the reaction

COAL (CARBON) + ________________ → ______________________

d) Name an impurity in coal that also oxidises *(reacts with oxygen)*, when coal burns.

....

....

e) When there is not enough *oxygen*, another substance is made.
What is the *name* of this substance?

....

f) Why is this substance *dangerous* to humans? ....

....

....

Methane (Natural Gas) is a compound made of carbon and hydrogen.

g) What *two* substances are formed when methane is burned in plenty of oxygen?

C.. and W..

h) Finish this equation for the reaction.

METHANE + ________________ → **CARBON DIOXIDE** + __________________

Questions on Fuels

Q2 Many of the fuels that we use today come from crude oil. This is a mixture of lots of different substances. We can draw a diagram showing how the crude oil is separated into different parts:

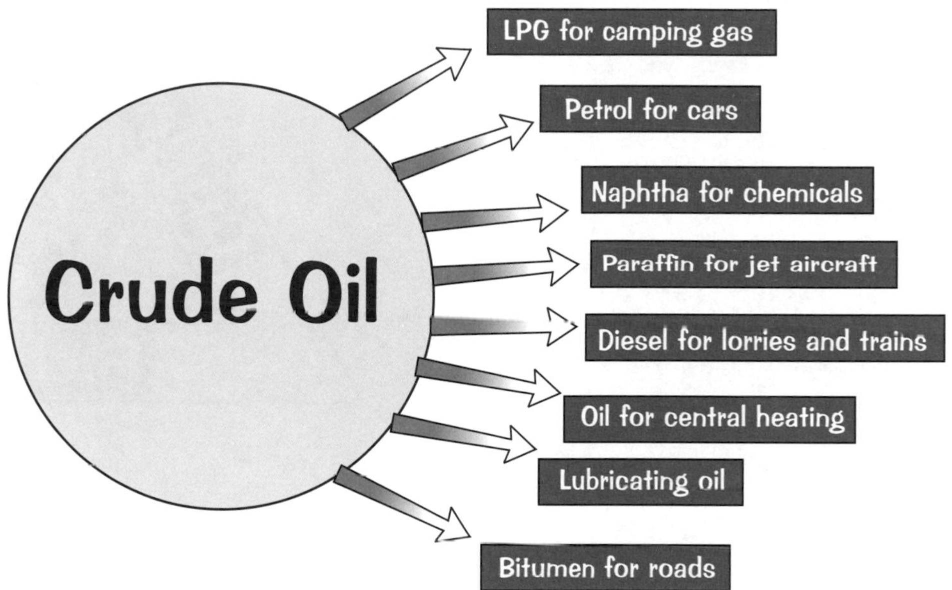

a) The fractions (different parts) are separated by a process called *fractional distillation*. What happens to a substance when it is *distilled*?

....

....

....

b) Fractional distillation works because the fractions have *different* boiling points. Which one of the *fractions* above has the *lowest* boiling point?

....

c) Two typical fractions are propane (C_3H_8) and octane (C_8H_{18}). Find out a use for each of these two fractions.

....

....

....

....

Questions on The Fire Triangle/Fire Extinguishers

Q1 This picture shows the fire triangle.

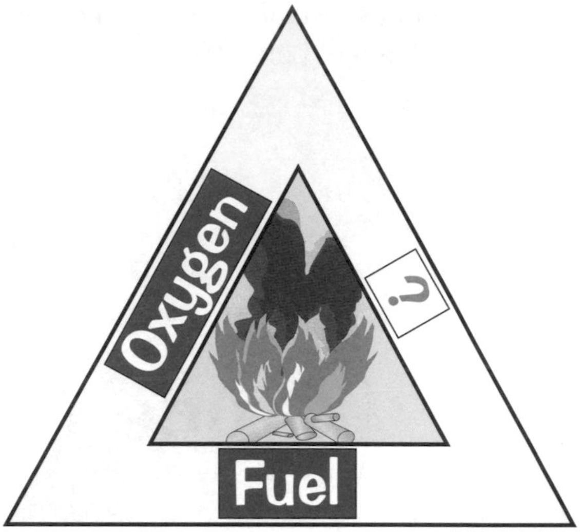

a) One side of the triangle has not been filled in. What should it *read*?

....

b) What is the effect of removing any of the 3 quantities shown in the triangle?

....

....

....

Oxygen

?

Fuel

Q2 The following are all ways of *minimising* injury or damage due to fire. For each one, indicate which *property* of the fire triangle is being removed.

a) If a child's clothing catches fire, roll them up in a *wet* blanket or towel.

....

b) Firemen protect buildings near a large fire by spraying the outsides of the buildings with *water.* ....

c) Pilots of planes that may be about to crash try to *dump* fuel over the sea.

....

d) If you suspect a room may contain a fire, it's best to leave the door *closed*.

....

e) If a chip pan catches fire, one of the things you should do is turn off the *power* to it.

....

f) Petrol stations have *"No Smoking"* signs. ....

g) Some fire extinguishers contain *Carbon Dioxide*. ....

....

Questions on The Fire Triangle/Fire Extinguishers

Q3 As part of a science experiment, Kenny and Fergus test the effect of dropping a red hot piece of metal onto different types of carpet.

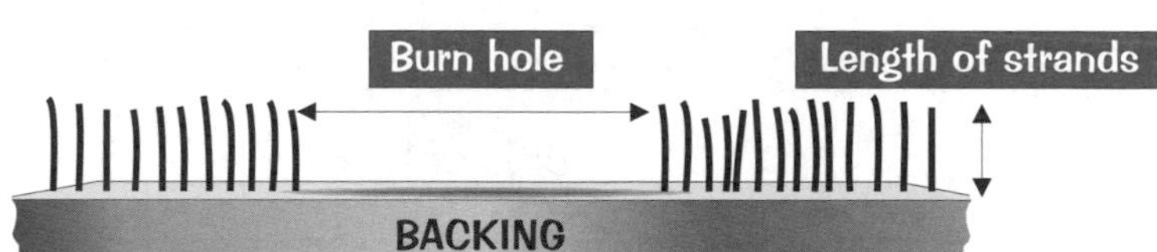

These are the *results* they got:

Material of carpet	Length of strands	Size of burn hole produced
Artificial	3mm	25mm
Artificial	9mm	125mm
Natural	3mm	12mm

a) What *effect* does the *strand length* have on the *size* of the *burn mark* produced?

....

b) What effect does the carpet *material* have on the *size* of *burn mark* produced?

....

c) By comparing the sizes of the artificial and natural carpet burn holes, estimate the size of the burn mark for a natural carpet having 9mm strands.

....

d) What *quantities* would they have to *control* to make it a fair test? ....

....

Q4 In another experiment, Kenny and Fergus light *one* side of some material and see how the flame *spreads*. Results are shown in the table opposite. Why do materials treated to be *flameproof* need treating again after several washes?

Untreated	Treated	Treated and washed
Immediate	12 seconds	9 seconds

....

....

....

....

Questions on Conservation of Energy

Q1 Fill in the blanks to complete this sentence.

The *principle* of *conservation of energy* states that *energy* can never be ____________ nor ___________, but is only _____________ from one form to another.

Q2 A device usually changes energy from one form to another, allowing it to do useful work for us.

a) Are any devices *perfect* converters of energy when they make these sorts of changes?

If so, give an example. ....

b) Usually, the *wasted* energy produced by a *useful device* comes out in *two* forms.

What are these two forms of energy? ....

c) Complete the following equation:

Total Energy INPUT = The USEFUL energy OUTPUT + ________________________

Q3 A can of paint is resting on a shelf 2 metres above the floor. When it was lifted from the floor onto the shelf, it gained 50 joules of potential energy. The can then falls from the shelf.

a) When the can is only 1 metre above the floor, how much potential energy has it *got?*

....

b) What is the *largest* amount of kinetic energy that it could have *1 metre* above the floor?

....

c) What happens to all the energy once the can has hit the floor and come to *rest?*

....

Q4 What is the useful energy and what is the wasted energy in the following items:

	Useful Energy	Wasted Energy
a) Light bulb	....	....
b) T.V.	....	....
c) Sheep running	....	....
d) Kettle	....	....

Answers

Section One — Life Processes and Cell Activity

Section One — Life Processes and Cell Activity

Page 1 — Questions on the Microscope

Q1 A — Eyepiece
B — Body tube
C — Rough focusing knob
D — Fine focusing knob
E — Low and high power objective
F — Stage
G — Iris diaphragm

Q2 A (Eyepiece) — Provides final magnification of image.
B (Body tube) — Supports a series of lenses.
C (Rough focusing knob) — Moves lenses rapidly, relative to the stage.
D (Fine focusing knob) — Allows fine adjustments to be made to the focus.
E (Low and high power objective) — Provides first magnification of image.
F (Stage) — Supports the object for viewing.
G (Iris diaphragm) — Controls the amount of light.

Page 2 — Questions on Life Processes

Q1 a)

N	O	I	T	C	U	D	O	R	P	E	R	G	N	C
W	U	V	P	G	Q	W	C	C	Q	N	C	O	C	D
V	E	L	J	I	L	B	K	G	P	E	I	M	N	U
T	D	K	T	H	E	B	Y	W	X	T	U	U	X	D
N	Z	O	C	L	Q	C	L	C	A	V	T	M	Z	H
E	S	C	L	J	X	M	R	R	T	R	M	K	F	V
M	F	C	J	I	G	E	I	W	I	Q	X	S	I	B
E	O	Y	Z	A	T	P	J	T	K	A	X	R	T	I
V	X	G	F	I	S	T	I	M	H	T	W	O	R	G
O	U	B	O	E	A	O	F	H	F	L	D	Y	T	I
M	S	N	R	I	N	N	P	E	I	K	J	P	B	H

b) sensitivity

Q2 Growth — The increase in size and complexity of an organism
Nutrition — The ability to take in food or raw materials to support other life processes
Respiration — The ability to take in oxygen and give out carbon dioxide to make energy
Excretion — The removal of waste materials which the cells have made and may be poisonous
Movement — The ability to move all or part of the organism
Sensitivity — The ability of an organism to respond
Reproduction — The ability to produce more of its kind

Pages 3-4 — Questions on Cells

Q1 A — cell wall
B — cell membrane
C — nucleus
D — cytoplasm
E — vacuole
F — chloroplast

Both cells have	Only plant cells have
1) cell membrane	1) cell wall
2) nucleus	2) chloroplasts
3) cytoplasm	3) vacuole (cell sap)

Q2 nucleus

Q3 chloroplasts

Q4

	Cytoplasm	Nucleus	Cell wall	Vacuole
Leaf mesophyll	✓	✓	✓	✓
Sperm	✓	✓		

Q5 a) red blood cell
b) It carries oxygen and carbon dioxide.
c) To increase the surface area.

Q6 a) root hair cell
b) It transports water and some minerals into the plant.
c) At the roots.

Q7 To receive, carry and pass on electrical impulses.

Page 5 — Questions on Specialised Cells

Q1 An epithelial cell with hairs on its outer membrane surface which waft or beat — These cells are found in the main body tubes like those near the lungs and help to trap germs and dust and clean the air
Contains the red chemical substance called haemoglobin — Carries oxygen around the body
Is a cell made with an extension (the tail) — After a journey it joins with an egg cell
Has a long cell cytoplasm and has many branches at the end/ends — Carries information (impulses) round the body and joins other impulses

Q2 a) i) red blood cell
ii) respiration
b) i) neurone
ii) sensitivity
c) i) sperm
ii) reproduction
d) i) root hair cell
ii) nutrition

Pages 6-7 — Questions on Plant Organs

Q1 S — flower — pollination / reproduction
T — leaf — photosynthesis / respiration
U — stem — support and liquid transportation
V — root hair — adsorption of water etc.
W — root tip — growth of root
X — tap root — anchorage and transportation of water

Q2 A — root hair cell
B — root
C — stem
D — shoot

Q3 a) flower
b) petal
c) leaf
d) stem
e) root

Q4 a) photosynthesis
b) carbon dioxide and water
c) oxygen and glucose
d) No. The energy required comes from light.
e) carbon dioxide + water $\xrightarrow{\text{(Sunlight)}}$ glucose + oxygen

Section Two — Humans as Organisms Part One

Pages 8-9 — Questions on Human Organ Systems

Q1 a) circulatory
b) respiratory
c) digestive
d) reproductive
Q2 a) brain — nervous
b) lung — respiratory
c) heart — circulatory
d) stomach — digestive
e) kidney — excretory
Q3 1. q
2. s
3. t
4. u
5. r
6. p
Q4 a) organ
b) organ-system
Q5 A — nervous system
B — digestive system
C — circulatory system
D a) — respiratory system
b) — excretory system

Section Two — Humans as Organisms Part One

Pages 10-11 — Questions on Nutrition

Q1 a)

Carbohydrates	proteins	Fats	minerals	vitamins
used like fuel for your body	Used for growth and repair	act as a store of energy	Usually needed in small amounts to help make certain parts of the body	A large group of substances needed in small amounts to prevent many diseases like scurvy

b) What we eat — intake of nourishing substances.
c) 75%
d) A disease directly resulting from a lack of essential nutrients.
e) You wouldn't get enough vitamins (e.g. vitamin C) in your diet and may show signs of vitamin deficiencies (e.g. scurvy).
Q2 a) Sausages contain mostly fat and protein which are not easily accessible energy sources.
b) water
Q3 a) carbohydrates
b) Hibran flakes
c) Fibre keeps your digestive system fit and healthy by giving it an internal workout.
d) No. Different food groups are needed in different amounts.
Q4 a) Any two of, e.g. growth / repair / movement / maintaining body temperature / reproduction.
b) A builder, because he/she is likely to be more active and so have the largest energy demands.
c) Food is used as a **fuel** for the process of **respiration** and as a raw material for **growth** and **repair**.

Pages 12-14 — Questions on Digestion

Q1 The process of **digestion** is the breakdown of food into **soluble** substances, and the passage into the **bloodstream**. The food molecules are too **large** to pass through the walls of the **small intestine** and need to be broken down by special chemicals called **enzymes**.
Q2 a) A — gullet — carries food from the mouth to the stomach
B — stomach — churns food, adds hydrochloric acid (HCl) to kill bacteria and promotes protease enzyme activity
C — pancreas — makes the enzymes protease, carbohydrase and lipase
D — small intestine — absorbs food through the gut wall into the blood
E — large intestine — absorbs water from the gut
F — liver — makes bile to emulsify fats and neutralise stomach acid
b) mouth — Salivary amylase
stomach — Proteases in acid, which digests protein
pancreas — Protease, carbohydrase and lipase
Q3 a) No. The molecules are too large to pass through the visking tubing.
b) The molecules/particles of glucose are small enough to pass through the microscopic holes in the visking tubing.
c) capillaries in the villi
d) blood
e) partly digested food
Q4 a) glucose
b) amylase (a carbohydrase enzyme contained in saliva)
c) glucose
d) amino acid
e) protease
f) amino acid
g) fatty acids
h) glycerol
i) lipase
j) fatty acid
k) glycerol
Q5 a) small intestine/gut
b) villi
c) Any two of, e.g. walls one cell thick / good blood supply / large surface area.

Page 15 — Questions on Absorption and the Kidneys

Q1 into the blood
Q2 absorption
Q3 large surface area, good blood supply and walls one cell thick.
Q4 a) egestion
b) anus
c) i) lungs
ii) kidneys
Q5 1. Fats — under the skin
2. Carbohydrates (glucose) — stored in the liver
Q6 a) Any two from, e.g. glucose / salts / water.
b) urea

Section Three — Growing Up

Pages 16-18 — Questions on the Circulatory System

Q1 Blood is the **transport** system of the body. It carries **nutrients** and **oxygen** to all parts of the body. It is pumped round the body by the **heart**. It also takes away **waste** products.

Q2 a) A — red blood cell — carries oxygen
B — white blood cell — kills off invading microbes
C — platelets — helps to clot the blood

b) Any two of, e.g. engulf invading microbes / produce antibodies / neutralise toxins.

c) plasma (carries the cells and platelets and contains a soup of digested food etc.)

Q3 Plasma — The liquid portion of the blood
Capillaries — Narrow blood tubes
Red blood cells — Contain haemoglobin
White blood cells — Fight against disease occurring
Antibodies — Can be produced by a certain type of blood cell
Platelets — Help the blood to clot and so prevents invaders
Heart — The body's blood pump

Q4 red blood cells

Q5 haemoglobin

Q6 Vessel A — Vein — thin muscle as blood is flowing at low pressure and valves to stop the blood flowing in the wrong direction.
Vessel B — Capillary — walls made of a single cell layer which is good for delivering oxygen and food.
Vessel C — Artery — thick muscle wall as blood is flowing at high pressure.

Q7 a) right

b) left

Q8 a) B, D, F, H, A, C, E, G

b)

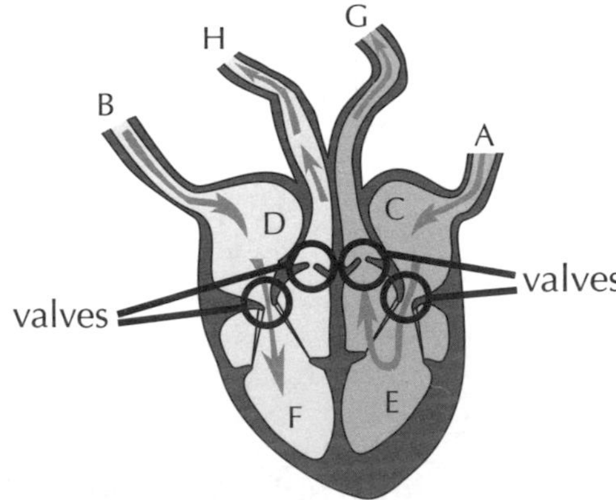

c) To stop the blood flowing backwards.

d) arteries

e) D — is the part of the heart where the deoxygenated blood comes first.
G — is the main artery in the body and carries blood with oxygen away from the heart.
C — is the left top part of the heart.
H — is the blood vessel which carries blood with carbon dioxide from the heart to the lungs to pick up oxygen and remove the carbon dioxide.
A — is the blood vessel which brings back blood with oxygen from the lungs to the heart.
E — is the part of the heart with the thickest walls to put the blood under the most pressure.
B — is the blood vessel which carries blood from the tissues to the heart.

Pages 19-21 — Questions on the Skeleton, Joints and Muscles

Q1 **bones**, **organs**, **movement**, **support**

Q2 a) B, D, C, A

b) 1. Skull — protects the brain
2. Ribs — support, protection and movement
3. Spine — support and protection
4. Humerus — movement
5. Legs — movement

Q3 a) i) To withstand impact.
ii) To allow efficient movement.

b) They are not attached to the sternum.

Q4 a) Vitamin D and calcium. They are found in eggs and milk.

b) A is a female pelvis because it's wider (which makes it more suitable for giving birth).

Q5 Wherever bones meet a **joint** is formed. Bones are held together by strong fibres called **ligaments**. The bones are prevented from rubbing on each other and wearing away by smooth **cartilage** and there is also a **fluid** which fills the joint.

Q6 a) i) E.g. spine
ii) E.g. skull

b) The bit covering each bone.

c) To stop bones wearing down.

d) E.g. cartilage problems

Q7 a) A — Humerus
B — Biceps muscle
C — Triceps muscle
D — Radius
E — Ulna
F — Elbow

b) B (biceps)

c) C (triceps)

d) tendons

Section Three — Growing Up

Pages 22-23 — Questions on Growing Up

Q1 Children, like all young animals cannot **reproduce** because their **sex organs** have not fully developed. In order to produce offspring the female **ovaries** must produce **eggs** and the male **testes** must produce **sperm**. The process of reproduction in humans is called **sexual** reproduction where the material in the male sex cells combines with that in the female sex cells when **fertilisation** occurs. The stage of life when human sex organs begin to develop is called **puberty**.

Q2 a) A — M
B — M
C — B
D — F
E — F
F — M
G — B
H — M
I — B
J — F
K — F
L — F
M — F
N — B
O — B
P — B

Section Four — Humans as Organisms Part Two

b) adolescence

Q3 puberty — The time when male and female sex organs begin to work.
ovaries — The female sex organs that produce eggs (ova).
testes — The male sex organs that produce sperm.
sex hormones — The chemicals which cause the changes at puberty.
adulthood — The period usually reached in the late teens or early twenties when boys and girls have grown up.

Q4

S	E	N	O	M	R	O	H	X	E	S
T	H	I	S	I	S	H	A	R	D	T
X	A	D	U	L	T	H	O	O	D	Y
J	B	A	D	C	E	F	V	G	U	H
J	P	H	Y	S	I	C	A	L	K	L
T	M	I	N	P	O	Q	R	S	T	U
V	E	W	E	X	Y	Z	I	A	C	E
B	A	S	C	P	U	B	E	R	T	Y
F	I	B	T	G	I	B	S	H	I	P
J	A	B	K	E	G	L	I	M	B	S
E	C	N	E	C	S	E	L	O	D	A

Pages 24-25 — Questions on the Menstrual Cycle

Q1 The egg cell is released normally from an **ovary** once a **month**. Each time an egg cell is released the **uterus** gets ready to grow a baby. A thick lining full of **blood** vessels slowly develops. If the egg is **fertilised** it passes into the uterus and becomes attached to it. The uterus grows a fresh new lining every time an egg is released because the environment in the uterus provides excellent conditions for **bacteria** to grow and so it must be replaced. If the egg is not fertilised the breakdown of the uterus lining occurs and this is called **menstruation**. The whole sequence of making a new uterus lining and an egg is called the **menstrual cycle**.

Q2 Ovary — The female organ which produces the egg
Uterus — The female organ which nurtures the fertilised egg
Menstruation — The breakdown of the uterus lining
Egg (Ovum) — The female sex cell
Menstrual cycle — The 4 week cycle of the female sex organ

Q3
1. D
2. B
3. C
4. D
5. A

Q4 a) To give a good blood supply for the fertilised egg to develop in.
b) 10 days
c) day 14

Pages 26-28 — Questions on Having a Baby

Q1 a) A — urethra
B — scrotum
C — testes
D — penis
E — foreskin
F — sperm duct
G — ovary
H — uterus
I — vagina
J — uterus lining
K — oviduct
b) The sperm must fuse with the egg.
c) Usually in the oviduct.
d) Information from the mother and father.

Q2 a) sexual intercourse
b) They die off.
c) A genetic mixture of the mother and father's genetic characteristics.

Q3 a) food, warmth and oxygen
b) A, C, B
c) A ball of cells.
d) pregnant
e) No. The lining is needed for the embryo so no menstruation happens.

Q4 A — Placenta
B — Umbilical cord
C — Amnion
D — Cervix
E — Amniotic fluid
F — Uterus
G — Vagina

Q5 No. They come very close to each other.

Q6 a) 9 months
b) No. Normally the head is born first (and the baby is still too small).
c) Umbilical cord
d) Placenta (afterbirth). It is removed later.

Q7

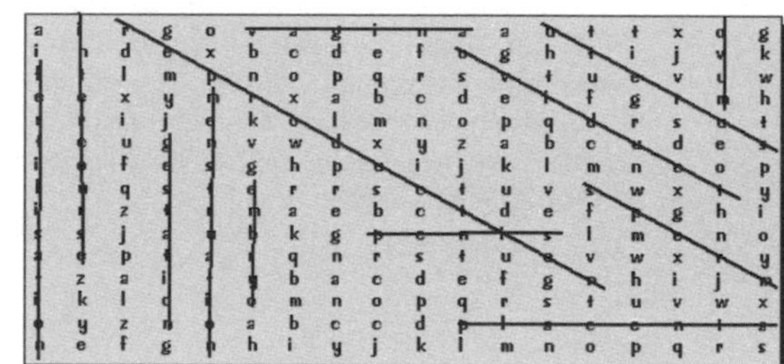

Section Four — Humans as Organisms Part Two

Pages 29-31 — Questions on Breathing

Q1 Lung — b
Windpipe (trachea) — a
Bronchus (plural: bronchi) — d
Alveoli — g
Diaphragm — c
Ribs — e
Rib muscles (intercostal muscles) — f

Section Four — Humans as Organisms Part Two

Q2 The **oxygen** we need to stay alive comes from the **air**. The waste gas, **carbon dioxide**, and water vapour go out of our body. This total process is called **breathing**. The important gas we take in enters our **blood** and is used with sugar in the cells to release **energy**.

Q3 Rib muscles contract — Rib cage moves upwards and outwards
Diaphragm contracts — Diaphragm becomes flatter
More space is formed in the chest — Air enters to fill the extra room
Rib muscles relax — Rib cage moves downwards and inwards
Diaphragm relaxes — Diaphragm becomes dome-shaped i.e. moves upwards
Less space is left in the chest — Air is forced out from the chest space

Q4 a) lungs
b) trachea (windpipe)
c) bronchi (bronchus)
d) rib muscles (intercostal muscles) and diaphragm muscle
e) diaphragm
f) thorax (chest cavity)
g) They fill with air.
h) inhalation

Q5 a) bronchioles
b) alveolus
c) blood capillaries
d) red blood cells
e) To increase the surface area of the lungs and increase the amount of gas exchange.
f) They both have walls only one cell thick to make it easier for gas exchange.
g) oxygen and carbon dioxide

Pages 32-33 — Questions on Smoking

Q1 The way in which we make sure we get good **air** into our **lungs** is to **clean** it first. To do this our **windpipe** has special cells which produce sticky **mucus** which trap dust. There are also tiny hairs called **cilia** to take the mixture back to the throat where it can be **swallowed**.

Q2
1. C
2. B
3. A
4. F
5. E
6. D

Q3 a) The mucus layer is thicker and there are less cilia.
b bronchitis
c) coughing
d) Any one of, e.g. oxygen content of blood may be reduced / poisons introduced.

Q4 a) cancer
b) emphysema and heart disease.
c) Breathing in smoke that others have exhaled.
d) carbon monoxide

Q5

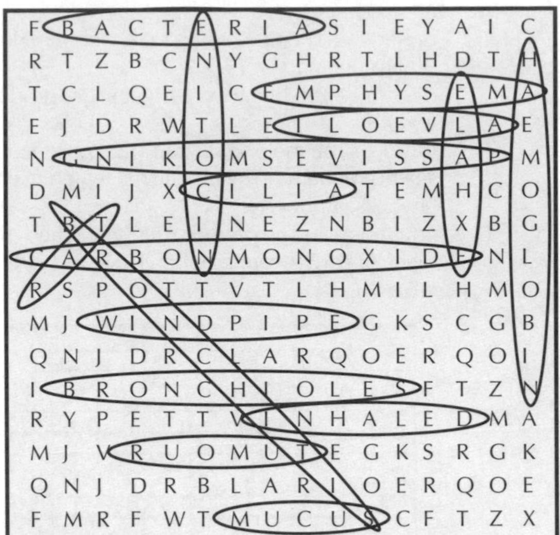

Pages 34-37 — Questions on Respiration

Q1 In this section we show how **glucose** is oxidised to produce **energy**. This process is called **respiration** and the glucose is broken down to make **carbon dioxide**, water and energy. All living things need energy for processes such as **growth/movement/ reproduction**, **growth/movement/reproduction**, and **growth/movement/reproduction**.

Q2 a) glucose and oxygen
b) carbon dioxide and water
c) Energy. Any three of, e.g. growth / movement / reproduction / repair / maintaining body temperature.
d)

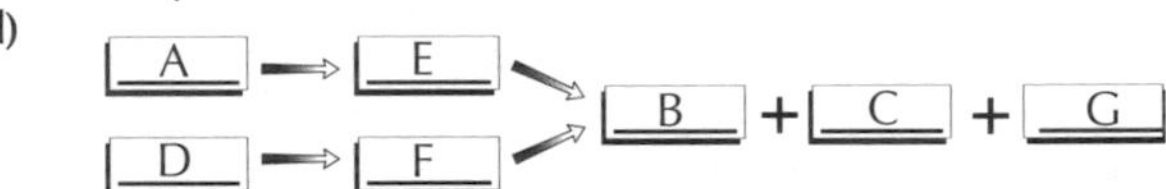

Q3 a) It is similar to glucose.
b) It goes cloudy.
c) Carbon dioxide is given off.
d) respiration
e) Oxygen to oxidise the sugar.
f) Energy. It is used for many purposes, e.g. growth, movement, reproduction, repair, maintaining body temperature.

Q4 a) E.g. muscles
b) Yes. The body can't store energy.
c) glucose + oxygen → carbon dioxide + water + energy
d) carbon dioxide and water — waste
energy — useful

Q5 a) nitrogen and oxygen
b) red blood cells
c) We go into oxygen debt when using anaerobic respiration. Glucose only gets partially oxidised and acids are produced which cause cramp.

Q6 a) All living organisms.
b) All living cells.
c) energy
d) It is used for many important purposes, e.g. growth, movement, reproduction, repair, transportation of stuff around the body and maintaining temperature.

Section Five — Plants as Organisms

Q7 a) A — **aerobic respiration**
B — **enzymes**
C — **energy**
D — **carbon dioxide**
E — **water**
F — **oxygen**
G — **glucose**
H — **nitrogen**
I — **limewater**
J — **aerobics**
b) aerobics

Pages 38-40 — Questions on Health

Q1 a) 4
b) 1
c) 2
d) 5
e) 3

Q2 a) Your body needs a regular supply of them.
b) Effects they have on the body other than those that they were taken for.

Q3 a) depressant
b) brain and liver
c) Reaction times are reduced so accidents are not avoided in time. Inhibitions are reduced so reckless driving is more likely.

Q4 a) solvent
b) E.g. paints, aerosols and glue.
c) i) Makes you sleepy
Makes you light headed
Gives hallucinations
Helps you to relax
ii) Stops the process of digestion
Can damage brain and lungs
Can cause damage to the eyes
Can cause damage to the nervous system

Q5 1. B
2. C
3. A

Q6 a) **Bacteria**, **viruses**
b) Bacteria — A, B, D, E
Viruses — C
c) viruses

Q7 a) When you breathe in, in food and through cuts in the skin.
b) Coughing and sneezing sprays tiny drops of water into the air which can contain microbes and infect others.
c) An infection.
d) Cholera
e) Any bacteria present in the food could still be alive. Cooking food properly kills bacteria.

Q8 A — ✓ correct
B — ✗ incorrect
C — ✗ incorrect
D — ✓ correct
E — ✗ incorrect
F — ✗ incorrect
G — ✓ correct
H — ✗ incorrect

Page 41 — Questions on Fighting Disease

Q1 The body has its own **natural defences** against disease but it can be helped by **medicine** and **immunisation**. The main armies of defence of the body are **antibodies** and **white blood cells** which are part of the body's **immune** system.

Q2 When the skin is cut, **bacteria** can enter and cause disease, so **platelets** in the blood seal the wound. During this process **white** blood cells come to the site of damage and either **eat** the bacteria or produce **antibodies** to fight them.

Q3 a) Eat/engulf them, produce antibodies and produce antitoxins.
b) **antibodies**, **immunity**

Q4 a) immunisation
b) vaccine or serum
c) It stimulates the production of antibodies.
d) vaccine
e) antibiotics

Section Five — Plants as Organisms

Pages 42-43 — Questions on Plant Nutrition

Q1 a) photosynthesis
b) It could become unable to produce food, so it could die.
c) support, anchorage, absorption
d) It may blow away / not take in enough nutrients.

Q2 Fertilisers are a source of mineral nutrients, not 'food' — plants make their own food.

Q3 Water and minerals are absorbed. Root hairs increase the surface area of the root to maximise absorption.

Q4 a) Potassium. Leaves become yellow with dead spots.
b) Phosphate. Roots didn't grow properly in beaker C.
c) yellowing of leaves and weakening of the stem
d) Eventually they would die.
e) i) Important for green leaves and strong stems.
ii) Important for good root development.

Q5 A — So they absorb as much light as possible.
B — So carbon dioxide in the air gets inside cells easily.
C — For water and glucose transportation.
D — To let carbon dioxide in / oxygen out.

Pages 44-47 — Questions on Photosynthesis

Q1 a) Both plants were watered regularly.
b) Swap plants over and repeat the test.
Repeat experiment with many plants.
c) The plant needs light to make food.
d) It will eventually die.
e) light, water

Q2 A — dark, B — light
Plants in the dark become long and spindly as they try to reach the light (etiolation).

Section Five — Plants as Organisms

Q3 a) The chlorophyll was removed from the plant.
b) Starch was present.
c) No colour change — there was no light for photosynthesis so the plant uses up its starch stores.
Q4 oxygen — it relit a glowing splint
Q5 Photosynthesis requires carbon dioxide.
Q6 a) carbon dioxide in, oxygen out
b) Green. It absorbs the energy of sunlight for photosynthesis.
c) It is needed for photosynthesis.
d) glucose/oxygen
e) carbon dioxide + water $\xrightarrow{\text{light}}$ Glucose + oxygen
f) Light provides the energy to drive the reaction.
Q7 No — light is needed.
Q8 a) carbon dioxide
b) oxygen (and water vapour)
c) water (and minerals — especially magnesium/ nitrates)
Q9 It provides oxygen and food.
Q10

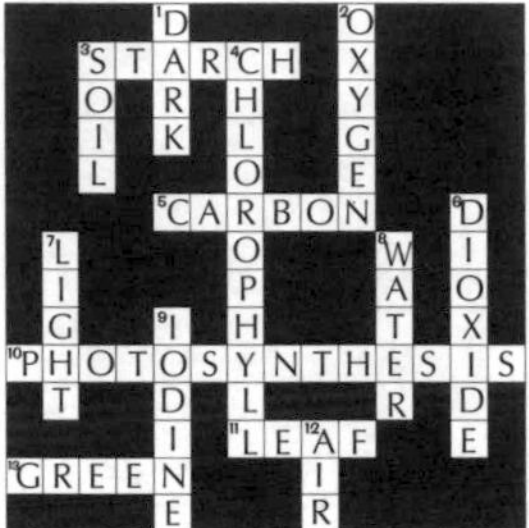

Page 48 — Questions on Plant Growth

Q1 Roots grow **away from** the light and **with** gravity.
Roots grow **towards** the light and **away from** gravity.
Q2 nitrogen is needed for — strong stems and green leaves
phosphorus is needed for — healthy root growth
photosynthesis is needed for — glucose and oxygen production
potassium is needed for — healthy green leaves
starch is made from — glucose
water and carbon dioxide are needed for — photosynthesis
Q3 a) Photosynthesis makes glucose, which is used for growth.
b) 4 units. No — it has reached its maximum rate of photosynthesis.
c) 40°C and 0°C
d) 25°C
e) E.g. buy a greenhouse / cover the plants with transparent plastic.

Pages 49-51 — Questions on Plant Reproduction

Q1 a) stem — Y, roots — Z, flower — W, leaf — X
b) absorbs water and minerals — Z
absorbs light for photosynthesis — X
anchors the plant — Z
contains the reproductive organs — W
makes food for the plant — X
supports the plant — Y
c) Roots: anchor the plant and absorb water and minerals.
Stem: supports the plant and carries liquids.
Leaves: make food and transpire.
Flowers: used for reproduction.
Q2 The **male** sex cells is the pollen, and the **female** sex cell is the **ovum**.
Q3 a) *See diagram for labels.* The filaments support the anther. The anther makes pollen.
b) *See diagram for labels.* The female sex organs.
c) *See diagram for labels.* The ovules/eggs.
d) *See diagram for labels.*

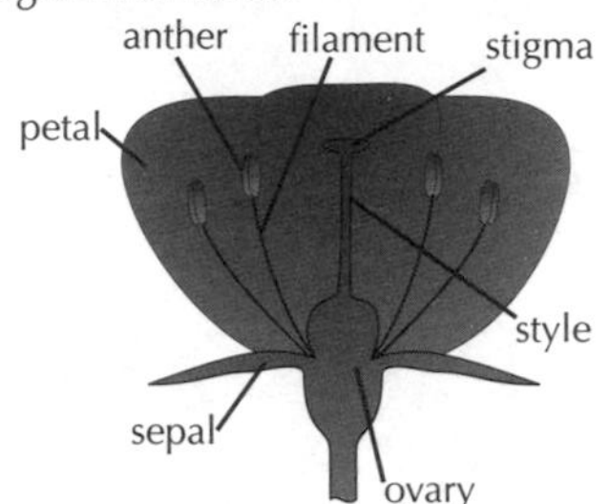

Q4 a) colour
b) They protect the budding flower.
c) They attract insects.
Q5 the female sex cell in plants is called — the ovule
the female sex organ in plants is called — the carpel
the female sex organ is made up from — the stigma, style and ovary
the male sex cell in plants is called — the pollen
the male sex organ in plants is called — the stamen
the male sex organ is made up from — the filament and anther
Q6 insect-pollinated — buttercup, dandelion, sunflower
wind-pollinated — grass, stinging nettle, willow tree
Q7

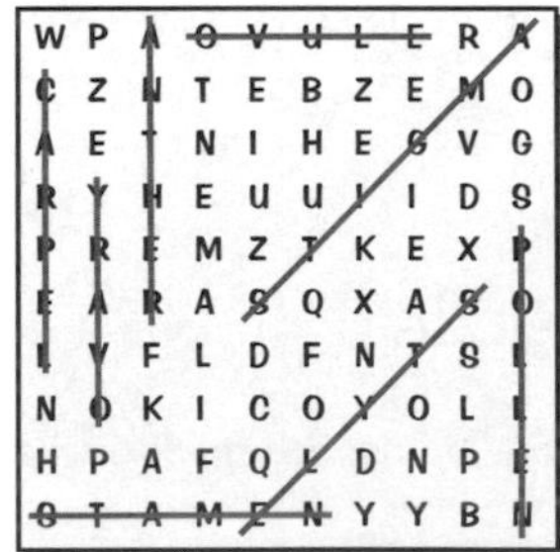

Q8 a) The travel of pollen from one plant to another.
b) B — e.g. anthers hanging outside the flower
c) A — e.g. brightly coloured petals, anthers inside flower
d) Lighter pollen is more easily carried by the wind.
Q9 a) In self-pollination only one plant is involved.
b) *Some plants only have male flowers, and others only have female flowers* — cross pollination is the only way of produced offspring.
The stamens and carpels mature at different times — so a plant can't pollinate itself.

Pages 52-53 — Questions on Fertilisation and Seed Formation

Q1 a) style
b) fertilisation

Section Six — Variation

c) ovary
d) scattered
e) germination

Q2 release of pollen → pollination → growth of pollen tube → fertilisation → seed production → dispersal → germination → growth of seedlings

Q3 a) dandelions — parachutes catch the wind
sycamore — blades spin and fly like a helicopter

b) The animal receives nutrients.

c) The animal will disperse the seeds and provide a dose of fertiliser.

d) tomato — needs to be eaten then spread via excrement
burdock — attaches to animal fur and gets carried around

e) E.g. apple (accept any sensible fruit). It is attractive because of the colour/smell/taste.

Pages 54-55 — Questions on The Carbon Cycle

Q1 a) oxygen
b) carbon dioxide
c) wood + **oxygen** → water + **carbon dioxide** + energy
d) oxygen, carbon dioxide
e) glucose + **oxygen** → water + **carbon dioxide** + energy
f) They are basically the same.
g) One is effectively the reverse of the other.

Q2 Process 1 — photosynthesis
Process 2 — burning
Process 3 — respiration

Q3 a) Herbivores eat plants and, in turn, are eaten by other animals.

b)

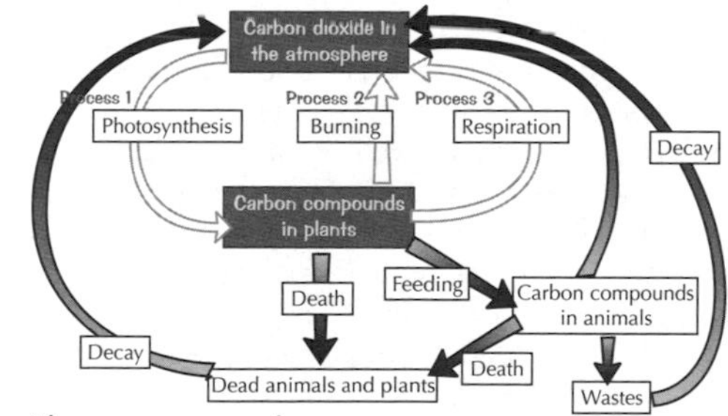

c) They are excreted as waste.
d) see diagram (Q3b)

Q4 bacterium, bird, dandelion, dog, fish, frog, human, seaweed, snake

Q5 see diagram (Q3b)

Pages 56-57 — Questions on The Nitrogen Cycle

Q1 a) Nitrogen and oxygen exist in the atmosphere but rarely react.
b) nitrogen oxides
c) Nitrogen oxides make acids which react with nitrates in the soil. These are absorbed by plants.
d) 2, 6, 3, 4, 7, 1, 5

Q2 a)

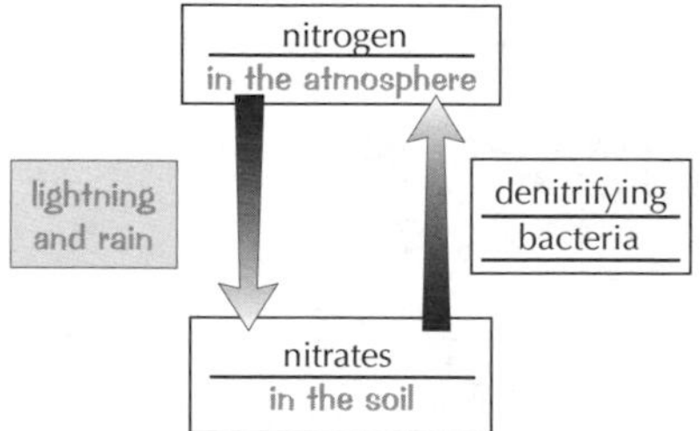

b) The process is cyclic.

Q3 a) nitrates
b) muscle/hair/nails
c)

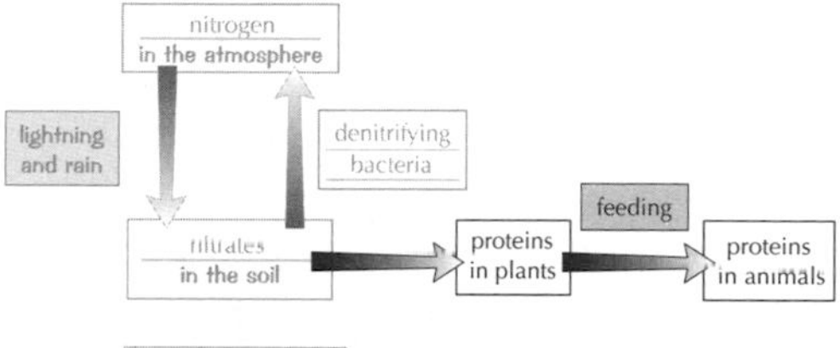

Q4

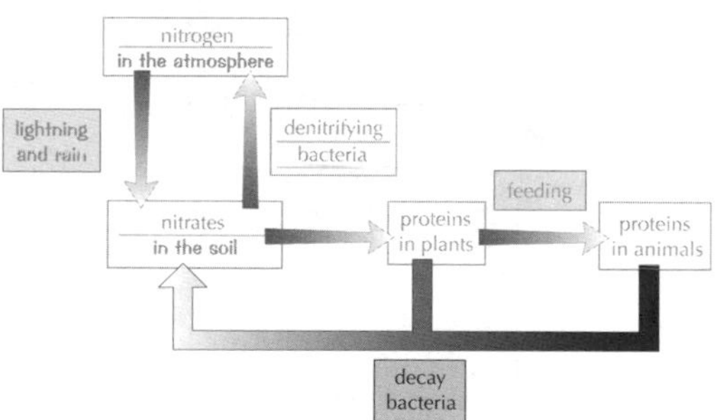

Q5 a) nitrogen fixation
b) denitrifying bacteria
c) One turns nitrates into nitrogen, the other turns proteins into nitrates.

Section Six — Variation

Pages 58-59 — Questions on Variation

Q1 a)

Colour of eyes	Number of children
Brown	9
Blue	12
Green	5
Hazel	6

b)

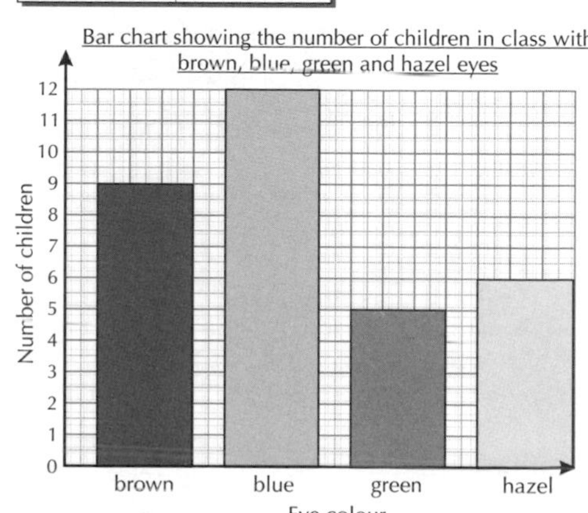

Section Seven — Organisms in Their Environment

c) 32 children were included.
Percentage with green eyes = (5 ÷ 32) × 100
= 15.625%

Q2 a)

Height range (cm)	Number of girls
135-139	| = 1
140-144	||| = 3
145-149	𝍸 | = 6
150-154	𝍸 ||| = 8
155-159	𝍸 || = 7
160-164	|||| = 4
165-169	| = 1

b) Bar chart showing the number of girls in class by height range

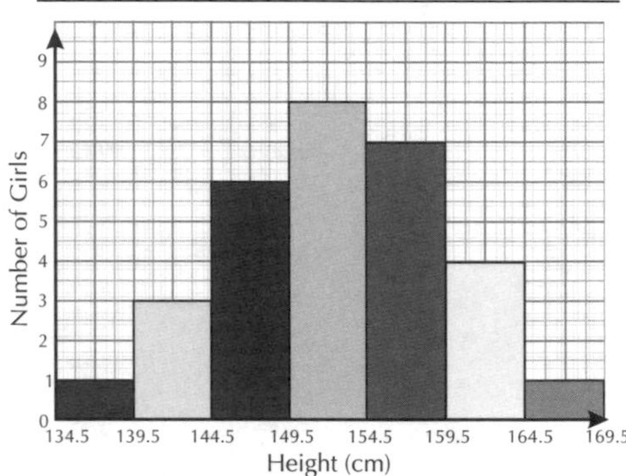

c) Amongst tallest: 160-169 cm.
Amongst shortest: 135-149 cm

d) E.g. weight and foot size.

Pages 60-61 — Questions on Environmental & Inherited Variation

Q1 a) E.g. trees have leaves, branches, seeds, green colour. E.g. both are alive.

b) E.g. chimps have shaggy hair, large jaws, short legs. E.g. both have fingers and toes, two arms and two legs, forward facing eyes.

c) **Differences:** E.g. eye/hair colour, height, weight, sex. **Similarities:** E.g. two arms and two legs, two eyes, five fingers on each hand.

d) a) all inherited
b) probably all inherited
c) inherited: eye/hair colour, sex
environment: hair style
inherited and environment: weight/height

Q2
1. Light — plants receiving less light will grow more slowly.
2. Temp — colder conditions will slow the rate of growth.
3. Soil — if soil lacks essential minerals plants grow badly.
4. Space — plants with lots of space grow more bushy.

Q3 inherited — 1) and 2)
environmental — 3), 4), 5), 6), and 7)

Pages 62-63 — Questions on Inheritance and Selective Breeding

Q1 a) Only bred from the largest birds and kept doing this for several years.

b) Some of the birds produced were too small. The longer he kept selecting, the fewer birds like this would be produced.

c) He chose which birds should be allowed to breed according to whether they had the desired feature or not.

d) Only bred from the large birds with beautiful beaks, and keep doing this for several years.

Q2 a) E.g. lots of fur / yellow fur / good nature / floppy ears.

b) E.g. short fur / short legs / barrel-shaped body / short nose / undershot jaw.

c) E.g. the physical characteristics of retrievers are too different from those of bulldogs. It would just take too long.

Q3 Wheat — short stems / thick stems / large heads. Could also select for flavour / disease resistance. Pig — no tusks / no hair / lots of meat. Could also select for fat content / speed of growing / good temper / flavour of meat.

Section Seven — Organisms in Their Environment

Pages 64-65 — Questions on Classification of Plants & Animals

Q1 E.g. plants make their own food. / Plants don't have a nervous system. / Plants store food as starch (not as fat or glycogen).

Q2 a) vertebrates

b) mammals — e.g. lion, mouse, human
birds — e.g. duck, eagle, ostrich

c) E.g. mammals have live young. / Mammals feed their babies milk. / Mammals don't have feathers.

d) E.g. they both have backbones / breathe with lungs / have a stable body temperature.

e) E.g. fish breathe with gills. / Fish have scales and fins. / Fish don't have a steady body temperature.

f) reptiles — e.g. lizard, alligator
amphibians — e.g. newt, frog
Differences — e.g. reptiles lay their eggs on land / have a dry scaly skin.

Q3 a) A — insects
B — arachnids
C — crustaceans
D — myriapods

b) Any four of, e.g. no backbone / hard body (external skeleton) / body divided into segments / legs / they are arthropods.

c) E.g. insects have six legs, whereas spiders have eight. / Insects' bodies have three segments, whereas spiders' have two.

d) an invertebrate with legs

Section Seven — Organisms in Their Environment

Q4 Mollusc, Flatworm, Roundworm, Slimy, Coelenterate, Invertebrate, Segmented, Shell

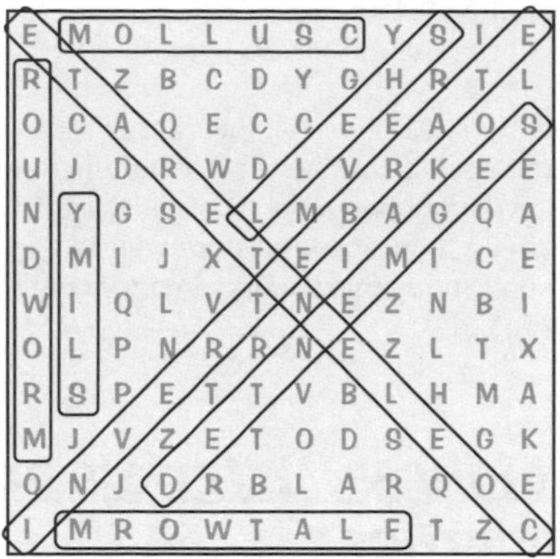

Pages 66-67 — Questions on Keys

Q1 A — triangle
B — square
C — rectangle
D — pentagon
E.g. insert these steps before the existing ones:
1) Does it have corners? YES go to 3, NO go to 2.
2) Is it longer than its height? YES ellipse, NO circle.

Q2 a) E.g. 1) Does it have a neck? YES go to 2, NO go to 3.
2) Does it have a flat bottom? YES conical flask, NO round-bottomed flask.
3) Does it have a spout? YES go to 4, NO test tube.
4) Is it tall and thin? YES measuring cylinder, NO beaker.

b) It would enable them to identify and name the laboratory equipment.

Q3

label	name
A	web spinner
B	sucking louse
C	thrip
D	termite
E	bird louse

Q4 (Students should produce a working key for a series of people, animals, plants, objects or places.)

Pages 68-69 — Questions on Adaptation

Q1 The place where something lives is called its **habitat**.
The conditions in a habitat are the **environment**.
Over millions of years, animals and plants become **adapted** to the environment.

Q2 a) leaves, stems and roots

b) leaves — to absorb sunlight
stems — support the leaves
roots — anchor the plant

c) It will be able to absorb more light if it can reach above plants and other obstacles.

d) The stem of the bladder wrack is not strong enough to hold it upright.

e) The air bladders will let the fronds float in the water and so hold the plant upright. When the tide comes in it will support the plant, holding it upright.

Q3 a) Long roots get water from deeper but require more resources to grow. Short roots can get water from dew but are vulnerable to grazers.

b) 1. Allows the plants to die when there is no water and new plants grow when water becomes available.
2. Plants do not need regular watering as they can store water when it rains.
3. Smaller surface area means lower water loss and thorns keep grazing animals away.

c) E.g. wide feet to spread weight on the sand. / Nostrils which close to stop sand getting in. / Sandy-coloured coat for camouflage. / It can drink a lot to make the most of water when it finds it. / Body fat is stored in its hump to help with heat loss from the rest of the body. / Can let its body temperature rise in the day and fall at night — doesn't need to sweat.

Pages 70-71 — Questions on Food Chains and Food Webs

Q1 carnivores — animals that eat other animals
omnivores — animals that can eat both plants and animals
herbivores — animals that eat plants
consumers — organisms that rely on other organisms for their food
producers — organisms that can make their own food

Q2 a) consumed by

b) herbivore — squid (eats plants)
carnivore — whale (eats animals)
producer — tiny plants (start of food chain)

Q3 Plants, e.g. lettuce, grass. They can produce food by photosynthesis.

Q4 carnivore, consumer, food chain, omnivore, producer, herbivore

E	P	C	O	N	S	U	M	E	R
R	R	F	O	I	D	C	H	A	O
O	E	O	O	A	E	R	B	M	I
V	C	O	M	H	I	V	N	C	A
I	U	D	A	C	H	I	N	G	R
B	D	C	E	D	V	O	R	E	S
R	O	H	S	O	K	I	Z	X	L
E	R	A	R	O	A	R	N	I	V
H	P	E	R	F	V	I	B	R	A
X	E	R	O	V	I	N	R	A	C

Q5 a) Blue tit, hawk, owl, fox. The blue tit is not a top carnivore.

b) blackberry — aphid — blue tit — hawk
blackberry — caterpillar — blue tit — hawk
blackberry — mouse — hawk

c) blackberry — mouse — owl

d) The number of rabbits and voles might increase because they have more food.

e) The number of owls might increase because the foxes would eat more of the voles and leave more mice to the owls.

f) There would be more blue tits because less would be eaten.

g) There would be fewer aphids because there would be more blue tits eating them.

Q6 true, false, false, false

Pages 72-73 — Questions on Number Pyramids

Q1 a)

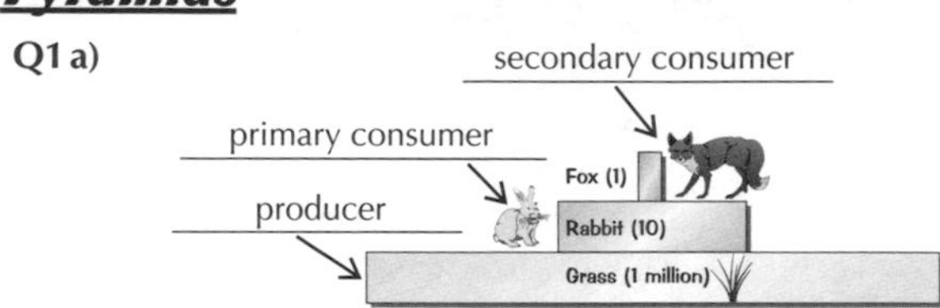

b) the number of organisms

Q2 **A)**

Owl (1)
Vole (10)
Grass (50)

Scale: e.g. 3mm = 1 organism

B)

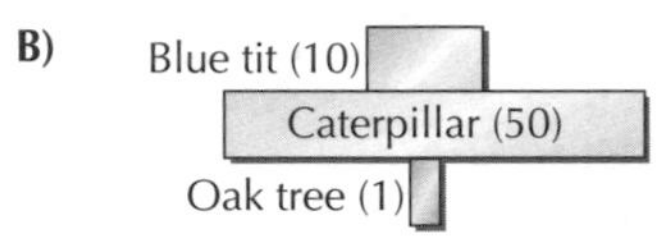

Scale: e.g. 3mm = 1 organism

B is not very pyramid shaped. It is this shape because one tree can support many caterpillars.

Q3 a) C. Lots of blackberries to support voles, fleas are very small.

b) A. Number of organisms decreases at each stage.

c) D. Oak trees are very large but there's only one of them. A lot of fleas can live off each bird.

d) B. The rose bush supports many aphids, bird eats many ladybirds.

Q4 a) food chain — from producer to consumer
pyramid of numbers — bottom to top

b) Trophic level. Energy is lost in respiration and waste.

Pages 74-76 — Questions on Survival

Q1 a) Slow rabbits are easier to catch by foxes and so don't get the chance to reproduce and pass on their genes.

b) Fast rabbits are more likely to escape predation by the foxes and so have more chance of reproducing successfully.

c) Only the fast rabbits can breed and pass on their genes to their offspring which inherit the fast genes.

d) The rabbit from the field with foxes should win. The other rabbit is more likely to be a slow rabbit as there are no foxes to apply a selection pressure. Slow rabbits will also breed as they are not eaten by foxes.

Q2 a) Key ideas should include camouflage, keen senses, speed or cunning, sharp teeth, claws, working in teams, setting traps.

b) Key ideas should include camouflage, keen senses, speed or cunning, team work, good defences (e.g. sharp teeth), poisons, warning signs, good hiding places, hard scales/skin.

c) Yes. Camouflage, keen senses, speed or cunning, sharp teeth, working in teams.

Q3 a) E.g. ability to climb trees / camouflage against trunks or leaves / ability to hop/jump/fly/glide from tree to tree.

b) E.g. gills / streamlined shape / fins / webbed feet / camouflage against the sea bottom / light lower surface dark upper surface / ability to swim.

c) E.g. ability to burrow and store water / wide feet to walk on sand / large surface area for heat loss / nocturnal.

Section Eight — Materials and their Properties

Pages 77-78 — Questions on Types of Materials

Q1 Things made of ceramic:
Plates
Bricks
Tiles
Jugs / cups
Things made of glass:
Windows
Drinking glasses
Lenses (any)
Ornaments
Things made of plastic:
Pipes and gutters
Car fittings
Cases for TV
Plates, lenses

Q2 Glass: transparency, low reactivity
Plastic: low density, low reactivity, ease of colouring
Ceramic: high melting point, low reactivity, ease of manufacture

Q3 E.g. Cups (ceramic) — low thermal conductivity.
Glasses (glass) — transparent and light.
Casing (plastic) — low electrical conductivity.

Q4 E.g. ceramic / plastic. Reasons include thermal insulation, strength (at 100 °C) and impermeability.

Q5 China cup — C
Lead crystal tumbler — G
Brick — C
Bin liner — P
Milk bottle — G
Kitchen tile — C or P (lino)

Q6 Friction heats nose — ceramics combine high melting point, good insulation and low reactivity.

Q7 E.g. glass fibre in resin for boat hulls. / Carbon fibre in resin for fishing rods.

Q8 It is stronger than plastic alone and less brittle than glass alone.

Q9 It has a high melting point and low reactivity. It is also hard. Disadvantages include low thermal conductivity and brittleness.

Section Nine — Solids, Liquids and Gases

Pages 79-80 — Questions on Raw Materials

Q1 E.g. petrol, pharmaceuticals, paints, lubricating oils, camping gas

Q2 E.g. copper — thermal conductivity / iron — thermal conductivity / aluminium — thermal conductivity and low density / wood — low thermal conductivity / plastic — low thermal conductivity.

Q3 Paper/wood/plant fibre
Ink

Q4 a) (window pane — sand)
b) rubber — crude oil
c) paper — wood
d) beer — water

Q5 An oak chair — N
A coffee cup — M
A book — N
A biro — M
A washing-up bowl — M
A kitchen sink — M
A T.V. — M
A mahogany chest — N
Paint — M
A cricket bat — N
A beer mug — M
A brick wall — M

Q6 E.g. pharmaceuticals / plastics (when oil runs out) / tar

Q7 O_2 — e.g. rocket motors
N_2 — e.g. Haber process
Ar — e.g. MIG+TIG welds
Ne — e.g. lights

Page 81 — Questions on Man-Made and Synthetic Materials

Q1 a) Cotton — polyester / nylon
Wood — aluminium / plastic
Hemp — nylon
Rubber — bunar / plastic
Silk — nylon

b)

Item	Material	Advantages	Disadvantages
Shirt	Cotton	Wears well, smooth	Expensive
	Nylon	Cheap, colourful	Scratchy, "sweaty"
Window	wood	looks nice	rots
	aluminium	long lasting	not easy to paint
Rope	hemp	strong	rots
	nylon	strong	few
Tyre	rubber	cheap	limited resource
	bunar	save rubber	expensive
Tie	silk	looks good	expensive
	nylon	cheap	naff

Q2 a) Re-using old things as raw materials.
b) Conserve stocks of raw material and can reduce energy waste.
c) Sand is abundant so recycling glass is energy saving and reduces the need for land fill.

Section Nine — Solids, Liquids and Gases

Pages 82-84 — Questions on Particle Theory

Q1 a) True
b) False
c) False
d) True
e) True
f) True
g) False
h) True

Q2

	Particles are close together	Particles are held in fixed positions	Particles are moving
Solid	✓	✓	✓
Liquid	✓		✓
Gas			✓

Q3 A — X
B — Z
C — Y

Q4 The forces between particles in solids are strong. The forces between particles in gases are very weak. The forces between particles in liquids are weaker than in solids but stronger than in gases.

Q5 a) Yes
b) No

Q6 Particles are close together but able to move around. Properties — e.g. constant volume, ability to flow, incompressibility.

Q7 closely, fixed, vibrate, move, fixed, volume, flow, compressed, closely, dense, small

Q8 Particles are strongly joined.

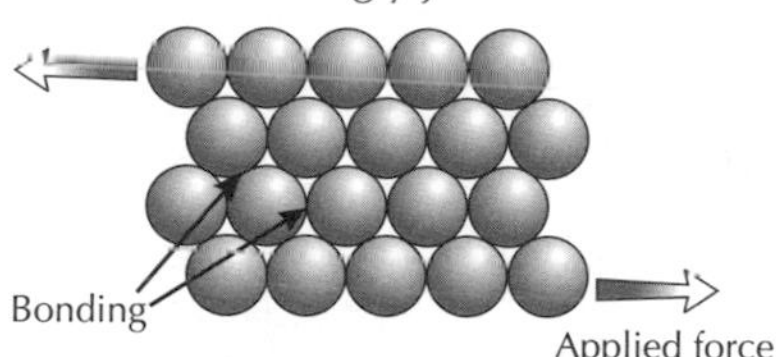

Q9 The following should be ticked:
Particles move fast.
Particles collide with the container.
No definite shape.
Very low density.

Section Nine — Solids, Liquids and Gases

Pages 85-87 — Questions on Melting and Boiling Points

Q1

(D I F F U S I O N)

Q2 a) A — Melting
B — Freezing
C — Boiling/Evaporation
D — Condensation
E — Sublimation

b) Most materials decrease slightly in density on melting.

Q3 a) Smaller distances of free travel — more collisions per gas particle per unit time. Lower surface area of container means more collisions per unit of area.

b) increases, squashed, smaller, more often, condensed, 100 °C, boiling point

Q4

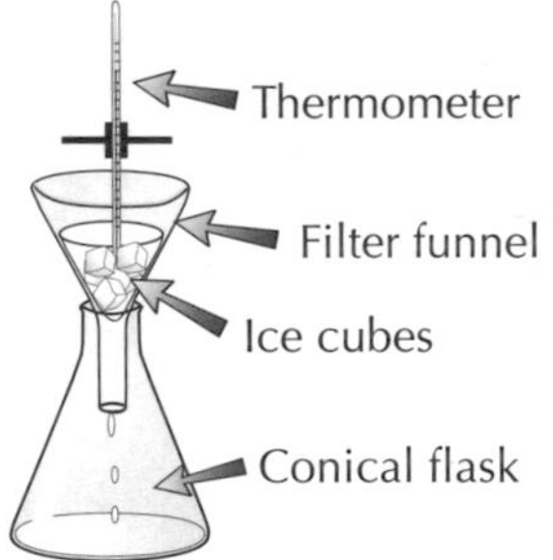

Wait until the ice begins to melt and read off the temperature on the thermometer.
Reading: 0 °C

Q5 a) 100 °C

b) salty water

Q6 Ice is more slippery than water and so salt makes roads safer by keeping water liquid.

Pages 88-89 — Questions on Density

Q1 a) $200 \div 10 = 20$ g/cm^3

b) $400 \div 10 = 40$ g/cm^3

c) $10\,000 \div 50 = 200$ g/cm^3

Q2 a) lead

b)

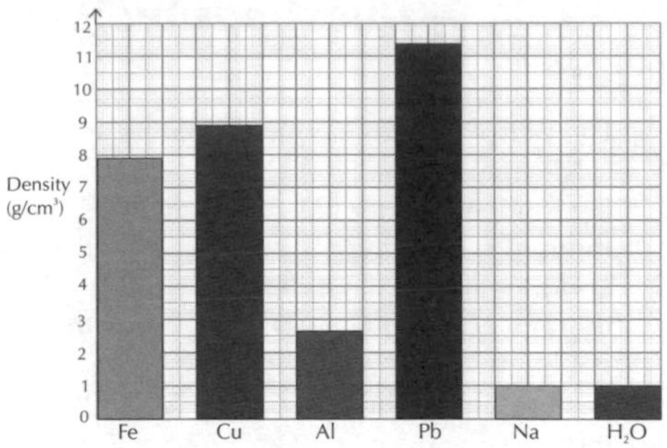

c) Sodium floats, all others sink.

Pages 90-91 — Questions on The Water Cycle

Q1 a)

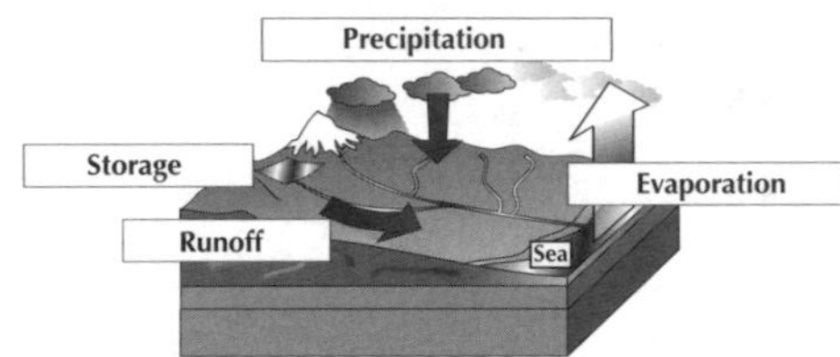

b) Rain, snow, etc.

c) Heat of the Sun.

d) clouds

e) They fall as rain.

Q2 Particles in the sea have a range energies due to the heat of the Sun. If a fast particle reaches the surface with enough energy to escape the liquid it evaporates.

Q3 B — warm moist air from low lying area or sea rises up steep mountains and water condenses out.

Q4

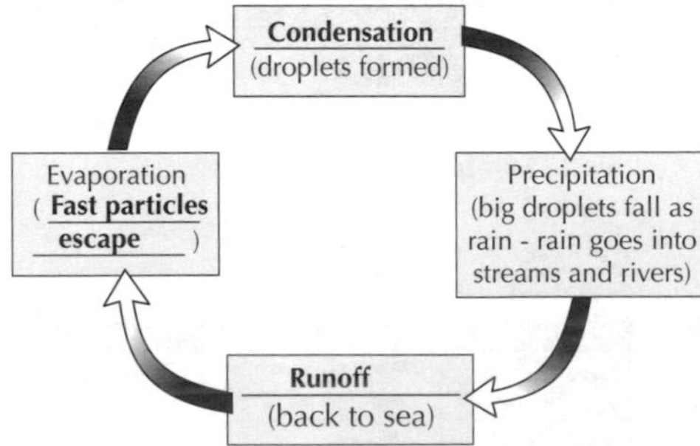

Q5 Energy from the sun — evaporates water from the — sea to form water vapour.
Water vapour rises — and cools forming droplets — which we see as clouds.
When clouds rise — they cool further — and form bigger droplets.
These bigger droplets — fall as rain sometimes — snow, sleet or hail.
Rain water flows into — steams and then rivers — and then back to the sea.
Not all water returns — directly into the sea — some is evaporated.
Some water is — taken up by the plants — and given out during transpiration.

Q6 E.g. snow, hail, sleet.

Q7 Into plants and animals and evaporation from land.

Section Ten — Elements, Mixtures and Compounds

Section Ten — Elements, Mixtures and Compounds

Pages 92-93 — Atoms, Elements and Compounds

Q1 elements
Q2 A column of elements.
Q3

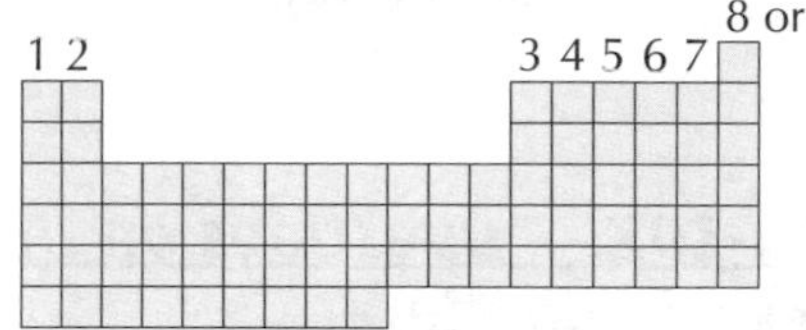

Any two of, e.g. I = alkali metals / II = alkali earth metals / VII = noble gases
Q4 A row of elements in the table.
Q5 Metals are to the left, non-metals are to the right.
Q6 a) Silicon is a non-metal.
b) Chlorine is a non-metal.
c) MgO as all others are Group 1 compounds.
d) CO as all the others are elements.
e) Hydrogen is not a gas.
f) Fe as it is not in Group 1.
g) Lithium is the only metal.
Q7 a) D
b) A
c) A
d) D
e) A
f) D
Q8 Elements: Lead, Sulphur, Oxygen, Helium, Calcium, Chlorine
Compounds: Sodium Chloride, Water, Methane, Sulphur dioxide, Propane, Carbon Monoxide, Magnesium Oxide, Carbon Monoxide, Sulphuric Acid.
Q9 a) 1 Cu, 1 S, 4 O
b) 1 Na, 1 Cl
c) 2 Fe, 3 O
d) 1 N, 3 H
e) 2 H, 1 O
f) 1 Cu, 1 O

Page 94 — Questions on Naming Substances

Q1 a) elements, ide
b) combine, oxygen, ate
c) doesn't
d) E.g. copper sulphate, zinc carbonate.
Q2 water — H_2O
iron oxide — Fe_2O_3
carbon dioxide — CO_2
methane — CH_4
carbon monoxide — CO
sodium chloride — NaCl
Q3 a) sodium chloride
b) sodium bromide
c) sodium oxide
Q4 a) calcium Ca, carbon C, oxygen O
b) calcium Ca, oxygen O
c) potassium K, hydrogen H, oxygen O
d) copper Cu, sulphur S, oxygen O

Pages 95-96 — Questions on Elements

Q1 a) carbon
b) chlorine
c) calcium
d) copper
e) sodium
f) fluorine
Q2 carbon, chlorine, fluorine
Q3 carbon, hydrogen (or holmium HO), oxygen, phosphorus, potassium, iodine, nitrogen, sulphur, calcium, iron.
Q4 b) helium
c) chlorine
d) argon
e) oxygen
f) iodine
Q5

I	O	D	I	N	E	N	N	V	M	U	I	S	S	A	T	O	P
R	C	F	Z	S	A	L	T	P	S	B	R	E	V	L	I	S	E
O	U	Q	M	L	I	C	N	I	Z	Y	F	A	X	U	V	W	D
N	U	S	A	M	L	L	U	E	C	H	L	O	R	I	N	E	I
S	M	R	T	U	L	L	I	T	P	N	U	G	O	K	L	L	X
U	U	M	U	I	C	L	A	C	I	H	O	F	F	L	M	T	O
L	I	L	O	I	J	E	H	R	O	I	R	S	E	E	R	I	R
P	L	D	P	A	L	K	G	J	S	N	I	D	D	A	S	N	E
H	E	I	H	H	Y	D	R	O	G	E	N	C	C	D	T	E	P
I	H	C	O	Y	U	R	M	M	N	O	E	Z	A	U	P	G	P
D	E	A	S	D	A	R	G	J	K	N	B	B	W	R	C	Y	O
E	Y	C	P	R	N	L	I	T	H	I	U	M	V	T	B	X	C
A	R	I	H	O	O	I	K	C	H	I	U	M	B	B	B	O	A
G	U	R	O	X	G	M	E	F	A	N	E	G	O	R	T	I	N
O	C	T	R	Y	R	E	F	G	U	C	R	I	H	O	O	P	O
L	R	I	U	P	A	L	U	M	I	N	I	U	M	D	K	F	R
D	E	N	S	O	D	I	U	M	N	N	M	D	L	Y	V	A	O
A	M	U	I	S	E	N	G	A	M	U	I	L	L	Y	R	E	B

Q6 a) copper
b) oxygen
c) mercury
d) sodium
e) sulphur

Pages 97-98 — Having Fun with Symbols

Q1 Pupils who work hard will do well in sats.
Q2 I love homework. More for me.
Q3 E.g. Beryllium. sulphur, (thorium hydrogen) / dysprosiumyttrium), oxygen / sulphur, oxygen, (manganese-nitrogen), (europium-uranium)/ tungsten, oxygen, rubidium-boron), potassium/ (molybdenum-oxygen), astatine, (einsteinium-sulphur), yttrium!

Page 99 — More Questions on Naming Substances

Q1 a) H_2O
b) SO_2
c) CuO
d) MgO_2

e) NaCl
f) $CuSO_4$
g) $CaCo_3$
h) NH_3
i) Cl_2
j) H_2SO_4
k) CO_2
l) CH_4

Q2 b) NH_3
c) carbon dioxide
d) H_2O water
e) N_2 nitrogen
f) HCl

Q3 a) copper sulphide, copper oxide, sulphur dioxide, carbon dioxide
b) copper, oxygen, sulphur, carbon
c) i) False
ii) True

Pages 100-101 — Questions on Separating Substances

Q1 coal — M, water — C, air — M, carbon dioxide — C, crude oil — M, a cup of tea — M, pure salt — C, concrete — M, ketchup — M, sulphur — E, bromine — E, rust — C, sugar — C, magnesium — E

Q2 In order: E, C, D, E, E, F and E

Q3 Weigh a sample of lawn sand and a dried filter funnel with its filter paper. Mix the sample with water. Filter. Wash the filtrate through with distilled water to remove all fertiliser. Dry the filter funnel, paper and sand taking care not to lose any sand. Reweigh to find weight of sand and calculate % of original sample. Repeat and average. Recrystallising fertiliser is an alternative method.

Q4 a) Y
b) It travelled the furthest.

Q5 a) 2
b) Kate, Simon, Theo, Chris
c) Paul
d) Paul's ink has the same colours as the note.

Section Eleven — Metals and Non-Metals

Pages 102-104 — Questions on the Properties of Metals

Q1 E.g. good thermal conductor, high melting point

Q2 Electrical conductivity, low density

Q3 Steel and tin/aluminium. Magnets could lift steel cans off conveyor belt. The property used is magnetism.

Q4 Brass: copper/zinc
Stainless steel: chromium/copper
Titanium alum: titanium/aluminium
Coinage silver: nickel/copper

Q5 a) i) oxide
ii) oxide
iii) oxide
iv) oxide
b) Blue/purple meaning pH is greater than 7.

Q6 sonority, rigidity, strength, density, electrical conductivity, reflects, thermal conductivity, ductility/strength

Q7 1. non-metallic
2. metallic
3. metallic

Q8 yes, yes, yes, yes, no, no

Q9 Metals would bend. Non-metals would break (posing threat to health + safety).

Pages 105-107 — Questions on the Properties of Non-Metals

Q1 a) and b)

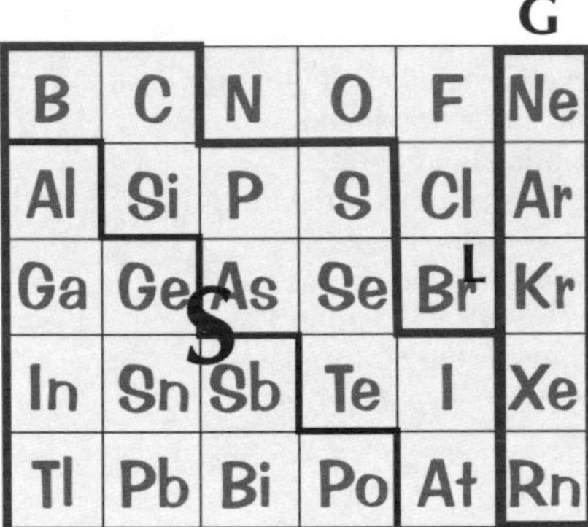

c) The densities of non-metals tends to be lower than those of metals.

Q2 a) carbon
b) It breaks.
c) Lack of ductility.
Layers of carbon atoms will slide past each other giving lubricating properties. It is also a good electrical conductor.

Q3 Sulphur — No, Carbon — No, Chloride — No, Silicon — No, Iodine — No

Q4 E.g. very strong/hard / high melting point.

Q5 It tends to be low.

Q6 yellow → red. Oxides are acidic.

Q7 a) Non metal — it has an acidic oxide, it is a non-conductor, it has a low melting point, it is brittle, it is non-magnetic.
b) Sulphur — as for Q
Iron:
A — conductor of electricity
B — ductile
C — no gaseous product
D — burnt fingers
E — magnetic

Section Twelve — Chemical Change

Pages 108-109 — Questions on Chemical Change

Q1 a) combustion
b) heat
c) endothermic
d) mass
e) ice

f) catalyst
g) alkali
h) limestone
i) copper sulphate
j) heat
k) aluminium
l) neutralise
m) glucose
n) electricity
The phrase is chemical change.

Q2 Melting is a physical change because it can easily be reversed.

Q3 a) 25 – 24.65 = 0.35g
b) It has lost weight.
c) Carbon dioxide is formed which escapes as a gas. This accounts for the change in mass.
d) calcium carbonate → calcium oxide + carbon dioxide
e) thermal decomposition
f) Delicate balances can be damaged by heat.

Q4 a) It is exothermic.
b) Not easily.

Page 110— Questions on Reduction of Metal Ores

Q1 a) carbon
b) **carbon** + iron oxide → **iron** + **carbon dioxide**
c) Reaction rates are high and the product is liquid.
d) Solid sand would remain in the iron, ruining it. Liquid slag floats on the iron and can be easily removed.
e) If the apparatus was set up as shown and heated strongly for 15-30 minutes, the bottom of the crucible will glow. After cooling, the contents can be examined for shiny lead.

Page 111— Questions on Combustion

Q1 a) A = thistle funnel
B= delivery tube
b) i) Causes condensation in U-tube
ii) Allows detection of carbon dioxide.
c) i) A clear liquid (water) which has condensed.
ii) It will go cloudy, showing that carbon dioxide is produced.
d) It shows that carbon dioxide is produced with something else that is probably water.
e) The same result.
f) Heat and light.

Pages 112-113— Questions on Useful Chemical Reactions

Q1 a) It produces a fair test and allows comparison of changes in volume.
b) Weights will remain almost unchanged as nothing is added and only a little CO_2 escapes.
c) The dough at 40 °C will rise the most and the dough in the ice will rise the least.
d) It is volatile and will boil off.
e) fermentation
f) Carbon dioxide is used in bread making. Carbon dioxide and alcohol are used in beer and wine making.

Q2
1. acid
2. neutralise
3. digest
4. kill
5. germs
6. enzymes
7. salt
8. water
9. alkaline
10. calcium hydroxide
11. burning

The mystery word is indigestion

Pages 114-115 — Questions on Equations

Q1 a) Reactants: magnesium, oxygen
b) Products: carbon dioxide
c) Reactants: lead oxide, carbon
Products: lead oxide, carbon dioxide
d) Reactants: sodium hydroxide, hydrochloric acid
Products: sodium chloride, water
e) Reactants: calcium carbonate
Products: calcium oxide, carbon dioxide

Q2 a) iron sulphide
b) iron oxide
c) magnesium oxide
d) sulphur dioxide
e) hydrogen dioxide
f) magnesium sulphide
g) aluminium chloride
h) hydrogen iodide
i) carbon dioxide
j) iron bromide

Q3 a) potassium + **chlorine** → potassium chloride
b) iron + **sulphur** → iron sulphide
c) **lead** + oxygen → lead oxide
d) **calcium** + oxygen → calcium oxide

Q4 a) **sodium** + **chlorine** → sodium chloride
b) **sodium** + **sulphur** → sodium sulphide
c) **magnesium** + oxygen → magnesium **oxide**
d) calcium + **oxygen** → **calcium** oxide

Section Thirteen — Reactivity of Metals

Pages 116-117 — Questions on Reactivity of Metals

Q1 potassium, magnesium, aluminium, zinc, iron, copper

Q2 a) In a fair test, only one variable should be altered at a time. Different metals are used so everything else must be the same.

Section Thirteen — Reactivity of Metals

b)

Metal in copper sulphate solution	Observation after half an hour
magnesium	lots of copper on Mg
copper	no change
iron	a little copper on Fe
zinc	some copper on Zn

c) zinc + copper sulphate → copper + zinc sulphate
d) magnesium
e) No change. Silver is less reactive than copper and will not displace it.

Q3 a)

Metal	Reaction with iron sulphate
(i) Magnesium	✓
(ii) Aluminium	✓
(iii) Iron	
(iv) Lead	
(v) Copper	

b) iron
c) aluminium oxide

Pages 118-119— Questions on Displacement Reactions

Q1 a) magnesium
b) iron
c) lead
d) reactive
e) colourless
f) iron
The mystery metal is silver.

Q2 a)

Metal ↓ / Salt solution →	magnesium sulphate	aluminium sulphate	zinc sulphate	iron sulphate	copper sulphate
magnesium		✓	✓	✓	✓
aluminium			✓	✓	✓
zinc				✓	✓
iron					✓
copper					

b) Salt solution of copper and silver.
c) From the table, magnesium is the most reactive. (From the reactivity series generally at this level potassium is the most reactive.)

Q3 a)

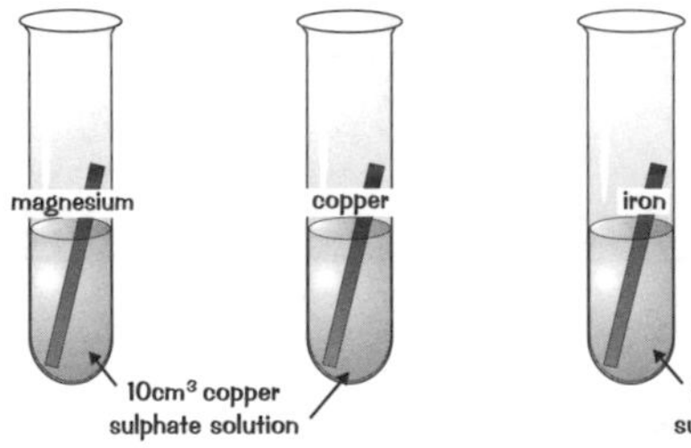

b) X — because they knew it was less reactive than iron so trying copper might yield more information.
c) lead
d) The copper was displaced from its salt.
e) magnesium, iron, X, copper

Pages 120-122 — Questions on Metal Extraction

Q1 iron — reduced by coke
copper — unreactive but purified by electrolysis
potassium — electrolysis
gold — very unreactive, found on its own
magnesium — electrolysis
Q2 C
Q3 It is rare and was adopted as the basis for monetary systems because of its rarity, appearance and low reactivity.
Q4 Patricia. Highly reactive metals are keener to remain as compounds and require more energy to convert them into metals.
Q5 a) compound
b) Order of apparatus — C, B, D, A
Labels:
i) delivery tube
ii) pestle and mortar
iii) lime water
iv) carbon dioxide
v) carbon
vi) clay poy tripod
vii) crucible
c) reduction
d) thermal decomposition
Q6 a) D, B, C, A
b) filtration, evaporation
c) anode and cathode
d) sodium and chlorine

Pages 123-125 — Questions on Rusting

Q1 a) red/brown
b) It had rusted.
c) i) 50.47 – 50.10 = **0.37 g**
increase
ii) The weight of oxygen and water incorporated into the rust.
d) iron + oxygen → **iron oxide**
e) oxidation/corrosion
Q2 Water at the bottom of the pool will not have much dissolved oxygen which is needed for rusting.
Q3 a) painting, plating
b) painting
c) plating
d) oiling
e) plating
f) plating, painting
g) alloying
Q4 They are lighter and last longer. They can also be left unpainted.
Q5 a) corrode
b) oxygen
c) paint
d) plastic
e) extracted
f) reactivity series
The word is copper.
Q6 a) E.g. use nails of the same sort. / Use the same amount of metal. / Use the same water.
b) The ones with copper and lead and possibly aluminium.
c) They are so reactive that they would corrode away too fast and might even be dangerously reactive.

Section Fourteen — Acids and Alkalis

Pages 126-129 — Questions on Reactions of Metals with Acids

Q1 a) A
b) The acid's juice will corrode the zinc.
c) Copper is lower in the reactivity series than hydrogen so does not react.
d) Zinc salt would have contaminated it.
e) copper

Q2 a)

Metal	Observation of reaction after		
	2 min	4min	6min
Zinc	Moderate reaction	Moderate reaction Gas given off	Moderate reaction
Magnesium	Fast reaction Gas evolved	Reaction slowing	Fast reaction now finished
Iron	Few bubbles Slow reaction	Few bubbles Slow reaction	Few bubbles Slow reaction
Copper	No reaction	No reaction	No reaction

b) magnesium
c) high temperature

Q3 a) i) bung
ii) thistle funnel
iii) delivery tube
iv) gas jar
b) i) 1.5 cm^3
ii) 4 cm^3
c) more quickly

Q4 a) The reaction will be so violent it will pose safety risks. Even touching the solution is dangerous.
b) Lots of bubbles and the gas ignites.
c) sodium + hydrochloric acid → **sodium chloride + hydrogen**
d) $NaCl_{(aq)}$

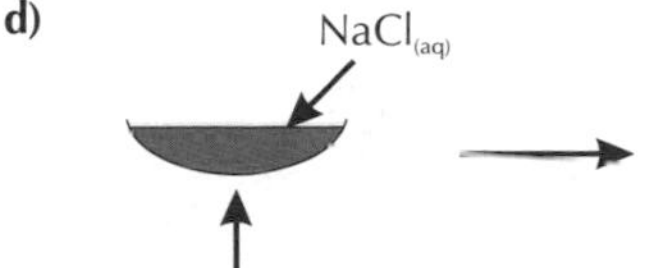

Crystalization

heat

Q5
1. potassium
2. sodium
3. calcium
4. magnesium
5. aluminium
6. zinc
7. iron

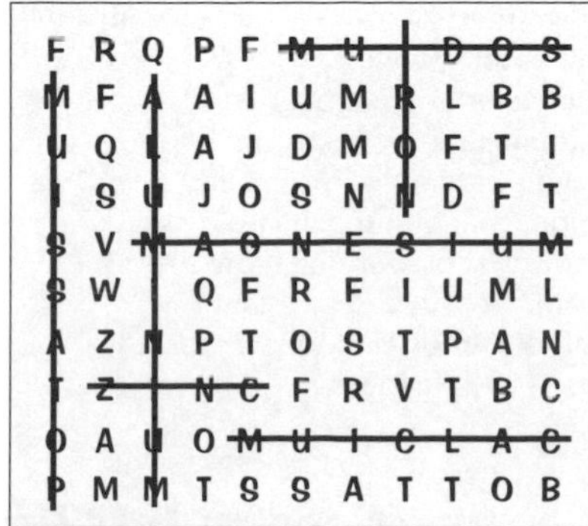

Q6

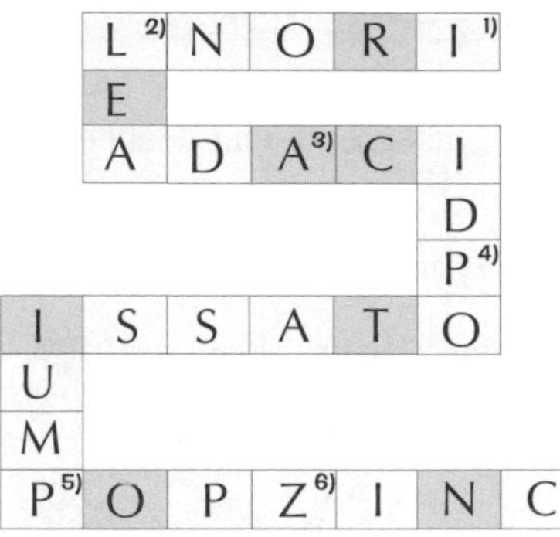

The mystery word is reaction.

Q7 a) Potassium + Sulphuric Acid → Potassium sulphate + water
b) Sodium + Hydrochloric Acid → Sodium chloride + water
c) Iron + Sulphuric Acid → Iron sulphate + hydrogen
d) Copper + Hydrochloric Acid → No reaction — metal too unreactive.
e) Magnesium + Sulphuric Acid → Magnesium sulphate + hydrogen

Section Fourteen — Acids and Alkalis

Pages 130-131 — Questions on Acids and Alkalis

Q1
Apple — acid
Orange — acid
Lemonade — acid
Bleach — alkali
Water — neutral
Washing powder — alkali

Q2

pH Scale	1	2	3	4	5	6	7	8	9	10	11	12	13	14
	i)				ii)		iii)			v)				iv)

Q3

Useful Substance	pH value	Colour with Universal Indicator	Acid, Alkaline or Neutral
a) Hydrochloric acid in stomach	pH1	red	strong acid
b) Smelling salts (phew!) ammonia	pH10	dark blue	medium alkali
c) Kitchen cleaner	pH13	purple	strong alkali
d) Tap water	pH7	green	neutral
e) Washing up liquid	pH8	blue	weak alkali

Q4 a) E.g. litmus — it is red in acids and blue in alkalis.
b) It gives the strength of the acid and alkali as well.

Q5 a) bacteria
b) high, hydrogen
c) hydrogen
d) corrosive
e) citric acid
f) sour
g) 1 and 6
h) 1
i) 6

Q6 a) False
b) False
c) True
d) False
e) False
f) False

Section Fourteen — Acids and Alkalis

Pages 132-133 — Reactions of Acids and Alkalis

Q1 a) The tube should not be in the liquid in Tube A.
b) i) limewater
ii) CO_2
c) Metal carbonate + acid → salt + **water** + **carbon dioxide**
Q2 a) The acid and alkali react to make a salt and water.
b) No, because they are both acids. You need an alkali to neutralise an acid.
Q3 a)

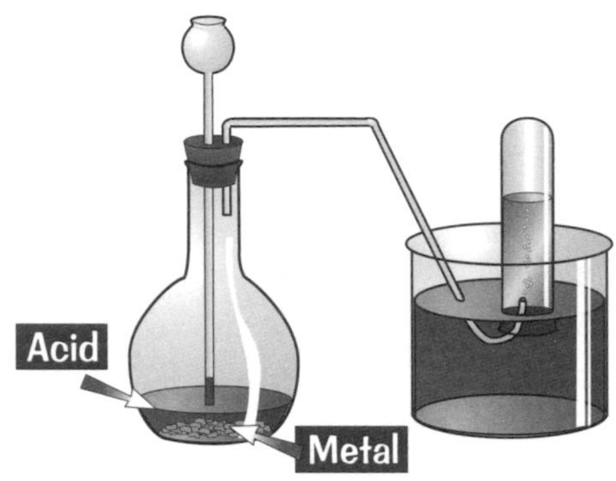

b) e.g. zinc
c) The 'squeaky pop' test.
Q4 a) corrosive, burn
b) 8, 14
c) 8
d) 14
e) bases, neutralise
f) bleach, soap flakes
Q5 sodium hydroxide, bleach, water, vinegar, hydrochloric acid
Q6 a) zinc + nitric acid → zinc nitrate + **hydrogen**
b) calcium carbonate + nitric acid → calcium nitrate + **carbon dioxide** + **water**
c) hydrochloric acid + sodium → **sodium chloride** + **hydrogen**

Pages 134-135 — Questions on Indigestion

Q1 a) i) To compare equal masses of all tablets to ensure a fair test.
ii) To make the tablets easier to dissolve.
iii) So that all the tablet can react with the acid — it mimics the conditions in the stomach.
b) They used equal amounts of water and the same masses of tablets in each experiment.
c) Universal Indicator
d) Indicator turns green when enough acid has been added.
e) Tablet X — 14.5
Tablet Y — 20
Tablet Z — 22.5
f) An average from two results is more reliable than the result from one.
g) Z — this one neutralises the largest amount of acid.
h) The strong alkali will kill the enzymes in the stomach.

Pages 136-137 — Questions on Useful Acid Reactions

Q1 a) **excess acid**
b) **neutralisation**
c) **enzymes**
d) **hydrochloric**
e) **metal**
f) **magnesium**
g) **salt**
The missing word is enzymes.
Q2 alkaline, acidic, rock, calcium carbonate, alkaline, acid, acidic, minerals, liming, neutralises
Q3 a)

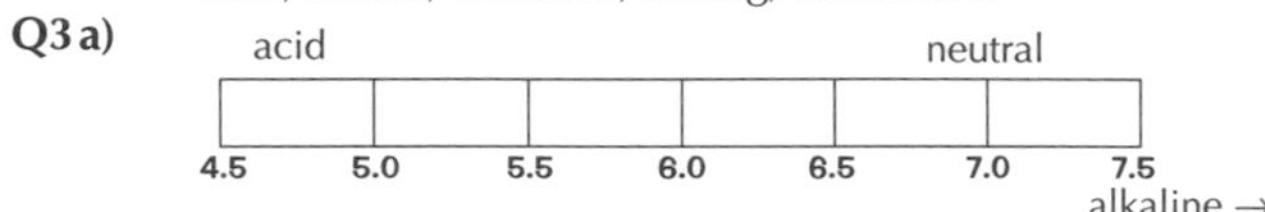

b) The soil is too acidic for onions to grow well, but the soil can be made neutral by adding lime to it.
Q4 a) Lime's pH is greater than 7.
b) It makes the soil more acidic so fewer plants will grow. It makes lakes more acidic, killing plants and animals.

Pages 138-140 — Questions on Acid Rain

Q1 marble, weathering, gases, sulphur dioxide, nitrogen, industry, car fumes, trees, plants, fish
Q2 a) limestone
b) carbon dioxide
c)

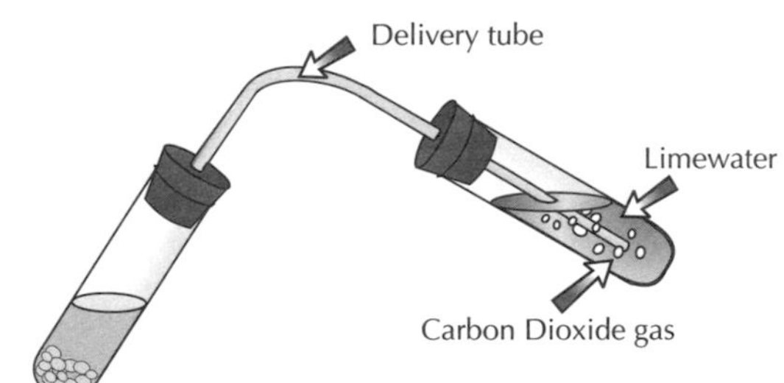

Q3 a) So that it is a fair comparison. All the graves will have been subjected to the same amount of weathering time.
b) Iron rusts and marble dissolves. Granite is resistant to weak acids.
c) Copper doesn't react very much with anything.
Q4 a) potatoes and parsley
b) broad beans and cabbage
c) By adding lime.
d) Eel and trout could live in fairly acidic water. Salmon, char and roach could not.
Q5 a) E.g. any one of, burning more fossil fuels / more volcanic activity / deforestation.
b) Levels of carbon dioxide will increase.

Page 141 — Questions on Less Useful Acid Reactions

Q1 a) The vinegar would react with the steel so the onions would taste bad.
b) i) To prevent the food from reacting with the steel.
ii) e.g. tin

Section Fifteen — Geological Change

Q2 a) To let light in to allow the cress grow.
b) The ensure a fair test and keep the soil damp.
c) Cress in A will grow more effectively than in B.
d) Acidic conditions restrict growth.
e) Water vapour in the air.

Pages 142-143 — Questions on Making Salts

Q1 a) neutralisation
b) pH7
c) i) Sodium hydroxide + **sulphuric acid** → sodium sulphate + water
ii) Sodium hydroxide + **nitric acid** → sodium nitrate + water
iii) Calcium hydroxide + **hydrochloric acid** → calcium chloride + water
iv) Calcium hydroxide + **sulphuric acid** → calcium sulphate + water
Q2 a) It helps the reaction happen.
b) To remove any remaining copper oxide.
c) Evaporate the water from the copper sulphate by gently heating the solution in an evaporating dish.
Q3 neutralisation, acid, alkali, water, alkali, indicator, Universal Indicator, green, sulphuric acid, chloride, nitrate
Q4 a) If a pure sample of salt is to be produced, then the right amounts of acid and alkali must be used.
b) Universal Indicator
c) You do not want the salt crystals to be green.
d) smaller, bigger

Section Fifteen — Geological Change

Pages 144-145 — Questions on Weathering Rocks

Q1 a) higher
b) The ice expands and the glass breaks.
Q2 a) they expand
b) they contract
c) the Sun
d) at night
e) the surfaces
f) onion skin weathering/exfoliation
g) Areas with great variations in temperature.
Q3 a) chemical
b) biological
c) physical
d) physical
e) biological
f) physical
Q4 a) There is more acidic rain in towns and cities.
b) The roots could grow through the foundations, causing damage.
c) Weathering breaks up cliffs.

Pages 146-147 — Questions on The Rock Cycle

Q1 a) transportation
b) exposure
c) depositing
d) weathering
e) burial/compression
f) melting
g) erosion
h) cooling
i) heat/pressure
Q2 a) True
b) True
c) False
d) False
e) False
f) True
g) True
h) False
i) False
Q3 a) Rocks formed from molten magma pushed up towards the surface.
b) Rocks formed from layers of sediment laid down in lakes and seas.
c) Rocks formed from existing rocks as a result of increased heat and pressure inside the Earth.
Q4

Type of rock or change	Number
IGNEOUS	1
SEDIMENTARY	10
METAMORPHIC	11
SEDIMENTS	8
MAGMA	13
Weathering	6
Transportation	7
Deposition	**14**
Exposure	**2**
Heat + pressure	3
Cooling	5
Melting	12
Burial + compression	9
Lava	4

Pages 148-149 — Questions on Rock Types

Q1 three, molten, cooled, volcano, crystals, minerals, randomly, layers, seas, millions, minerals, fossils, age, older, changes, heat, pressure, long, crystals, layers
Q2 uplift and weathering
Q3 Igneous rocks are formed from interlocking crystals. Sedimentary rocks are only cemented together so are less resistant to weathering.

Q4

Rock	Igneous	Sedimentary	Metamorphic
Basalt	✓		
Chalk		✓	
Slate			✓
Grit		✓	
Granite	✓		
Marble			✓
Breccia		✓	
Obsidian	✓		
Pumice	✓		
Sandstone		✓	
Marl		✓	
Quartzite			✓

Pages 150-152 — Questions on Recognising Rock Types

Q1 a) Layers of eroded rock are laid down over millions of years and compressed/buried and cemented together.
b) 1 — it's on the surface.
c) 5 — it's the deepest layer.
d) From molten magma which has cooled.
e) Basalt — it has the smallest average size crystals.
f) Basalt — near the surface.
Rhyolite — medium distance from the surface.
Syenite — furthest from the surface.
g) i) extrusive igneous rock
ii) intrusive igneous rock
h) E.g. bubbles would be seen / a reaction would take place.
i) Yes. It is chemically identical so it would react with the acid.
j) metamorphic rock
k) marble
l) calcium carbonate + hydrochloric acid → calcium chloride + water + carbon dioxide

Section Sixteen — Basic Skills

Page 153 — Questions on Common Physics Apparatus

Q1 B
Q2 J
Q3 D
Q4 A
Q5 H
Q6 C
Q7 I
Q8 E
Q9 K
Q10 F
Q11 B
Q12 G

Pages 154-155 — Questions on Reading Scales

Q1 a) 0.8 A
b) 0.7 V
Q2 a) 6203 J
b) 6 kJ
Q3 a) Pa
b) 177 Pa
Q4 a) 1.5 kPa
b) It is still measuring atmospheric pressure.
Q5 a) 8 N
b) gravity
Q6 a) 14 minutes, 10 seconds
b) 5 minutes, 50 seconds
Q7 a) 4 kN
b) 3 minutes
c) 133 mm
d) 2 MW
e) 13 J
f) 9854 kA

Page 156 — Questions on Units and Equations

Q1

Quantity	Voltage	Force	Speed	Frequency	Current
Standard Unit	volt	newton	m/s	hertz	amp

Q2

Standard Unit	ohms	joules	kilograms	pascals	seconds
Quantity	resistance	energy	mass	pressure	time

Q3 a) kilometres, km
b) milliwatt, mW
c) megajoule, MJ
d) millisecond, ms
e) newton, N
f) kilovolt, kV

Q4

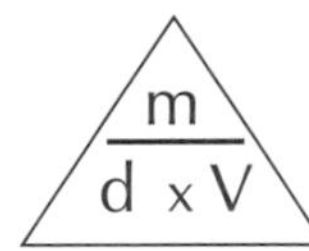

Section Seventeen — Electricity

Page 157 — Questions on Electricity and Conductors

Q1 Any five of, e.g. toaster / kettle / iron / fridge / TV / HiFi.
Q2 E.g. toaster, kettle, iron and fridge convert electrical to heat / TV is electrical to light and sound / HiFi is electrical to sound.
Q3 Candle. It converts chemical energy not electrical.
Q4 Any one of, e.g. battery / dynamo.
Q5 a) Electricity will only flow if you have a **complete** circuit.
b) A complete circuit has **no** gaps in it.
c) Electricity can only flow through **a conductor**.
Q6 All **metals** are conductors, but not all **conductors** are metals.

Section Seventeen — Electricity

Q7 A working circuit must contain a power supply or battery.
A complete circuit does not have an open switch in it.

Q8 Electric current is the flow of charge like the flow of water.

Pages 158-159 — Questions on Static Charge

Q1 a) Materials that you can charge up by rubbing are types of **insulator**.
b) Rubbing causes **friction** between a duster and a polythene rod.
c) There are **two** types of charge.
d) The names of different types of charge are **positive** and **negative**.
e) Positively charged objects will attract **negatively** charged objects.

Q2 Place the plastic rod over little bits of paper and see if they are attracted to the rod. If they are, the rod is charged.

Q3 a) True
b) False
c) False
d) True
e) True
f) False
g) False
h) True

Q4 It is negatively charged.

Q5

	Charge 1	Charge 2	Force between
1	Positive	Positive	Repel
2	Positive	Negative	Attract
3	Positive	Uncharged	Attract
4	Negative	Positive	Attract
5	Negative	Negative	Repel
6	Negative	Uncharged	Attract

a) It is the same as the second row.
b) Likes charges **repel**, unlike charges **attract**.

Q6 a) The rod is charged and it attracts the uncharged pieces of paper.
b) The balloon is charged and it attracts the uncharged wall.
c) A charge opposite to that of the object is induced on the electroscope plate. The leaf is left with the same charge as the object, so they separate due to repulsion.

Pages 160-162 — Questions on Electric Current in Circuits

Q1

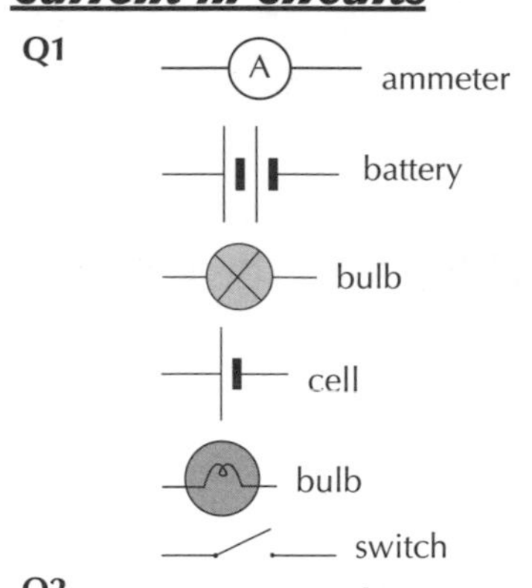

Q2

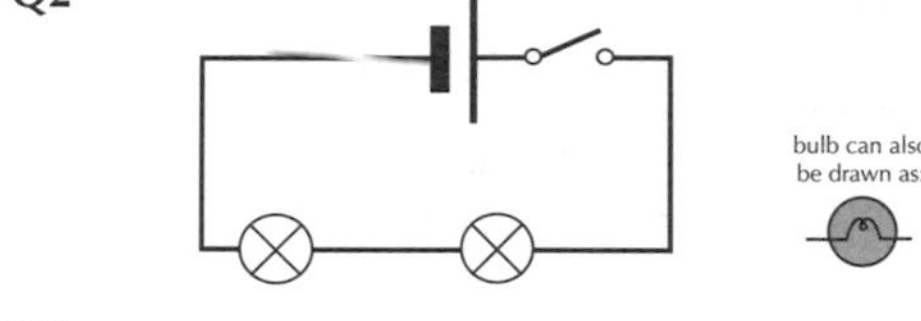

Q3

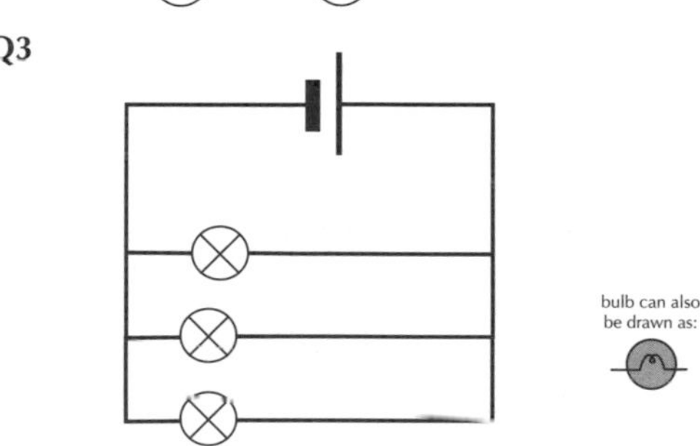

Q4 see diagram above
Q5 the amp (ampere)
Q6 A
Q7 ammeter
Q8

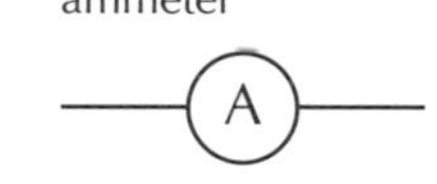

Q9

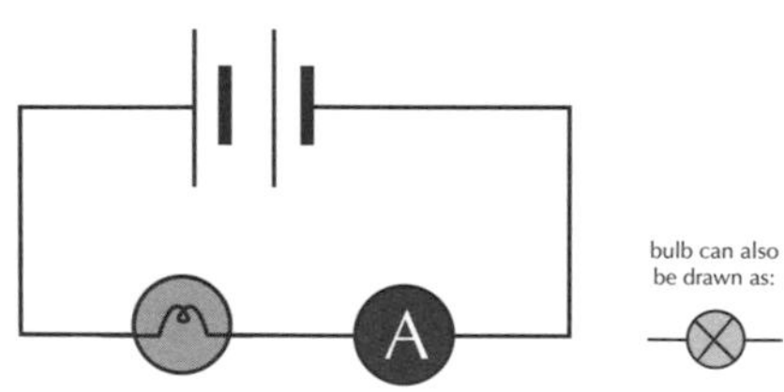

Q10 series
Q11 It would be increased.
Q12a) They are dimmer.
b) It would stay the same.
Q13a) False
b) True
c) True
d) True
e) False
Q14 Conventional current flows from positive to negative, but electrons flow the opposite way.
a) parallel
b) series

Section Seventeen — Electricity

Q15 Pump — Battery
Pipes — Wires
Water Flow — Electric current
Radiator — Heater

Q16 We are paying for the energy of moving electrons.

Q4 a) 6 A
b) 3 A
c) Resistance due to different filament thicknesses.
d) 4 V
e) i) False
ii) True
iii) False

Pages 163-164 — Questions on Series Circuits

Q1 a) cell
b) wires
c) switch
d) ammeter
e) bulb
Q2 a) cell — provides the electricity
b) wires — complete the circuit
c) switch — turns circuit on and off
d) ammeter — measures current through the circuit
e) bulb — provides light
Q3 2 A
Q4 2 A
Q5 The current is the same at all points in the series circuit.
Q6 The bulbs would be dimmer.
Q7 The bulbs would be brighter.
Q8 More **voltage** in a series circuit means there is more push for the charge and so **more** current flows, making the bulb **brighter**. More bulbs in a series circuit means there is more **resistance** to the flow of current, so **less** current flows, making the bulb **dimmer**.
Q9 dimmer, the same, brighter
Q10
1. 2 A
2. 4 A
3. 1 A
4. 6 A

Q11 insulator
Q12 To measure current passing through a component.
Q13 more = brighter, less = dimmer

Pages 165-166 — Questions on Parallel Circuits

Q1 a) No
b) Yes
c) No
d) Yes
e) Yes
f) short circuit
g) same
Q2 a) The other lamp is normal.
b) A and B are bright.
c) A and B are normal.
Q3 a) False
b) False
c) True
d) True
e) False

Pages 167-170 — Questions on Magnets

Q1 a) Any one of, e.g. a nail made from iron / a coin made from nickel / a spring made from steel.
b) Any one of, e.g. a pencil made from wood / a ring made of gold / a bracelet made of copper.
c) Set C
Q2 any one of, e.g. nickel / iron / steel / cobalt / zinc
Q3 It retains its magnetism.
Q4 Test all with a magnet — the coins attracted contain nickel.
Q5 Materials which are attracted to a magnet are called m**agnetic** materials. They all contain one of three elements: **iron**, **cobalt** or **nickel**. If a magnetic material is magnetised it becomes a **magnet**.
Q6 magnetic material, e.g. iron filings
Q7 bar magnet

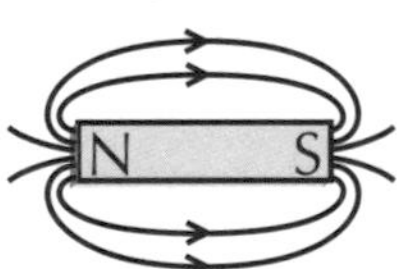

Q8 a) iron filings
b) compass
c) strong field
Q9

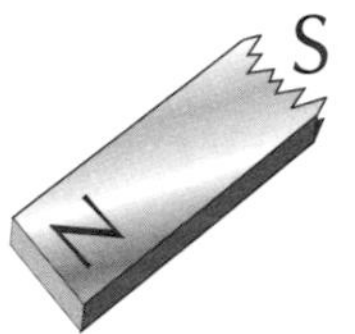

Magnetic poles always come in p**airs**.
The broken ends of the magnet will a**ttract** each other.
The broken end of one piece will **repel** the unbroken end of the other.

Q10 A N-pole with attract a S-pole.
A N-pole will attract a piece of unmagnetised steel.
A S-pole will attract a N-pole.
Q11 Put the engine both ways around on the south end. If it repels then it's magnetised and is an S disc.
Q12 Any magnet has **two** "ends" called **poles**. Opposite poles **attract** but like poles **repel**. The area around a magnet is known as the magnetic **field**. The stronger the magnet, the **stronger** the field.
Q13 It's a south pole.
Q14 You only need a magnet and a piece of magnetic material for the two to be **pulled** together. For two magnets to **attract/repel** or **repel/attract** each other, they must be suitably orientated.

Section Eighteen — Forces

Q15 1. A — north, B — south
2. A — south, B — north
3. A — south, B — north

Q16 1. c
2. b
3. a

Pages 171-173 — Questions on Electromagnets

Q1 a) a bar magnet
b) It would reverse.
c) It would increase.
d) The field lines would be closer together.
Q2 Inserting an iron metal core will increase the strength of the magnetic field.
Changing the direction of the current will swap the poles of the magnetic field.
Increasing the number of coils of wire will increase the strength of the magnetic field.
Increasing the current flow will make the magnetic field stronger.
Q3 Electromagnets can be turned on and off.
Q4 Toaster — heating
Drill — magnetic
Iron — heating
Light bulb — heating
Blender — magnetic
Q5 b) This causes a **current** to flow in the **input** circuit.
c) This makes the coil become an **electromagnet**.
d) The coil then **attracts** the iron lever.
e) The lever tips and the contacts **touch** each other.
f) This causes a **circuit** to flow in the **output** circuit.
g) This current makes the **heater** work.
Q6 A relay uses a **small** current in one circuit to switch on a much **larger** current in another circuit.
Q7 b) There is a **current** in the coil.
c) The coil becomes an **electromagnet**.
d) The electromagnet **attracts** the spring armature.
e) The clanger moves away from the **bell**.
f) The contacts separate and the circuit is **broken**.
g) The armature **springs** back and the clanger hits the bell.
h) The contacts **close** the circuit.
i) Current then **flows** in the circuit.
j) And then the process **repeats** itself.
Q8 **Nickel**, **Repel**, **Strength**, **Core**, **South**, **Iron**, **North**, **Motor**, **Relay**, **Filings**, **Needle**, **Field**, **Cobalt**.
Word — electromagnet

Section Eighteen — Forces

Pages 174-177 — Questions on Forces

Q1 a) Forces are measured in **newtons**.
b) **Weight** is the name given to the force of gravity acting on you.
c) A plastic rod will **attract** bits of paper because of an **electrostatic** force.
d) The force which makes things float is called **buoyancy**.
e) The force between two magnets is a **magnetic** force and can make them **attract/repel** or **repel/attract**.
f) Water droplets are held together by **surface tension**.
g) **Friction** between a moving object and the surface it moves on is a force which slows the object down.
Q2 a) accelerates
b) slows down
c) accelerates
d) stationary
e) steady speed
f) slows down
Q3 If an object has an unbalanced force acting on it, it will **speed** up, **slow** down, or change **direction**. If an object has **balanced** forces acting on it, it will either move at a **constant** speed in the same **direction**, or, if it was stationary to start with, it will remain **stationary**.
Q4 The object would begin to rotate.
Q5 a) Mass is measured in **kg**.
b) Weight is a **force** and is measured in **N**.
c) One kilogram weighs approximately **10** newtons on earth.
Q6

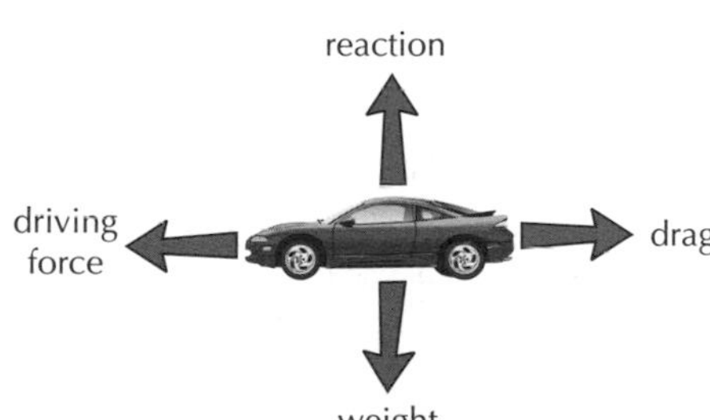

Q7 a)

Mass on Earth	Weight on Earth (N)	Mass on the Moon	Weight on the Moon (N)
2kg	2 × 10 = 20 N	2 kg	2 × 1.6 = 3.2 N
0.1kg	1 N	0.1 kg	0.16 N
500g	5 N	500 g	0.8 N
1000kg	10 000 N	1000 kg	1600 N
10g	0.1 N	10 g	0.016 N

b) The force of gravity is greater on the Earth than the Moon.
c) 12.5 N
d) D
e) A
f) The satellite would move in a straight line if balanced forces acted on it.
Q8 Tension, compression and shear.
When an object is being stretched it is said to be in **tension**.
When an object is being squashed it is said to be in **compression**.

Section Eighteen — Forces

Q9

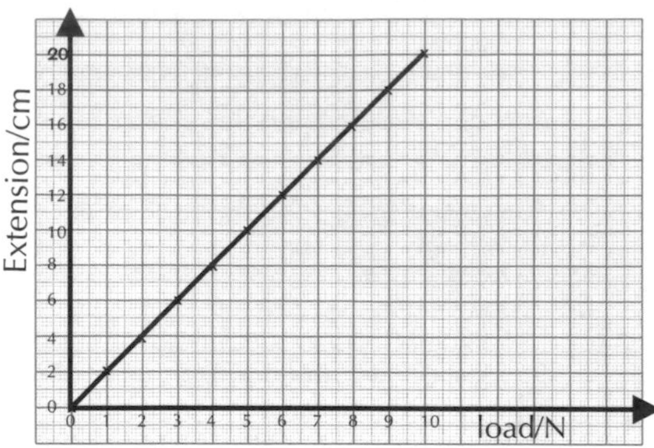

The larger the load, the **larger the extension**.

Pages 178-180 — Questions on Speed

Q1 a) Speed is usually measured in **m/s**.
b) Average speed is worked out from dividing **distance** by **time**.
c) An increase in speed is called **acceleration**.
d) A decrease in speed is called **deceleration**.
e) To change speed you need to have an **unbalanced** force acting.
Q2 The average speed over the whole journey was 40 mph, but at any specific time the car could have been stopped or going above 40 mph, etc.
Q3 speed = distance × time — s = d ÷ t
time = distance ÷ speed — t = d ÷ s
distance = speed × time — d = s × t
Q4 Velocity is speed in a named direction. Speed has no specific direction.
Q5

DISTANCE (m)	TIME (s)	SPEED (m/s)
10	5	2
0.5	2	0.25
1,000	10	100
20	0.1	200
500	50	10
48	4	12
1	0.01	100
10	50	0.2
225	15	15
200	10 000	0.02

Q6

DISTANCE	TIME	SPEED
50km	18 000 s	10km/h
2m	100 years	2cm per year
150,000,000km	500s	300 000 km/s
1km	333 s	3m/s
9.46 × 10 m	1 year	300,000,000m/s
1km	20 s	50m/s
600m	1 minute	10 m/s
72km	2h	10 m/s
360km	3600 s	100m/s
360km	60 minutes	100m/s

Q7 a) The object is stationary.
b) The object is moving at a constant speed.
c) The cat is moving at 0.5 m/s.
The cat is stationary.
The cat is moving at 1 m/s.
The car is moving at 2 m/s backwards.

Pages 181-183 — Questions on Air Resistance and Friction

Q1 a) Friction is a type of **force**.
b) The force of friction is measured in **newtons**.
c) Friction always acts to make moving objects travel more **slowly**.
d) Friction occurs when two **rough** surfaces rub together.
e) Air and water both exert **decelerating** forces upon moving objects.
f) When an object moves through air the force of friction is called **drag**.
g) Friction forces in a fluid increases as an object travels more **quickly** through it.
h) As an object accelerates through the air, the force of friction will **increase**.
Q2 When the force of friction equals the accelerating force the object will **continue at the same speed**.
Q3 The chains give more friction between the wheels and the road, stopping the car from sliding on the ice.
Q4

Example of Friction	Friction should be...
A car tyre in contact with a road surface	high
A skater moving over the ice	low
Brake blocks pressing against a wheel rim	high
Rock climbing boots in contact with the rock	high

Q5 a) driving force
b) It will increase.
c) The frictional force has increased.
d) driving force
e) balanced
f) The speed is constant.
g) One of the forces must change.
h) Weight and the reaction from the ground.
Q6 a) The driving force can be decreased.
b) decrease
c) The car would need to be made more pointed, like a dart.
Q7 a) weight
b) drag
c) no
d) Drag increases with increasing speed.
e) B (drag)
f) It will decrease.
g) It will be constant.
Q8 a) They must have the same mass.
b) It is more viscous, causing slower speeds which are easier to time.
c) B. It is more aerodynamic than the others.

Pages 184-187 — Questions on Moments (Force and Rotation)

Q1 a) Any three of, e.g. car wheels, wind turbine blades, roundabout at a fayre.
b) The sails are rotating which means that they are moving in a **circle**.
c) The end of the sail travels f**aster** than the centre of it.
d) Each part of the sails takes the s**ame** time to complete one rotation.
e) The sails are rotating about a f**ulcrum**.
f) Another name for this point is a p**ivot**.

Section Eighteen — Forces

g) Overall the forces on the sails must be un**balanced**. The sails are rotating, implying an acceleration. This implies a force.

Q2

It will accelerate to the left.
It will accelerate downwards.
It will rotate anticlockwise.
It will rotate clockwise.
It will accelerate to the right.
It will accelerate upwards.

Q3 a) Moments are a measure of the **turning** effect of a force.

b) The moment is increased as the size of the force is **increased.**

c) The moment is also increased if the force acts at a **greater** distance from the **pivot**.

d) Moments are calculated using:
Moment = **F**orce x **D**istance

e) Moments are measured in **Nm**.

Q4 Multiply the force by the perpendicular distance from the pivot.

Q5 a) friction

b) Easier. A larger disc gives a larger moment which means the friction will be more effective.

Q6 a) 30 kg

b) 300 N

c) 300 N × 2 m = **600 Nm**

d) 400 N

e) 400 N × 2 m = **800 Nm**

f) clockwise

g) Aarun should move towards the pivot.

h) A seesaw will balance if the cl**ockwise** and anti-cl**ockwise** moments are equal.

Q7 It would be easier at the edge. Moment = force × distance, so if the DJ exerts the same force at both points, the further his fingers are from the middle, the greater the moment.

Q8 a) effort

b) weight (load)

c) pivot

d) 200 N

e) 10 cm = 0.1 m

f) 200 N × 0.1 m = **20 Nm**

g) 20 Nm

h) Effort = 20 Nm ÷ 0.5 m = **40 N** (to balance). To lift, the effort needs to be more than 40 N.

Q9

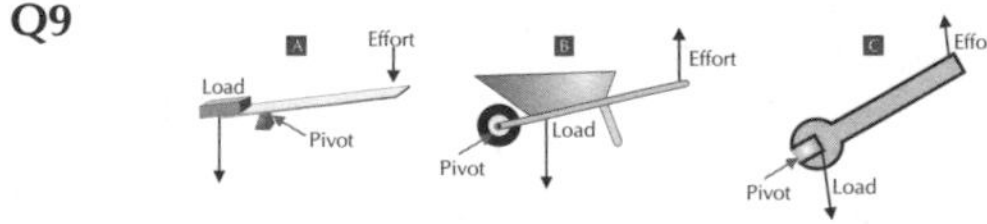

Pages 188-191 — Questions on Pressure

Q1 a) Pressure measures the **force** per unit **area**.

b) The more force there is the **greater** the pressure.

c) The greater the area over which the force acts, the **smaller** the pressure.

d) Pressure is worked out from dividing **force** by **area**.

e) Force is measured in **newtons**.

f) Area is measured in **m²**.

g) Pressure is measured in **pascals**.

Q2 a) She has not taken into account the shape of her shoes.

b) too big

c) For both her feet.

d) Area = 2 × 0.2 × 0.05 = **0.02 m²**
Pressure = (50 × 10) ÷ 0.02 = **25 000 Pa**

e) She could measure her shoes more accurately.

Q3 Pressure = Force ÷ Area
A = F ÷ p
Force = Pressure × Area

Q4 a) 120 N

b) 2 m × 3 m = **6 m²**

c) Pressure = 120 N ÷ 6 m² = **20 Pa**

d) Pressure = 100 N ÷ 2 m² = **50 Pa**

e) Smallest area = 1 m × 2 m = **2 m²**
Pressure = 120 N ÷ 2 m² = **60 Pa**

f) Smallest area = 1 m × 0.5 m = **0.5 m²**
Pressure = 100 N ÷ 0.5 m² = **200 Pa**

g) Total force = 120 N + 100 N = **220 N**
Pressure = 220 N ÷ 2 m² = **110 Pa**

Q5 a) For a given force, blunt scissors have a greater area so they give a lower pressure.

b) In the first case, there is a low pressure. In the second there is a high pressure and the finger is not a strong as the pin, resulting in an injury.

c) Caterpillar tracks have a large surface area compared to wheels, so the weight of the vehicle is spread over a larger area. This means a lower pressure and so the vehicle is less likely to sink.

Q6

Object	Area should be: (small / large)	Pressure will be: (small / large)
A knife to cut meat	small	large
Shoe heels that don't damage floors	large	small
A sewing needle	small	large
Tractor tyres for use on soft ground	large	small
Snow skis	large	small

Q7 Pressure = 900 N ÷ 0.1 m² = **9000 Pa**

Q8 a) The forces on a stationary object are **balanced.**

b) A name for the highest speed when falling is **terminal** velocity.

c) Force is measured in n**ewtons**.

d) The force of gravity on an object is its w**eight**.

e) A stretched spring is said to be in t**ension**.

f) A moment is the t**urning** effect of a force.

g) A force which slows things down is f**riction**.

h) Gases and liquids are both f**luids**.

i) Pressure = force ÷ a**rea**

j) The force that keeps boats afloat is buoyancy.

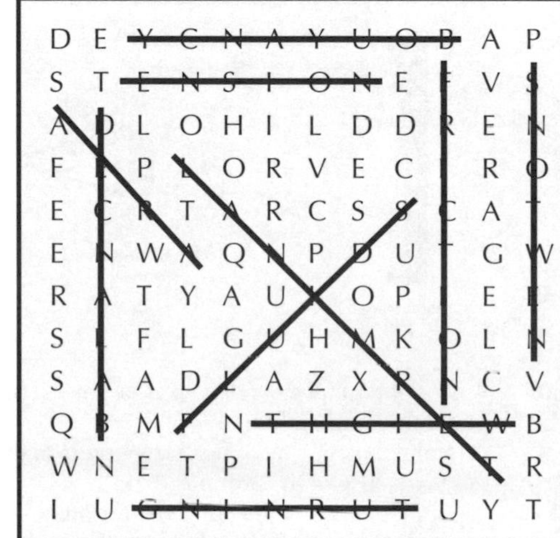

Section Nineteen — Light and Sound

Section Nineteen — Light and Sound

Pages 192-194 — Questions on Light

Q1 a) Light travels in s**traight** lines.
b) Light travels as a type of electromagnetic r**adiation**.
c) Light travels at a speed that is f**aster** than that of sound.
d) The speed of light in a vacuum is **300 000 000** m/s.
e) Some things can be seen through. These are said to be t**ransparent**.
f) Some things just don't let light through at all. These are called o**paque** materials.
g) Some things give out their own light. These are said to be l**uminous**.
h) All other things we see because they r**eflect** light.
i) For us to see something, light from it must enter our e**ye**.
j) Areas where light can't reach because something is in the way are called s**hadows**.
Q2 a) A window is **transparent**.
b) A mirror is **opaque**, **shiny**.
c) The Sun is **opaque**, **luminous**.
d) The Moon is **opaque**.
e) Air is **transparent**.
f) Greaseproof paper is **translucent**.
g) Water is **transparent**.
h) Carpet is **opaque**, **dull**.
i) Aluminium foil is **opaque**, **shiny**.
Q3 a) Most things are able to be seen because they **reflect** light into our eyes.
b) Objects with rough surfaces give a **diffuse** reflection.
c) Objects with smooth surfaces give a **regular** reflection.
d) Usually we think of using a flat mirror. This sort of mirror is called a **plane** mirror.
e) When we are thinking about reflections in a mirror, we are interested in two angles, the angle of **incidence** and the angle of **reflection**.
f) These angles are not measured from the mirror but from the **normal** line.
g) This line is at **90°** degrees to the mirror's surface.
Q4 a) It must block all or some of the light falling on it.
b) Light travels in straight lines.
Q5

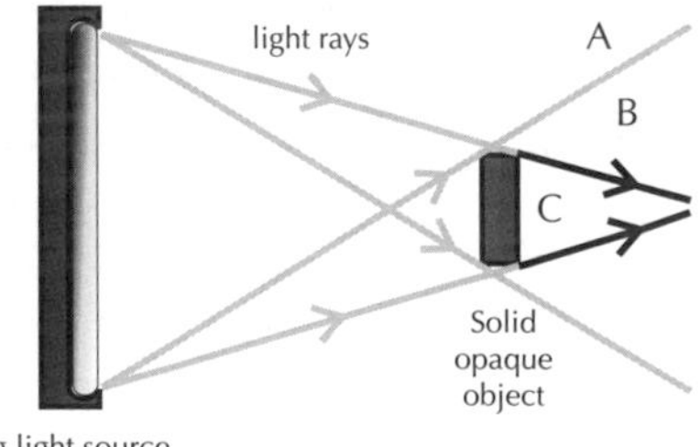

a) A is brighter than B and C. B is brighter than C.
b) penumbra and umbra
Q6 a) A total eclipse of the Sun. The Moon exactly covers the Sun's disc. On Earth it is dark.
b) A partial eclipse of the Sun. The Moon covers part of the Sun's disc. On Earth it is twilight.

Q7

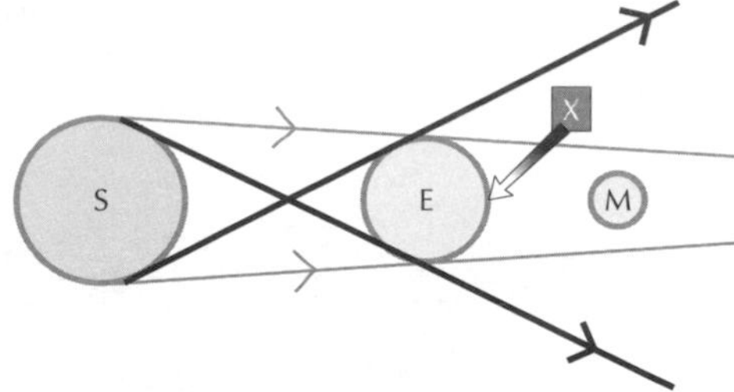

a) The full moon will look very dark (or copper).
b) The Moon.
Q8 The Moon moves through penumbra (turns pale) and then into umbra (turns dark). It appears copper from refracted sunlight.

Pages 195-196 — Questions on Reflection

Q1 a) Reflection of light and transmission of light.
b) Transparent objects transmit most light but opaque objects transmit none and reflect some (unless they are black). Shiny objects are smooth and reflect some light.
Q2 a) clouds (of small water droplets)
b) infrared radiation
c) On clear nights, heat (IR) escapes into space. A cloud layer reflects this heat back to Earth so the temperature drop is less.
Q3

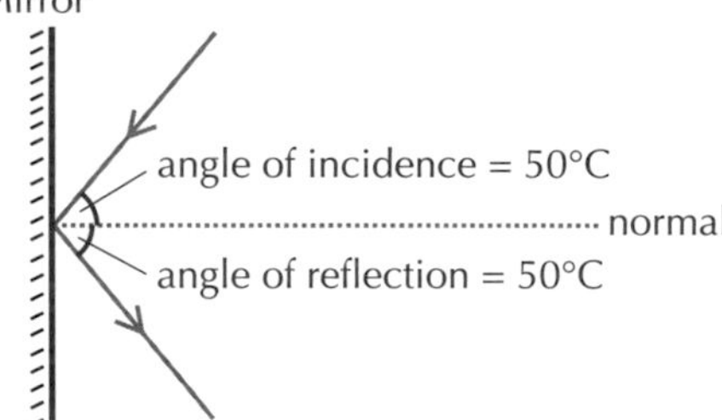

Pages 197-199 — Questions on Refraction

Q1 When light is travelling through a medium it travels in a **straight** line. When light moves from one medium into another, its speed **is** changed. In the new medium it continues to travel in a **straight** line, but with a new direction. This change happens because the speed of light is **different** in different materials. The name given to this effect is **refraction**.
Q2 B and D
Q3 When light moves from air to glass it will bend **towards** the normal. When it moves from glass to air it will bend **away from** the normal. If the light is travelling along the normal its direction **will not** be changed.

Section Nineteen — Light and Sound

Q4 a) and b)

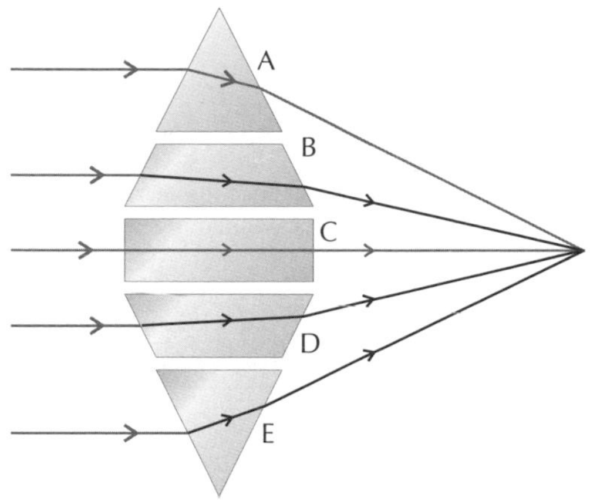

c) E.g. telescope, magnifying glass, spectacles, microscope, camera

Q5 **pRism**, **lEns**, **reFract**, **Ray**, **Angle**, **vaCuum**, **Towards**, **incIdence**, **nOrmal**, **deNsity**

Q6

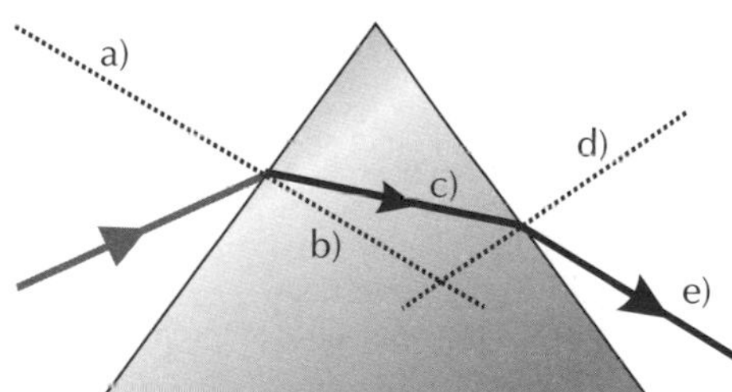

f) The light you see appears to come from the direction of the emergent ray, but it has really come from the direction it entered the prism.

Q7 He has shown the light ray from the fish bending towards the normal with the water surface. The ray should bend away from the normal.

Pages 200-203 — Questions on Colour

Q1 a) Light from the Sun and light bulbs is often called **white** light.

b) This light is made up from **many** different colours.

c) Different colours are caused by light having different **frequencies** and **wavelengths**.

d) The main colours making up sunlight are **red**, **orange**, **yellow**, **green**, **blue**, **indigo** and **violet**.

e) Light can be split into its colours using a **prism**.

f) This splitting is called **dispersion**.

g) The pattern of colours made like this is called a **spectrum**.

h) Our eyes can be fooled into seeing any of the different colours by mixing different amounts of just three of them. These three colours are **red**, **blue** and **green**.

i) These three colours are called the **primary** colours.

j) Mixing these three colours in equal amounts gives **white** light.

Q2 A post box is red because the paint on it **reflects** red light and **absorbs** all the other colours. A dandelion appears yellow because it absorbs **blue** light but reflects **red/green** and **green/red** light.

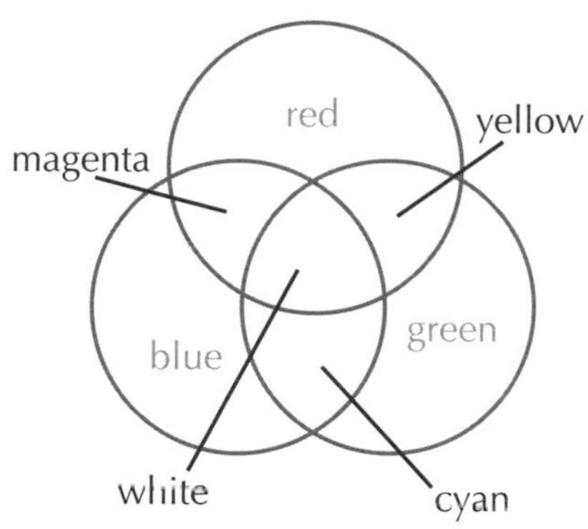

Q3 a) secondary colours

b) magenta

c) complimentary colours

Q4 a) They 'filter out' (absorb) certain colours in the light that pass through them.

b) Red filter **transmits** and **reflects** red light, but **absorbs** all other colours.

c)

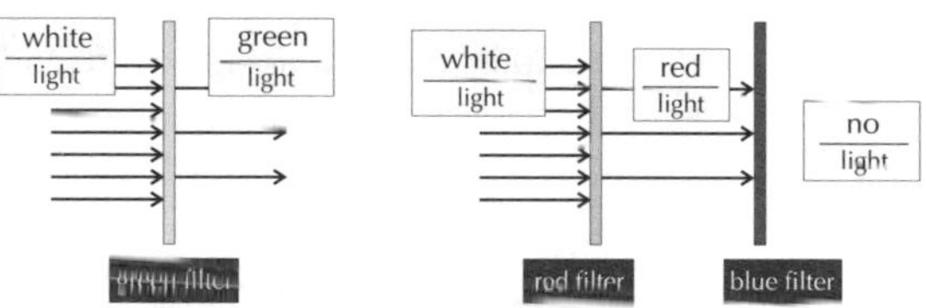

Q5 a)

Colour of cube	Colour of light	Colour cube seems to be
white	Red	Red
	Blue	Blue
	Green	Green
Red	Red	red
	blue	Black
	Green	black
Blue	red	Black
	blue	Blue
	Green	black
yellow	Red	Red
	Blue	Black
	Green	Green
Green	Red	black
	Blue	black
	Green	green

b) Yes. A filter only lets through light of a specific colour. E.g. a red cube illuminated by white light, seen through a blue filter will appear black.

c) Only red cars and yellow cars will appear the right colour under this light. E.g. blue cars will look black and white cars will look orange.

Q6 diffraction, incidence, dispersion, primary, luminous, reflection, transparent, plane, cyan, opaque, shadow, blue

Section Twenty — Earth and Beyond

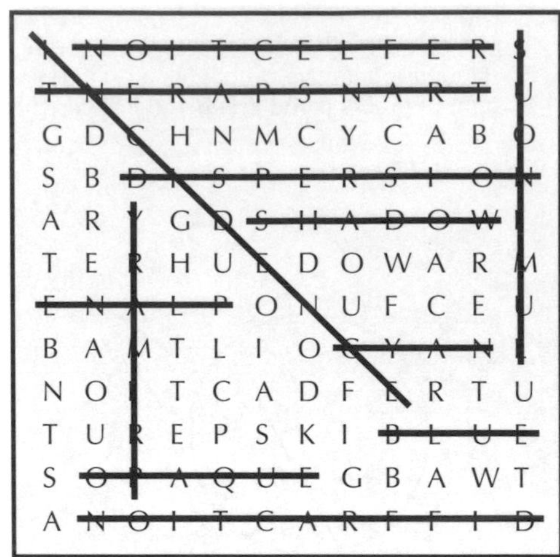

Pages 204-207 — Questions on Sound

Q1 a) The propagation of sound can be described in terms of motion of a **wave**.
b) Sound cannot travel through a **vacuum**.
c) Sound can travel through gases, **liquids/solids** and **solids/liquids**.
d) A high **frequency** of vibration makes a **high** pitched sound.
e) A large **amplitude** of vibration makes a **loud** sound.
f) Sound travels **less** quickly than light.
g) The speed of sound in air is about **330** m/s.
h) We hear sound when a sound wave causes our **eardrums** to vibrate.
i) Some sounds have too **high** a frequency to hear. These are called **ultrasound**.

Q2 Drum — drum skin
Guitar — guitar string
Flute — air
Keyboard — speakers (paper membrane)

Q3 a) It will vibrate faster (with a greater frequency).
b) It will vibrate faster (with a greater frequency).
c) Increasing the length decreases the frequency (and vice versa).
The pitch is lowered.
d) A high pitched note has a **high** frequency of vibration. A string will vibrate faster if it has **more** tension, is **shorter** or has **less** mass.

Q4 a) The vacuum pump removes air. The foam block stops sound from passing through the base.
b) As more air is removed, the sound of the bell gets quieter.
c) Sound cannot travel through a vacuum. In this case it needs air.

Q5 a) It will damage the fork.
b) The paper hums.
c) Ripples are made.
d) The glass may break.
e) It damages teeth.
f) A smaller fork will have a higher pitch.
g) Thinner prongs move faster.
h) They move too fast.
i) Reverberation of the air inside the box leads to amplification of the sound.
j) A — Long fork with box
B — Short fork with box
C — Short fork with no box
D — Long fork with no box

Q6 a) electrical
b) To produce sound.
c) That it is the same for each frequency.
d) To check that they really do hear sound when it is turned on.
e) Show them the oscilloscope reading.
f) A 20 - 20 000 Hz hearing range.

Pages 208-209 — Questions on Hearing

Q1 A — pinna
B — ear canal
C — eardrum
D — ossicles
E — semi-circular canals
F — cochlea
G — eustachian tube

Q2 a) It collects sound.
b) It channels sound to the eardrum.
c) It makes hearing more difficult.
d) a skin membrane
e) Semi-circular canals. It is responsible for our sense of balance.
f) To the back of the mouth/throat.

Q3 a) decibels (units of loudness)
b) E.g. noisy apparatus / people moving around.
c) P.E. and technology
d) Teachers are exposed to the noise all day.
e) Older people can't hear high frequencies as well as children.
f) Wooden surfaces do not absorb much sound. Sound is reflected around the room for longer than if other materials were used.

Section Twenty — Earth and Beyond

Pages 210-212 — Questions on Day, Night and the Four Seasons

Q1 a) D
b) K
c) J
d) G
e) Earth's rotation
f) higher

Q2 a) June 21st
b) Dec 21st
c) March/Sept 21st
d) June 21st
e) March 30th
f) June 21st
g) March 21st and Sept 21st

Q3 a) The height of the sun at noon increases.
b) 4.9 metres
c) longer
d) northwards

Q4 a) P and R
b) Q and U
c) U

Section Twenty One — Energy

Q5 a) false
b) true
c) true
d) false
e) false
f) true
g) false
h) true
i) true

Q6 a) The Earth spins on its **axis** in 24 hours.
b) We call this time one **day**.
c) It takes a **year** for the Earth to complete one revolution of the Sun.
d) We call the track followed by the Earth an **orbit**.
e) The tilt of the Earth's axis causes the **seasons**.
f) In summer, **days** last longer than **nights**.
g) There are **four** seasons every year.
h) In parts of Australia, some people eat their Christmas dinner on the **beach** because it's so warm there at that time.

Page 213 — Questions on the Moon

Q1 a) it reflects light from the Sun
b)

c) 5
d) 7
e) evening

Page 214 — Questions on Satellites and Gravity

Q1 a) C, D and F
b) no
c) the military, sailing, air travel and climbing

Q2 a) B
b) It is the same strength, but acts in the opposite direction.

Q3 a) 1
b) 2

Pages 215-216 — Questions on the Solar System

Q1 a) Uranus
b) Earth
c) Saturn
d) Mars
e) Mercury
f) Neptune
g) Mercury, Earth, Mars, Saturn, Uranus, Neptune
h) Venus and Jupiter
i) Jupiter

Q2 a) Saturn
b) Venus
c) Neptune
d) Earth
e) Uranus

Q3 A) — ii)
B) — iii)
C) — iv)
D) — i)

Q4 a) Jupiter, Saturn
b) Mercury, Mars, Venus
c) two
d) Jupiter, Saturn, Uranus, Neptune
e) Neptune

Q5 The Sun shines because **nuclear** reactions inside it produce huge amounts of **heat** and light. This energy radiates out from the Sun and some of the light **reflects** off the planets, allowing us to see them. Sunlight also causes comets to warm up when they approach the inner Solar System, making them produce huge tails of **gas** and dust.

Q6 a) orbit
b) ellipse
c) Stars generate their own light whereas planets only reflect light.

Page 217 — Questions on the Solar System and Beyond

Q1 The are eight planets in the Solar System. The most massive planet is **Jupiter** and the least massive is **Mercury**. The time taken for a planet to orbit the Sun **increases** the further out you go, while the gravitational pull of the Sun **decreases** the further out you go. The inner planets Mercury, Venus, Earth and Mars are made mainly from **rock**, while the rest are made up mostly from **gas**.

Q2 a) iii) A galaxy
b) yes
c) Billions

Q3 a) —
b) visible, inside the Solar System
c) visible, inside the Solar System
d) visible, inside the Solar System
e) visible
f) visible

Section Twenty One — Energy

Page 218 — Questions on Different Types of Energy

Q1 a) light
b) elastic
c) sound
d) potential
e) thermal
f) electrical
g) kinetic
h) chemical

Q2 a) kinetic
b) electrical
c) potential
d) light
e) elastic

Section Twenty One — Energy

f) chemical
g) sound
h) thermal

Q3

Statement	Applies to heat	Applies to temperature
measures how hot something is		✓
is a form of energy	✓	
measured in °C		✓
measured in joules	✓	
a difference in this causes heat to flow		✓
a flow of this causes a change in temperature	✓	

Page 219 — Questions on Generating Electricity

Q1

Problem	Coal	Oil	Gas	Nuclear
Release of CO_2 adding to the Greenhouse Effect	✓	✓	✓	
Acid rain production	✓			
Devastation of landscape caused by mining	✓			
Production of dangerous, long lasting waste				✓
Danger of major catastrophe due to human error				✓

Q2 a) coal, oil, natural gas
b) uranium
c) biomass/geothermal
Q3 a) no
b) Petrol is too valuable to use when more abundant, cheaper fractions will do.
Q4 a) Any one of: coal/oil/gas/biomass.
b) nuclear
c) coal

Pages 220-221 — Questions on Transfer of Energy

Q1 b) chemical → heat (+light)
c) electrical → light (+heat)
d) sound → electrical
e) chemical → heat +light
f) light → electrical
g) kinetic → heat + sound
h) potential → kinetic
i) electrical → sound
j) kinetic → electrical
k) chemical → light
Q2 a) False
b) True
c) True
d) False
e) False
f) True
g) True
Q3 a) kinetic, heat, sound
b) kinetic, heat, sound
c) light, heat
d) light, heat
e) heat, sound
f) light, heat
g) kinetic, heat, sound

Q4 **Heat** is produced most often. It is less useful than other types of energy as it is difficult to collect for other uses.
Q5 Method 1: Loft insulation — reduces convection and conduction
Method 2: Double glazing — reduces convection and conduction
Method 3: Cavity wall insulation — reduces conduction, radiation and convection.

Pages 222-223 — Questions on Energy Resources

Q1 The Sun produces a great deal of **light** energy and heat energy. Some of this reaches the Earth. **Plants** can trap this energy and change it by a process called **photosynthesis**. Some of the energy becomes locked in them, in the form of **chemical** energy. Over many years, loads and loads of plants grew. Some were **buried** underground. Their energy became trapped as they were turned into **coal**. Tiny **creatures** can feed on plants and absorb some of the energy. This happened **millions** of years ago. They then fell to the bottom of the seas. They were buried under **sediment** and chemical changes occurred to make **oil** and **natural gas**. We call fuels formed from living things in this way **fossil** fuels.
Q2 a) food, biomass, wind, waves
b) the Sun
c) Any one of, e.g. coal/oil/gas/biomass.
d) Any two of, e.g. wind/waves/tidal/geothermal/nuclear/solar.
Q3 a) chemical
b) heat
c) turbine
d) kinetic
e) generator
f) grid
Q4 Condensing waste steam before it is recycled.
Q5 Be more energy efficient. Use alternative energy resources.
Q6 Rate of use is much greater than the rate of creation, so fossil fuel will eventually run out / CO_2 levels in air will also rise.
Q7 The Sun will continue to give out energy for millions of years, so we can ignore the fact that it will eventually run out of fuel.

Pages 224-225 — Questions on Fuels

Q1 a) oxygen
b) carbon dioxide
c) oxygen, carbon dioxide
d) sulphur
e) carbon monoxide

SHW30M